Essentials of WRAML3 and EMS Assessment

Essentials of Psychological Assessment Series
Series Editors, Alan S. Kaufman and Nadeen L. Kaufman

Essentials of 16PF Assessment*
by Heather E. P. Cattell and James M. Schuerger

Essentials of Adaptive Behavior Assessment of Neurodevelopmental Disorders
by Celine A. Saulnier and Cheryl Klaiman

Essentials of ADHD Assessment for Children and Adolescents
by Elizabeth P. Sparrow and Drew Erhardt

Essentials of Assessing, Preventing, and Overcoming Reading Difficulties
by David A. Kilpatrick

Essentials of Assessment Report Writing, Second Edition
by W. Joel Schneider, Elizabeth O. Lichtenberger, Nancy Mather, Nadeen L. Kaufman, and Alan S. Kaufman

Essentials of Assessment with Brief Intelligence Tests
by Susan R. Homack and Cecil R. Reynolds

Essentials of Autism Spectrum Disorders Evaluation and Assessment
by Celine A. Saulnier and Pamela E. Ventola

Essentials of Bayley Scales of Infant Development-II Assessment
by Maureen M. Black and Kathleen Matula

Essentials of Behavioral Assessment
by Michael C. Ramsay, Cecil R. Reynolds, and R. W. Kamphaus

Essentials of Career Interest Assessment
by Jeffrey P. Prince and Lisa J. Heiser

Essentials of CAS2 Assessment
by Jack A. Naglieri and Tulio M. Otero

Essentials of Child and Adolescent Psychopathology, Second Edition
by Linda Wilmshurst

Essentials of Cognitive Assessment with KAIT and Other Kaufman Measures
by Elizabeth O. Lichtenberger, Debra Y. Broadbooks, and Alan S. Kaufman

Essentials of Conners Behavior Assessments™
by Elizabeth P. Sparrow

Essentials of Creativity Assessment
by James C. Kaufman, Jonathan A. Plucker, and John Baer

Essentials of Cross-Battery Assessment, Third Edition
by Dawn P. Flanagan, Samuel O. Ortiz, and Vincent C. Alfonso

Essentials of DAS-II Assessment*
by Ron Dumont, John O. Willis, and Colin D. Elliott

Essentials of Dyslexia Assessment and Intervention
by Nancy Mather and Barbara J. Wendling

Essentials of Evidence-Based Academic Interventions
by Barbara J. Wendling and Nancy Mather

Essentials of Executive Functions Assessment
by George McCloskey and Lisa A. Perkins

Essentials of Forensic Psychological Assessment, Second Edition
by Marc J. Ackerman

Essentials of Gifted Assessment
by Steven I. Pfeiffer

Essentials of IDEA for Assessment Professionals
by Guy McBride, Ron Dumont, and John O. Willis

Essentials of Individual Achievement Assessment
by Douglas K. Smith

Essentials of Intellectual Disability Assessment and Identification
by Alan W. Brue and Linda Wilmshurst

Essentials of KABC-II Assessment
by Alan S. Kaufman, Elizabeth O. Lichtenberger, Elaine Fletcher-Janzen, and Nadeen L. Kaufman

Essentials of KTEA™-3 and WIAT-III Assessment*
by Kristina C. Breaux and Elizabeth O. Lichtenberger

Essentials of MCMI-IV Assessment*
by Seth D. Grossman and Blaise Amendolace

Essentials of Millon™ Inventories Assessment, Third Edition
by Stephen Strack

Essentials of MMPI-A™ Assessment
by Robert P. Archer and Radhika Krishnamurthy

Essentials of MMPI-2 Assessment, Second Edition*
by David S. Nichols

Essentials of Myers-Briggs Type Indicator Assessment, Second Edition*
by Naomi L. Quenk

Essentials of NEPSY-II Assessment*
by Sally L. Kemp and Marit Korkman

Essentials of Neuropsychological Assessment, Second Edition
by Nancy Hebben and William Milberg

Essentials of Nonverbal Assessment
by Steve McCallum, Bruce Bracken, and John Wasserman

Essentials of PAI® Assessment
by Leslie C. Morey

Essentials of Planning, Selecting, and Tailoring Interventions for Unique Learners
by Jennifer T. Mascolo, Vincent C. Alfonso, and Dawn P. Flanagan

Essentials of Processing Assessment, Second Edition
by Milton J. Dehn

Essentials of Psychological Assessment Supervision
by A. Jordan Wright

Essentials of Psychological Testing, Second Edition
by Susana Urbina

Essentials of Response to Intervention
by Amanda M. VanDerHeyden and Matthew K. Burns

Essentials of Rorschach® Assessment
by Tara Rose, Michael P. Maloney, and Nancy Kaser-Boyd

Essentials of Rorschach Assessment: Comprehensive System and R-PAS
by Jessica R. Gurley

Essentials of School Neuropsychological Assessment, Third Edition
by Daniel C. Miller and Denise E. Maricle

Essentials of Specific Learning Disability Identification, Second Edition
by Vincent C. Alfonso and Dawn P. Flanagan

Essentials of Stanford-Binet Intelligence Scales (SB5) Assessment
by Gale H. Roid and R. Andrew Barram

Essentials of TAT and Other Storytelling Assessments, Second Edition
by Hedwig Teglasi

Essentials of Temperament Assessment
by Diana Joyce

Essentials of Trauma-Informed Assessment and Interventions in School and Community Settings
by Kirby L. Wycoff and Bettina Franzese

Essentials of Treatment Planning, Second Edition
by Mark E. Maruish

Essentials of WAIS®-IV Assessment, Second Edition
by Elizabeth O. Lichtenberger and Alan S. Kaufman

Essentials of WISC®-IV Assessment, Second Edition
by Dawn P. Flanagan and Alan S. Kaufman

Essentials of WISC-V® Assessment
by Dawn P. Flanagan and Vincent C. Alfonso

Essentials of WISC-V Integrated Assessment
by Susan Engi Raiford

Essentials of WJ IV® Cognitive Abilities Assessment
by Fredrick A. Schrank, Scott L. Decker, and John M. Garruto

Essentials of WJ IV® Tests of Achievement
by Nancy Mather and Barbara J. Wendling

Essentials of WMS®-IV Assessment
by Lisa Whipple Drozdick, James A. Holdnack, and Robin C. Hilsabeck

Essentials of WNV™ Assessment
by Kimberly A. Brunnert, Jack A. Naglieri, and Steven T. Hardy-Braz

Essentials of Working Memory Assessment and Intervention
by Milton J. Dehn

Essentials of WPPSI™-IV Assessment
by Susan Engi Raiford and Diane L. Coalson

Essentials of WRAML2 and TOMAL-2 Assessment
by Wayne Adams and Cecil R. Reynolds

Essentials of WRAML3 and EMS Assessment
by Wayne V. Adams, David V. Sheslow, and Trevor A. Hall

Essentials

of WRAML3 and EMS

Assessment

Wayne V. Adams
David V. Sheslow
Trevor A. Hall

WILEY

Copyright © 2024 by John Wiley & Sons, Inc. All rights reserved.

Published by John Wiley & Sons, Inc., Hoboken, New Jersey.
Published simultaneously in Canada.

No part of this publication may be reproduced, stored in a retrieval system, or transmitted in any form or by any means, electronic, mechanical, photocopying, recording, scanning, or otherwise, except as permitted under Section 107 or 108 of the 1976 United States Copyright Act, without either the prior written permission of the Publisher, or authorization through payment of the appropriate per-copy fee to the Copyright Clearance Center, Inc., 222 Rosewood Drive, Danvers, MA 01923, (978) 750-8400, fax (978) 750-4470, or on the web at www.copyright.com. Requests to the Publisher for permission should be addressed to the Permissions Department, John Wiley & Sons, Inc., 111 River Street, Hoboken, NJ 07030, (201) 748-6011, fax (201) 748-6008, or online at http://www.wiley.com/go/permission.

Trademarks: Wiley and the Wiley logo are trademarks or registered trademarks of John Wiley & Sons, Inc. and/or its affiliates in the United States and other countries and may not be used without written permission. All other trademarks are the property of their respective owners. John Wiley & Sons, Inc. is not associated with any product or vendor mentioned in this book.

Limit of Liability/Disclaimer of Warranty: While the publisher and author have used their best efforts in preparing this book, they make no representations or warranties with respect to the accuracy or completeness of the contents of this book and specifically disclaim any implied warranties of merchantability or fitness for a particular purpose. No warranty may be created or extended by sales representatives or written sales materials. The advice and strategies contained herein may not be suitable for your situation. You should consult with a professional where appropriate. Further, readers should be aware that websites listed in this work may have changed or disappeared between when this work was written and when it is read. Neither the publisher nor authors shall be liable for any loss of profit or any other commercial damages, including but not limited to special, incidental, consequential, or other damages.

For general information on our other products and services or for technical support, please contact our Customer Care Department within the United States at (800) 762-2974, outside the United States at (317) 572-3993 or fax (317) 572-4002.

Wiley also publishes its books in a variety of electronic formats. Some content that appears in print may not be available in electronic formats. For more information about Wiley products, visit our web site at www.wiley.com.

Library of Congress Cataloging-in-Publication Data is Applied for:
Paperback ISBN: 9781119987819

Cover Design: Wiley
Cover Image: © Robert/Adobe Stock Photos

Set in 11.5/14pt Adobe Garamond Pro by Straive, Pondicherry, India

SKY10070020_032124

DEDICATION

To you who have provided and continue to provide such wonderful
memories: Nora, Jen, Elizabeth, Scott, Paul, Cana, Ellie,
Aurora, and Elyse!
Wayne

I am filled with gratitude for all the sustained wonderful memories
authored by my children, Annie and Paul, and, of course, my longest
and best memory author, my wife, Liz.
David

To Carrie, Jadon, and Ian for lovingly residing in all my best
memories!
Trevor

CONTENTS

	Series Preface	xi
	Acknowledgments	xiv
One	Essentials of Memory Measurement Using the WRAML3 and the EMS: Introduction and Overview	1
Two	Measuring Memory: Foundations	9
Three	Overview of the WRAML3	35
Four	Interpreting WRAML3 Subtests, Indexes, and Process Scores	71
Five	WRAML3 Interpretation: Levels of Analysis	148
Six	WRAML3 Abbreviated Formats	165
Seven	Integrated Interpretation of the WRAML3	181
Eight	Everyday Memory Survey: Overview, Administration, and Scoring	220

x CONTENTS

Nine	Uses and Interpretive Considerations for the Everyday Memory Survey	233
Ten	Q&A with the Authors	249
	References	266
	About the Authors	276
	Index	279

SERIES PREFACE

In the *Essentials of Psychological Assessment Series*, we have attempted to provide the reader with books that deliver key practical information in the most efficient and accessible manner. Many books in the series feature specific topics in a variety of domains, such as specific learning disabilities, social-emotional learning, neuropsychological assessment, cross-battery assessment, and adaptive behavior assessment. Books in this category are intended for professionals in psychology and education – and for graduate students in these or related disciplines – who are involved with any aspect of assessment and intervention. A second category of books in this series, such as *Essentials of Bayley TM–4 Assessment,* is devoted to a single test. Books in this category offer a concise yet thorough review of an instrument, with special attention given to the details of administration, scoring, interpretation, application, and tips for best practice of the test. Students can rely on series books in both categories for a clear and concise overview of the important assessment tools and key topics in which they must become proficient to practice skillfully, efficiently, and ethically in their chosen fields. Experienced clinicians will feel equally at home with this series in their efforts to remain on the cutting edge of new research and new instruments (including revisions of old ones) in an array of diverse fields.

Wherever feasible, visual cues highlighting key points are utilized alongside systematic, step-by-step guidelines. Chapters are focused and succinct. Topics are organized for an easy understanding of the essential material related to a particular test or topic. Theory and research are continually woven into the fabric of each book, but always to enhance the practical application of the material, rather than to sidetrack or overwhelm readers. With this series, we aim to challenge and assist readers interested in psychological assessment to aspire to the highest level of competency by arming them with the tools they need for knowledgeable, informed practice. We have long been advocates of "intelligent" testing – the notion that numbers are meaningless unless they are brought to life by the clinical acumen and expertise of examiners. Assessment must be used to make a difference in the child's life or the adult's life or why bother to test? All books in the series – whether devoted to specific tests or general topics – are consistent with this credo. We want this series to help our readers, novice and veteran alike, to benefit from the intelligent assessment approaches of the authors of each book.

In Essentials of WRAML3 and EMS Assessment, Drs. Adams, Sheslow, and Hall provide important insights into memory and memory testing alongside substantive guidance in administering and interpreting these two tests. The WRAML3 builds on the strong foundation of the test's two prior versions, continuing to provide a psychometrically sound memory assessment tool that can be used with children and adults, including older adults. Among other enhancements, the third edition of WRAML includes an embedded Performance Validity measure, greater emphasis on Delayed recall and Working Memory, additional process scores that allow more nuanced interpretation, and an additional abbreviated format. Both beginning and seasoned practitioners familiar with assessment in general, and memory assessment in particular, will find useful material that goes well beyond that found in the WRAML3 administration and technical manuals. While the WRAML3 is a complex instrument, the approach found in these very readable chapters provides users a means to evaluate their technical and clinical competency, especially useful for those new to the instrument and for those supervising students and colleagues.

Further, the inclusion of the EMS in this volume helps readers become aware of a means to contrast individually administered test results with self- and observer-subjective estimates of a given adult's performance in everyday tasks, such as remembering the location of a new office recently visited, or the content of a phone message. Everyday memory (i.e. memory performance outside of the clinician's office) is often overlooked. This volume shows how to use EMS results to generate practical, meaningful, and person-centered recommendations in combination with formal testing results (e.g. the WRAML3). This volume, therefore, will provide sound professional, practical guidance in how to conduct tailored, user-friendly, and functionally meaningful memory assessments.

Alan S. Kaufman, PhD, and Nadeen L. Kaufman, EdD, Series Editors
Neag School of Education, University of Connecticut

ACKNOWLEDGMENTS

The original WRAML appeared in 1990, which is before some reading this were born! Over the years, we would like to feel that the test has been on a path of steady improvement and greater helpfulness. Accordingly, we would be remiss not to express sincere gratitude for our associations with those at Wide Range, Inc. and our more recent friends at Pearson, as well as for the many WRAML users, clients, students, and colleagues who, over the years, have been sources of learning, encouragement, challenge, and useful suggestions. Good memories!

One

ESSENTIALS OF MEMORY MEASUREMENT USING THE WRAML3 AND THE EMS: INTRODUCTION AND OVERVIEW

Memory is fundamental in determining who we are, what we become and what we perceive our past to have been. It is sometimes overlooked that activities as varied as psychotherapy, job training, and forming friendships are dependent on reasonably intact memory systems for such interactions to succeed. Those who pause to reflect on it usually marvel that the phenomenon of recall is a "by-product" of electrical connections and chemical interactions within our brains. Many have awe for those few who can remember with complete clarity the activities of a day randomly chosen from many years ago or correctly reproduce days or weeks later material only briefly perused. Less dramatically, we ourselves can recount events such as annual holiday get-togethers over the last few years, with only slight distortions of the differing locations and happenings of those times. We can also be stunned when we evaluate someone and discover after a mid-session break that they do not remember meeting us or the tasks just completed.

Essentials of WRAML3 and EMS Assessment, First Edition.
Wayne V. Adams, David V. Sheslow, and Trevor A. Hall.
© 2024 John Wiley & Sons, Inc. Published 2024 by John Wiley & Sons, Inc.

Memory is so fundamental to cognition that it received prominent attention early by both test pioneers, Binet and Wechsler. It may be surprising to learn that Wechsler developed a memory scale (i.e., the *Wechsler Memory Scale* [Wechsler, 1945b]) before any of his standardized child- or adult-focused intelligence instruments! This book focuses on two recent additions to the long list of increasingly sophisticated memory tests that have since evolved. In the pages that follow, it is the intent of the authors to provide a solid understanding of the *Wide Range Assessment of Memory and Learning, Third Edition* (WRAML3) (Adams & Sheslow, 2021) and the *Everyday Memory Survey* (EMS) (Hall et al., 2021) so that their purpose, administration, and interpretation are clearly understood. Whether used as stand-alone measures or parts of a comprehensive testing battery, it is hoped that users will be able to better address relevant referral questions with greater diagnostic sophistication, leading to meaningful recommendations that bring about a better quality of life for those at the center of the assessment, as well as those working with them.

IS MEMORY ASSESSMENT NEEDED?

Is memory assessment really needed? That is a reasonable question to ask at the outset of this book. After all, psychologists have no shortage of test instruments available, but most users have a shortage of available time. When have you heard a trainee or seasoned clinician say, "I have too much time to evaluate this client?"

In the "real world," memory is largely an ignored phenomenon unless it is not working properly. Teachers who have had a severely brain-injured student return to the classroom, or families with an aging parent entering dementia know only too well the transformative impact of altered memory, not only on the affected persons but also on those who know and interact with them. And as discussed in Chapter 2, the paradox about memory is that while it has been studied for centuries, we still have limited understanding of how it actually works.

The increasing impact of neuroscience on psychology and the lay public (e.g., ads for medications that purport to have a positive impact on memory loss, and almost daily news stories around memory loss) have led to an increased awareness that memory is a critical aspect of human cognitive functioning. Rapid Reference 1.1 lists common

≡ Rapid Reference 1.1

A Sampling of Common Pediatric and Adult Conditions Triggering Referrals for Psychological Assessments which Often Uncover Memory Deficits

Typical Common Referrals for Children and Adolescents	Typical Common Referrals for Adults
Traumatic Brain Injury	Traumatic Brain Injury
Sports Injuries	Sports Injuries
Motor Vehicle Accidents	Motor Vehicle Accidents
Abuse	Falls
Acquired Brain Injury	Acquired Brain Injury
Stroke	Stroke
Infectious/Inflammatory Conditions	Infectious/Inflammatory Conditions
Near Drowning	Near Drowning
Cardiac Arrest	Cardiac Arrest
Critical Care Intervention	Critical Care Intervention
Attention Deficit/Hyperactivity Disorder	Attention Deficit/Hyperactivity Disorder
Brain Tumor	Brain Tumor
Cancer Treatment	Cancer Treatment
Brain Infections	Brain Infections
Prenatal Alcohol/Substance Exposure	Alcoholism and Other Substance Abuse
Seizure Disorders	Seizure Disorders
Intellectual Disability	Thyroid Disorders
Autism Spectrum Disorder	Kidney Disorders
Genetic Disorders	Liver Disorders
Learning Disability	Hypoxia (e.g., cardiac arrest)
Substance Abuse	Medication Side Effects
	Dementia
	Mild Cognitive Impairment
	Normal Pressure Hydrocephalus

referral conditions that often lead to assessments typically yielding results showing that memory has been negatively impacted. Triggered by acute events or chronic conditions, the importance of obtaining an estimate of memory functioning as part of any comprehensive psychological assessment should not be underestimated.

To further press the argument that some kind of memory assessment in many cases is a reasonable inclusion, let us take a look at the very common referrals of Developmental Learning Disorder (LD) and Attention Deficit/Hyperactivity Disorder (ADHD). Such referrals of children and adults are made every day in schools, and to agencies and to those in private practices across the country, yet, few psycho-educational assessments typically include much by the way of memory assessment other than possibly a few short-term memory tasks. A dissertation study (Weniger & Adams, 2006), however, suggests that for those with LD or ADHD, memory deficits are fairly common, and for those with both conditions, memory deficits may be pervasive and even profound. Figure 1.1 shows the results of that study using the WRAML2. (Given the degree of overlap between WRAML2 and WRAML3, it is reasonable to expect similar results, but that assumption needs empirical replication.) You can see that for those with ADHD, generally immediate verbal memory performance is not that different than matched controls. As expected, the Attention/Concentration Index is lower than controls, and Visual Immediate Memory is a bit lower, primarily from lower performance on a task making perceptual-motor demands, a common finding in the literature (Ek et al., 2007; Pitcher et al., 2003). Of even more interest are the results for children with Developmental Reading Disorder; those children show uniformly lower performance on all the immediate memory indexes, including Working Memory. Of greatest interest though are the dramatically lower results of those children with both disorders (about 40% of those who present with ADHD), and these results were replicated even on the recognition memory tasks that assess a rather robust form of memory storage. If these data can be replicated, it would suggest that an ADHD or LD assessment that does not include some in-depth memory assessment is incomplete, especially given the academic

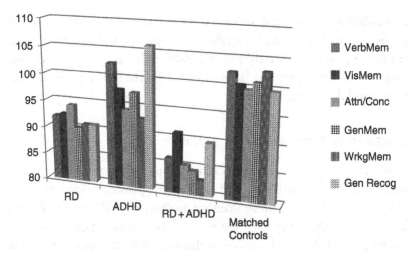

Figure 1.1 WRAML3 Standard Score performance of children with ADHD, RD (reading disorder), and both disorders, compared to matched controls.

Note: RD = reading disorder, ADHD = attention deficit hyperactivity disorder, RD + ADHD = having both the prior conditions, VerbMem = Verbal Immediate Memory Index, VisMem = Visual Immediate Memory Index, WrkgMem = Working Memory Index, and Gen Recog = General Recognition Index.

concerns (which are heavily memory related) that trigger most of these assessments. How often are memory compensatory strategies part of the recommendations for helping ADHD children (or adults) with reading delays?

On the other end of the population demographic are older individuals who are living longer than their parents and, as such, present with a higher frequency of concerns around potential effects of dementia, especially of the Alzheimer's type, as well as mild cognitive impairment. Unique to the older age group is the need for repeated assessments over time to tease apart "normal" decline in memory function vs. that possibly related to an additional degenerative process. Accordingly, comprehensive as well as abbreviated batteries of memory tests have increasingly become part of the older adult's assessment experience.

Because of the health and safety importance of turning neuropsychological test data into useful recommendations related to everyday functioning, as noted above, this book also includes the EMS, a standardized self- and other-report survey of everyday memory performance. When used together, the authors feel confident that combining each test's results will greatly enhance the number and usefulness of the recommendations included in the typical psychological report and debriefing session.

ORGANIZATION OF THIS BOOK

In the chapters that follow, the authors hope to better familiarize you with both the WRAML3 and EMS. Chapter 2 provides a brief overview of research with which those assessing memory should have familiarity, both for appreciating the empirical basis upon which memory assessment was founded, as well as the neurological basics involved in this core set of cognitive processes. The subsequent chapters are devoted to the use of the WRAML3 and EMS, highlighting interpretation more than administration or psychometric details of the instruments since those are covered thoroughly in their respective manuals. As the chapters progress, you will find that the interpretive focus becomes more complex eventually including several case vignettes for illustration and discussion. Relatively few conventional case studies have been included since full psychological assessments tend to be lengthy, and therefore their case studies also tend to be lengthy and, at times, tedious, therefore often skimmed or skipped by the reader. Hopefully, including shorter vignettes will be easier to follow.

A later section of the book is devoted to the EMS that, as the name suggests, focuses upon perceived capability with memory tasks of everyday life. (Readers wondering why a pediatric version is not available will find the answer in the introductory EMS chapter!) The EMS is a measure intended to be used in conjunction with a formal memory test measure such as WRAML3, and provides a brief, structured opportunity for the client and their significant other to each furnish input on how well typical memory-laden daily life experiences are performed. The scale is intentionally concrete and grounded in everyday experiences to which almost all people can relate. By using EMS input from both the client and someone who knows the client well, areas of perceived memory concern can be flagged. Once substantiated, tailored remediation recommendations can be offered in areas of identified concern, based on EMS findings, memory test results, and other relevant data uncovered during a comprehensive evaluation. One of the most common complaints heard from laypeople and especially from other professionals when sent a psychological report is, despite many pages of test results, there are few practical and specific recommendations that can be used to remediate the deficits that triggered the referral. For those working with adults, using the EMS and WRAML3 together will provide useful test results on a broad array of memory functions as well as provide ecologically meaningful targets for useful recommendations; hopefully, that will address the justifiable criticism.

The book concludes with a selection of common WRAML3 and EMS questions which have been presented to the authors by trainees, colleagues, or users contacting us personally or by email.

The authors have deliberately tried to keep the tone and content of this volume practical for both the experienced clinician as well as someone just starting a professional career in assessment. The reader will notice inclusion of the supplemental helps that those using the *Essentials* series have come to expect such as "Rapid Reference," "Don't Forget," "Caution," and "Test Yourself" inset boxes. In addition, the authors have included subtest administration checklists that can be used to help establish and maintain WRAML3 administration competency; these are especially intended for use by supervisors or the professionals themselves as they video and review practice administrations as is commonplace in therapy training, but, curiously, occurs much less in learning assessment skills.

Readers of this book will encounter several terms used for those being evaluated (e.g., client, patient, examinee, and participant) and those doing the evaluation (e.g., clinician, examiner, evaluator, and test user); in the pages that follow, the terms are used interchangeably reflecting terminology found in various clinical settings.

The authors have mercifully made no attempt to be exhaustive in their topical discussions other than those related directly to the two test instruments. For them, there is a thorough emphasis on practical content and clinical utility. It is hoped that by utilizing this volume, the reader will become increasingly confident in how to use and interpret the WRAML3 and/or EMS, as well as feel more able to exploit the instruments' strengths and clinical subtleties to better assist those who are referred with suspected or known memory and learning issues.

Finally, the authors are aware that most readers will not pick up this book and read it from cover to cover in one sitting! Instead, it is more likely that on many occasions, specific chapters or subsections of chapters will be selected to answer specific questions or gain more background or understanding of some specific part of the WRAML3 or EMS. Consequently, there is some redundancy found whenever a section depends on principles or content stated earlier but is needed again for clarity for those who did not read the earlier narrative or for whom that reading occurred a while ago. We ask some forbearance from those whose interest will be so captured that they will read this volume right through from beginning to end. To their advantage, repetition is a proven vehicle for improving recall!

Two

MEASURING MEMORY: FOUNDATIONS

Generating meaning from these words is a notable memory achievement. You have to remember procedural aspects, like where to start on the page and to use your eyes to scan in the direction common for your written language. You also need to remember what the various letter configurations and word combinations represent spatially, phonetically, and holistically. Then you need to remember what meaning to assign those many phonetic and spatial combinations. You also need to remember the meaning from the beginning of a sentence until the end of the sentence, and the beginning of the paragraph until its end. Obviously, without memory, reading would be impossible; and actually, without memory, life as we know it could not exist.

As a central feature of human cognition, memory is represented in nearly all day-to-day functions, be they intellectual, emotional, academic, social, vocational, or recreational. Memory provides meaning

---

Essentials of WRAML3 and EMS Assessment, First Edition.
Wayne V. Adams, David V. Sheslow, and Trevor A. Hall.
© 2024 John Wiley & Sons, Inc. Published 2024 by John Wiley & Sons, Inc.

in terms of who we are and it preserves our identity. Without the ability to recall our personal history, we would be in a near state of confusion and constant dilemma. Indeed, the greatest tragedy of most dementias is that they eventually take from us who we are and what we know of ourselves and others. Memory allows us to acquire skills and knowledge to perform our jobs and to recognize and respond appropriately to our loved ones. Simply stated, memory is a ubiquitous necessity for a life most would consider a quality existence.

While memory is a central cognitive process, it is also a vulnerable brain function due to its being highly interconnected and dependent on other aspects of cognition. Various injuries and illnesses, minor or devastating, can affect the efficiency of the brain's storing new memories and/or retrieving those already stored. Generally speaking, if there is going to be some cognitive compromise resulting from an injury or illness to the brain, it is highly likely that memory in some form will be among those processes negatively impacted. It is well known that difficulties with memory and attention are the two most common complaints following a brain injury, even if that injury is mild. Therefore, and akin to intellectual functioning, memory prowess is widely variable across individuals, from very impaired to highly advanced, with such differences apparent even in early childhood. There are also variable developmental trajectories associated with age; for example, visual memory seems to develop more rapidly and show decline in adulthood earlier than verbal (more about developmental trajectories in Chapter 10). Consequently, it should not be surprising that psychologists, neuropsychologists, neuroscientists, and physicians have devoted, and continue to devote much attention to memory and its measurement.

As noted in Chapter 1, a good portion of this book features the WRAML3, one of the most utilized comprehensive memory batteries currently available for assessment of memory functions from childhood to older adulthood. This volume also includes the introduction of a new complementary assessment tool, the *Everyday Memory Survey*. The WRAML3 is intended to reliably sample a variety of memory functions that are of clinical and theoretical importance for children, adolescents,

MEASURING MEMORY: FOUNDATIONS   11

and adults. The EMS provides reliable subjective personal accounts of memory performance demanded in navigating daily life; both the client and another familiar with the client contribute their opinions about how much challenge is posed performing specific everyday, functional recall tasks. Incidentally, the EMS was developed and normed at the same time as the WRAML3, sharing a significant portion of cases. By sharing standardization samples in this way, the authors used a psychometrically sound manner to bring together two important arenas that are often left disconnected, namely formal test performance of memory (i.e., the WRAML3) and perceived capacity to perform everyday memory demands (i.e., the EMS). When the WRAML3 and the EMS are used in concert, the evaluator has an empirical basis to comment on memory performance demonstrated both in the clinic and in the everyday world.

Memory can be broken down into a multitude of forms, or *types*, each of which has a seemingly endless number of variations of task, process, and stimuli. Depending upon one's theoretical orientation, distinctions among memory processes may carry such labels as abstract, meaningful, verbal, figural, spatial, associative, free recall, cued, sequential, recognition, short-term, long-term, rote, retrieval, procedural, episodic, working, semantic, and ecological—among others. There is no uniformly accepted terminology used to describe the subprocesses of memory. This diversity in memory terminology is rivaled only by the hundreds of terms designed to reflect specific aptitudes and personality characteristics.

> ## DON'T FORGET
> ....
> The WRAML3 formally measures memory and learning using a traditional one-to-one testing format. The EMS provides a subjective estimate of clients' perception of how well they are performing everyday life tasks that make memory demands, and validation (or lack of it) of that perception from a caregiver.

A single task may carry multiple classifications legitimately because of the complexity of memory and the corresponding theories of memory, and their terminology often overlaps. Some have even considered the classic definition of *learning* as also defining *memory* (e.g., see Kolb & Whishaw, 2021). However, although the distinction may be to some degree artificial (anything recalled must have been *learned*), the WRAML3 distinguishes between memory and learning by providing two subtests that allow the examiner to actually witness new visual and verbal learning occurring over multiple learning trials. The EMS, by design, captures estimates of perceived competency in recall involved in everyday demands that are also often impacted more by situational factors beyond memory alone. Although clinical utility was emphasized in the development of the WRAML3 and EMS, and is an important focus throughout this volume, researchers will also find both tests valuable because of their sound psychometric qualities, as well as content coverage of more varied memory functions across a broader age range than is available in most, if not all, other standardized instruments.

What follows in the remainder of this chapter are two sections that might be labelled, "what all clinicians using memory tests should know." The first looks at our memory-testing legacy and the second focuses on basic neuroanatomy of memory. Such background will hopefully serve as a useful backdrop to appreciate how the areas have evolved, as well as provide a foundation for better understanding (and interpreting) the cognitive process these tests are measuring.

> ### DON'T FORGET
>
> The EMS, by design, captures estimates of perceived competency in recall involved in everyday demands that are also often impacted by other factors beyond memory alone.

HISTORICAL FOUNDATIONS

Unlike some domains of psychological testing, memory assessment had a relatively strong empirical base upon which to build. That foundation has had many contributors. Hans Ebbinghaus is generally recognized as among the first to study memory. His now classic "forgetting curve" was published as part of numerous findings related to more than a decade of research on memory and forgetting (Ebbinghaus, 1885). Ebbinghaus operationalized what we now think of as *immediate memory* using digit span and nonsense syllable tasks. He showed that the amount to be remembered affects performance and having a way to *chunk* information improved performance. The meaningfulness of the information to the learner was shown to positively impact retention too.

A contemporary of Ebbinghaus was Alfred Binet, famous for creating the first measures of intellectual ability. Less known is Binet's interest in many facets of memory. This focus is perhaps one reason that 20% of his first intelligence test (the 1905 Binet-Simon Scale) consisted of questions directly assessing immediate verbal and visual memory abilities.

While Sigmund Freud did not investigate memory per se, his revolutionary theory was heavily reliant on assumed and diverse memory mechanisms. Later, Karl Lashley (1950) (long-term memory), George Miller (1956) (and his "7 ± 2" rule), Alexander Luria (2006) (the case of S and his unlimited long-term memory), and many others contributed an enormous amount of research that helps us better understand memory. A lengthier treatment of research "pioneers" who contributed both directly and indirectly to memory assessment can be found in comprehensive sources like Haberlandt (1997); Squire and Schacter (2002); and Kolb and Whishaw (2021).

Memory research continues, embracing new technologies, such as using fMRI imaging techniques, focusing on such contemporary and applied topics as investigating the impact of blast injuries on memory of soldiers (Newsome et al., 2015); memory impairment following pediatric intensive care admission (Leonard et al., 2022); estimating performance validity when assessing learning and memory (Nayar et al., 2022); memory as is related to central nervous system disease or injury (Backman et al., 2005; Baron, Fennell, & Voeller, 1995; Cullum, Kuck, & Ruff, 1990; Cytowic, 1996; Gillberg, 1995; Knight, 1992; Lezak et al., 2019; Mapou & Spector, 1995; Mitchell, 2008; Reeves & Wedding, 1994; Weissberger et al., 2017); and memory decline as it impacts activities of daily living (Farias et al., 2003; Jefferson et al., 2006; Mlinac & Feng, 2016).

Yet, despite over a century of research on the topic of memory, the clinical assessment of developmentally typical and disordered memory

14 ESSENTIALS OF WRAML3 AND EMS ASSESSMENT

> **DON'T FORGET**
>
> The two most common complaints of individuals following a closed head injury are difficulties with attention and memory, so both should be assessed.

has been fraught with problems (Fuster, 1995; Miller, Bigler, & Adams, 2003; Prigatano, 1978; Riccio & Reynolds, 1998), many of which stem from difficulties separating intertwined constructs such as executive functioning, attention, and mood regulation from memory, as well as distinguishing immediate memory from short-term and longer-term memory (see especially Fuster, 1995; Miller, Bigler, & Adams, 2003; Riccio & Reynolds, 1998; Riccio, Reynolds, & Lowe, 2001), and understanding the differential effects brain insults have on memory at different developmental stages.

We have known for a long time that certain neurological disorders of adulthood tend to occur in the elderly but as noted in Table 2.1, may also appear as early as 30 years of age. These "senior disorders" typically have a profound impact on memory, and the type of memory loss that a person displays may have diagnostic implications for that disorder. Table 2.1 lists the four most common forms of dementia which differ in how much and when memory is impacted, especially in their early stages of onset. Determining the presence and severity of dementia is a common reason for referral for those doing memory testing. While there are four discrete columns, in reality, there are probably different subtypes of each form of dementia, and people can have more than one kind and at different stages.

> **PUTTING IT INTO PRACTICE**
>
> Prescribed medication use and its inadvertent mistaken ingestion are common contributors to memory difficulties, so should be examined carefully when gathering history, especially in adults.

Also, in obtaining a thorough history, examiners should be looking for conditions such as those found in Rapid Reference 2.1 even for referrals not explicitly focused on memory concerns. If any are part of the "current status" or "past history" of the client, at least a memory screening may be indicated.

Table 2.1 A Sampling of Cognitive Effects Found in Common Kinds of Dementias[a]

Associated symptoms having a cognitive basis	Alzheimer's Disease	Lewy Body Dementia	Vascular Dementia	Frontotemporal Dementia
	Memory loss that disrupts daily life.	Visual hallucinations	Difficulty performing tasks that used to be easy.	Problems planning and sequencing (thinking through which steps come first, second, etc.).
	Poor judgment, leading to bad decisions.	Unpredictable changes in concentration, attention, alertness, and wakefulness from day to day and sometimes throughout the day	Trouble following instructions or learning new information and routines.	Difficulty prioritizing tasks or activities
	Loss of spontaneity and sense of initiative.	Ideas may be disorganized, unclear, or illogical	Forgetting current or past events.	Repeating the same activity or saying the same word over and over.
	Losing track of dates or knowing current location.	These kinds of changes are common and may help distinguish it from Alzheimer's.	Misplacing items.	Acting impulsively or saying or doing inappropriate things without considering how others perceive the behavior.
	Taking longer to complete normal daily tasks.	Slowness in starting and maintaining movement	Getting lost on familiar routes.	
	Repeating questions or forgetting recently learned information.	Severe loss of thinking abilities that interfere with daily activities.	Problems with language, such as finding the right word or using the wrong word.	Becoming disinterested in family or activities previously cared about.
	Trouble handling money and paying bills.		Changes in sleep patterns.	

(*continued*)

Table 2.1 (continued)

Associated symptoms having a cognitive basis	Alzheimer's Disease	Lewy Body Dementia	Vascular Dementia	Frontotemporal Dementia
	Challenges in planning or solving problems.	Memory problems may not be evident at first but often arise as the disease progresses.	Difficulty reading and writing.	Personality changes more apparent in early stages, while memory decline comes in later stages
	Wandering and getting lost.		Loss of interest in things or people.	
	Losing things or misplacing them in odd places.	Other changes related to thinking may include poor judgment, confusion about time and place, and difficulty with language and numbers.	Changes in personality, behavior, and mood, such as depression, agitation, and anger.	Movement disorders (balance, tremor)
	Difficulty completing tasks such as bathing.			Difficulty with speech and language
	Mood and personality changes.		Hallucinations or delusions	
	Increased anxiety and/or aggression.	Insomnia	Poor judgment and loss of ability to perceive danger.	
		Long staring spells		
Incidence among dementia cases	50–75%	10–15%	10–20%	1–3%
Typical age(s) of onset (yrs.)	Mid 60s (although rare cases as young as 30)	50 and older	65 and older	45–64

[a] Adapted from the National Institute on Aging (2022).

MEASURING MEMORY: FOUNDATIONS 17

> ### ⇒ *Rapid Reference 2.1*
>
> **Common Medical Contributors to Memory Loss**
>
> • Traumatic Brain Injury
> • Drug abuse including regular alcohol consumption
> • Prescribed medication use, especially anti-convulsants which are often prescribed for bipolar disorder, mania, migraine prevention, and mood disorders
> • Inadvertent client errors with prescribed Medication (e.g., dosage or schedule)
> • Hypothyroidism

Prescribed medication is mentioned twice since its prescribed use and its inadvertent mistaken ingestion (e.g., incorrect medicine, wrong dosage, or schedule) are both common contributors to memory difficulties.

Numerous neurological disorders of children and adolescents (including epilepsy, brain infection and trauma, most of the more than 600 known degenerative neurological disorders, and neoplasms) also have implications for memory, but they have less predictable and often more global effects on memory than with adults. As partly illustrated in the prior chapter, children diagnosed with a developmental learning disorder, whether viewed as a neuropsychological syndrome or not, commonly show a variety of memory problems (Reynolds & Fletcher-Janzen, 1997; Riccio & Reynolds, 1998; Riccio & Wolfe, 2003).

As part of their standard exam dating back to the beginning of the last century, neurologists have always asked the patient memory questions concerning the date, current news items, and some recall of letters, words, or sentences as a crude attempt to establish whether memory was within expected functional levels. Such a screening assumed that individuals free of neurological disease or disorder would have no difficulty recalling such simple items, in contrast to neurologically compromised individuals who would display some type of impairment. However, it became evident that neurological disorders impacted memory with such variability that more elaborate assessment methods were necessary. Neuropsychiatric and psychological problems (e.g., depression and anxiety) are also known to sometimes affect memory subsystems differentially across the age range; therefore, psychiatrists, among others, also routinely include informal memory tasks when working with children, adolescents, and adults, but again, given the complexity of memory, more nuanced assessments are typically needed. In part, this is because memory is paradoxical in certain regards in that it is both fragile and robust. Even slight, seemingly inconsequential blows to the head may cause substantial memory problems. Others with significant brain injury, early-in-life neuronal infections, or even hydrocephalus resulting in greatly reduced neural tissue, can exhibit minimal memory compromise (Hall et al., 2022). Consequently, systematic evaluation is often required to detect subtleties of memory dysfunction, typically using standardized testing such as the WRAML3 and the EMS.

> **DON'T FORGET**
>
> Children diagnosed with a developmental learning disorder commonly show a variety of memory deficits.

Years ago, recognizing the need to go beyond the common neurological and psychiatric memory exam, Luria (1966) devised a more thorough and insightful evaluation, but he adhered to a clinical tradition that was difficult to subject to quantification. Similar to neurologists of his day, Luria would often employ impromptu methods to assess a particular patient suspected of impaired memory. Again, the diagnostic assumption was that the patient would either be *impaired* or *not impaired*. Such a dichotomous and idiosyncratic approach in clinical practice, while sometimes creative, did not reflect the evolving nuances being reported within memory research, nor did it provide an approach that easily allowed standardized procedures or empirical validation. Further, while qualitative approaches provided a certain richness and flexibility diagnostically, they often did not detect milder deficits or identify areas of differential memory strengths. Also, qualitative approaches require many years of experience, lengthy supervision, and exposure to a wide range of pathology, not to mention immense creativity, a command of the literature, and careful theoretical reflection. In contrast, Western psychology, with its tradition of quantification, strongly influenced neuropsychological and other forms of assessment to proceed in a more psychometrically exacting direction.

Much of the evolution in modern neuropsychology in the United States can be attributed to events associated with World War II. With dramatically improved emergency medicine in field hospitals, for the first time in the history of warfare, many soldiers survived brain injury; not surprisingly, many of these demonstrated memory problems. Consequently, the need for some type of standardized *battery* of memory tests became obvious. Such a battery would allow findings to be reliably relayed from one health specialist to another. With the success of the (unnormed) *Wechsler-Bellevue Intelligence Test* in 1939, David Wechsler developed the *Wechsler Memory Scale* (WMS) as a "rapid, simple, and practical" measure of memory (Wechsler, 1945a, 1945b, p. 16). The WMS was quickly incorporated into clinical practice and by the 1950s and 1960s was entrenched as the only measure of adult memory that could be compared with an intelligence quotient. However, the WMS and its subsequent revisions (WMS-R, WMS-III, and WMS-IV, and soon, as of this writing, WMS-V) are primarily adult measures, beginning at the middle age range of adolescence. Memory problems in children and their impact on development, learning, and behavior simply were not emphasized or even recognized to the same extent that adult memory symptoms were.

During this same period of time (1940–1960), other less extensive tests of memory had been developed, most notably, *Rey-Osterrieth Complex Figure Test* (Rey, 1941), the *Benton Visual Retention Test* (Benton, 1946), and the *Rey Auditory Verbal Learning Test* (Rey, 1958) (RAVLT). The RAVLT is a list-learning task in which 15 words were presented to the patient over 5 trials. This would permit creation of a learning curve in the Ebbinghaus tradition; by using an interference procedure one could also examine forgetting—a factor particularly important in certain neurological disorders (Lezak et al., 2019). Additionally, the words could be embedded in a paragraph so that recognition memory could be assessed. Although widely used as a clinical test, the RAVLT was never fully standardized and normed using recognized psychometric standards. However, the RAVLT is now one of the instruments found in the NIH Toolbox Cognitive Battery (Fox et al., 2022), and, as such, is accumulating normative data from users. Since the RAVLT originally did not permit a detailed evaluation of storage and retrieval of information, Buschke and Fuld (1974) developed the *Selective Reminding Test*. With this procedure, the individual is told only the words that "failed" on the previous trial, thereby allowing another method of studying longer- and short-term retrieval.

From a historical perspective, visual memory has been typically assessed by the *Benton Visual Retention Test* (Benton, 1974) or the *Rey-Osterrieth Complex Figure Test* (Rey, 1941). Both have the problem of requiring the examinee to use reasonably well-developed fine-motor abilities, limiting its use with younger children as well as those with motor impairments. The *Benton Visual Retention Test* has sound psychometric properties for older children and adolescents but has not been fully standardized in the lower age ranges. The Rey-Osterrieth Figure Test is complicated and somewhat difficult to score, and this has presented obstacles in its clinical utility. Also, the delayed recall feature of the Rey-Osterrieth has never been fully standardized and normed, even though numerous methods for assessing delayed recall have been suggested (Zhang et al., 2021). Further, both of these measures have been criticized because each invites an element of verbal problem-solving to be used in a task intended to primarily measure visual memory.

As it developed since the late 1940s, memory testing continued to be focused primarily on adults. Nevertheless, some pediatric focus was evident. The various versions of the *Halstead* (and *Halstead-Reitan*) *Neuropsychological Test Batteries* (e.g., Reitan & Wolfson, 1985) routinely included several brief memory measures for children 6–14 years of age. Even so, if suspicions were raised of memory problems on these tasks or from memory performance on intelligence batteries, psychologists were often forced to use informal techniques, such as a *recall* segment following administration of the nonstandardized *Bender-Gestalt Test*

(Bender, 1938). Dorothea McCarthy (1972), a developmental psycholinguist, placed a Memory Index on the *McCarthy Scales of Children's Abilities*, but even this scale overlapped other cognitive processes and was very narrow in its coverage. It was not until the 1990s that the first comprehensive, pediatric-focused memory measures appeared—specifically the original version of the WRAML (Sheslow & Adams, 1990). In addition, recent history has given rise to measures targeting constructs like procedural memory via tests designed to measure performance on overlearned activities in cognitive, motor, and perceptual domains (Churchill et al., 2003; Mochizuki-Kawai, 2008; Steidl, Mohiuddin, & Anderson, 2006). Rating forms aimed at codifying the multidimensional construct of everyday memory have also emerged. Consequently, it can be said that from the growing sophistication over the past century, there are now more quality testing options available for those evaluating memory in children and adults.

It is also of interest to note that by the late 1980s, 80% of a sample of various testing experts noted memory as an important aspect of a cognitive assessment (Snyderman & Rothman, 1987). Yet, despite the recognized importance of memory assessment and the inclusion of brief recall tasks on most popular IQ tests since the early 1900s, widespread adoption of comprehensive memory batteries was not seen until the beginning of the 21st century.

Rapid Reference 2.2 lists the evolution of instruments used in clinical memory testing, and Rapid Reference 2.3 lists credible memory phenomena identified by various researchers over the last 150 years. Most terms in Rapid Reference 2.3 have been formative in determining the content of contemporary memory tests, and so are readily recognized by most psychologists. Those memory phenomena found within the subtests of the WRAML3 are also noted in Rapid Reference 2.3 The meaning of the terms can be found in almost any introductory

> **DON'T FORGET**
>
> It was near the mid-20th century when the first comprehensive memory measure for adults appeared, but availability of pediatric memory batteries, like the WRAML, was not common until decades later.

22 ESSENTIALS OF WRAML3 AND EMS ASSESSMENT

≡ Rapid Reference 2.2

A Chronology of Normed Memory Tests

1941.	Rey-Osterrieth Complex Figure Test
1945.	Wechsler Memory Scale
1946.	Benton Visual Retention Test
1958.	Rey Verbal Learning Test
1974.	Selective Reminding Task
1987.	California Verbal Learning Test
1987.	Wechsler Memory Scale-Second Edition
1990.	Wide Range Assessment of Memory and Learning
1994.	California Verbal Learning Test–Children's Edition
1994.	Test of Memory and Learning
1997.	Children's Memory Scale
1997.	Wechsler Memory Scale-Third Edition
2000.	California Verbal Learning Test–Second Edition
2003.	Wide Range Assessment of Memory and Learning–Second Edition
2007.	Test of Memory and Learning–Second Edition
2009.	Wechsler Memory Scale-Fourth Edition
2015.	Children and Adolescent Memory Profile
2017.	California Verbal Learning Third–Second Edition
2021.	Wide Range Assessment of Memory and Learning–Third Edition
2021.	Everyday Memory Survey

≡ Rapid Reference 2.3

Memory Phenomena that have Emerged from Past Research and Which are Found on WRAML3

Memory Phenomenon	On WRAML3?	Memory Phenomenon	On WRAML3?
Anterograde amnesia	Yes	Recognition memory	Yes
Retrograde amnesia	No	Meaningful vs. rote information	Yes

Memory Phenomenon	On WRAML3?	Memory Phenomenon	On WRAML3?
Episodic memory	No	Developmental changes with age	Yes
Semantic memory	Yes	Working memory	Yes
Explicit memory	Yes	Visual memory contrasted with verbal memory	Yes
Short-term (immediate) memory	Yes	Learning curve (new learning over trials)	Yes
Longer-term (delayed) memory	Yes	Immediate, delayed, and recognition comparisons	Yes
Eidetic memory	No	Working memory	Yes
Procedural memory	No	Primacy and recency	Yes

psychology or cognitive psychology text, and those assessing memory should be familiar with each as it pertains to testing as well as everyday life.

You will note that even though the delayed recall subtests on the WRAML3 utilize an aspect of long-term memory, they do not capture the construct fully. In fact, there are no normed, psychometrically sound measures of long-term memory. This, obviously, is not because long-term memory is

CAUTION

Tailored cognitive batteries are common in psychological assessment. Care should be exercised when comparing or integrating scores from different instruments since norms are likely based on different samples gathered at different times, and subject to different sampling techniques.

not an important aspect of our memory systems, but rather due to the difficulty of creating such a scale. In part, this is because everyone's background is different, and so creating a scale not biased to one or more cultural backgrounds would be challenging. Further, item difficulties of a long-term memory scale likely would change frequently. Questions like, "Who was Catherine the Great"? or "What country has the largest population?" can change in difficulty if a movie, videogame, or breaking news story happens to highlight this information. Accordingly, a scale made up of such questions would eventually have unknown validity as time passes after its standardization. This quandary could be circumvented using novel content, but for it to be a real long-term memory measure, testing would need to be completed months or years later, posing a situation most clinicians (and test developers) find impractical. Therefore, because of these numerous dilemmas, long-term memory, while important, is a domain of memory not typically assessed in memory batteries.

To conclude this section that focused on the research and historical underpinnings of memory assessment, the reader should note that a bibliography citing research completed specifically on WRAML2 with various clinical populations is included in the introductory chapter of the *WRAML3 Technical* manual. Research on WRAML3 is just beginning but should be increasingly available; using a platform like *Google Scholar* or *PubMed*, inserting the test's name as a search term will allow the reader to stay current as additional research is added. Findings in a domain of particular interest to you should be of value in developing WRAML background that will aid your own targeted understanding with the instrument and maybe also inspire your own research efforts in contributing to the memory literature using specific clinical populations.

ANATOMY OF MEMORY

Another avenue of investigation that contributed significantly to our understanding of memory is neuroanatomical research. Although a comprehensive review of the neurobiology of memory is well beyond

MEASURING MEMORY: FOUNDATIONS   25

the scope of this chapter, a brief discussion of the neural substrates of memory systems will provide an important backdrop to a discussion of memory assessment. For more in-depth discussions, excellent reviews, and clinical case examples, see Squire and Schacter (2002); Kolb and Whishaw (2021); and Blumenfeld (2021). Knowledge of the neurological aspects of memory and its pathology is important in guiding understanding and interpretation of clinical observations and test findings.

For memories to be formed, the individual must experience internal or environmental sensations; conscious awareness is not necessary. While memories can be formed and retrieved using any of our sense modalities, within our culture, visual and auditory systems are central. Therefore, historically, assessment of memory focused on these two modalities, with a greater emphasis placed on verbal recall. The verbal versus visual memory distinction provides an important heuristic for the clinician in that the left hemisphere is more oriented toward processing language-based memory and the right toward visuospatial memory (Zillmer, Spiers, & Culberston, 2008). It follows then that bilateral damage often affects both verbal and visual memory, whereas left hemispheric insult generally affects verbal memory more, and right hemispheric compromise tends to impact visual memory more. These are generalizations and need a number of qualifiers for precision, but the left-right localization notion just expressed for memory is good as a "rule of thumb."

Regardless of the sensory modality, several critical brain structures are involved in the development of memories, including the hippocampus, fornix, mamillary bodies, diverse thalamic nuclei, and distributed regions of the neocortex (see Figures 2.1, 2.2, and 2.3). Briefly, neural impulses travel from the sensory organs, primary cortex, and association neocortex to the medial temporal lobe regions including the hippocampal formation (Figure 2.1). The hippocampus and nearby structures (e.g., fornix, mamillary body, anterior thalamus) seem to be the location where associations are formed between new incoming information and previously processed information. (Figures 2.2 and 2.3 show increasingly greater detail of this important area of the brain.) Contemporary research

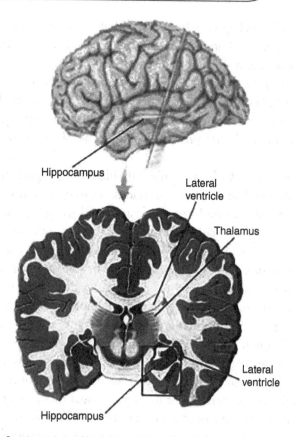

Figure 2.1 A coronal section of the brain showing the location of the hippocampus and related structures of both hemispheres. (McGill University / www.thebrain.mcgill ca / last accessed 27 September 2023).

of neuroscientists is examining functions of smaller and smaller areas within this region [e.g., the dentate gyrus, subiculum] and discovering yet greater complexity of memory storage and retrieval functions. For example, even synapses themselves are now thought to have information processing capacity (Maass & Markram, 2002). Relatedly, recent research seems to demonstrate that astrocytes can manage the limited space in the brain's hippocampus by pruning unwanted synapses, or the connections between neurons which can cause problems and lead to neurodegeneration (Koeppen, 2018).

MEASURING MEMORY: FOUNDATIONS 27

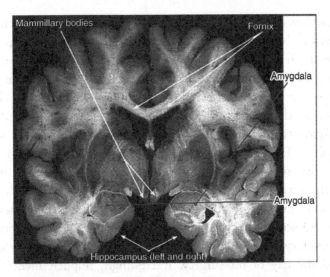

Figure 2.2 Hippocampus, fornix, and amygdala: bilateral, medial temporal lobe structures of the brain–coronal presentation. (BrainInfo / http://braininfo.org/ / last accessed 27 September 2023).

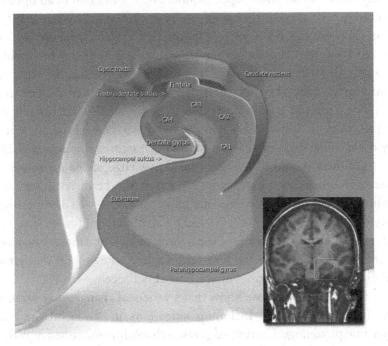

Figure 2.3 Some of the important hippocampal structures that are essential for laying down new memories. (Courtesy of Dr. Frank Gaillard).

Regardless of the source, insult to the hippocampal region can result in a person's being able to recall immediately a brief stimulus such as a picture or short sentence, but seconds later that information is less available to the person because the compromised region cannot fully participate in processes involved for storing new information. This was dramatically discovered from a patient who in the mid-1950s underwent the surgical removal of much of the hippocampal structures in both hemispheres in order to remedy his intractable seizures (Corkin, 2002). While the surgery successfully eliminated most of the seizures, unfortunately, it rendered the man, known as HM, mostly unable to lay down new memories. HM's old memories remained available, but despite IQ scores in the average range, he was unable to function in contemporary society because his "conscious life" never progressed beyond the day of his surgery. Interestingly, implicit memory (i.e., memory not dependent on conscious learning) was less impaired for HM. Squire presents a good overview related to the legacy of HM to neuroscience in his 2009 paper (Squire, 2009) and again in an updated volume on the science of human memory since (Squire & Wixted, 2011). Ongoing research has regularly shown that unilateral lesions seldom produce severe global memory impairment. But dominant hemisphere (usually the left) lesions in the hippocampal region can, as expected, cause more noticeable deficits in laying down new verbal memories, whereas unilateral lesions of the nondominant hemisphere (usually the right) tend to cause deficits in laying down new visual memories (Corkin, 2002; Papagno & Trojano, 2018; Schurgin & Flombaum, 2018).

Examiners should have some basic knowledge of the neurology of memory because insult to various parts of the brain resulting from injury or illness, or even genetic malformations, may well disrupt memory function in a variety of ways and by involvement of more than one mechanism. In a discussion of the neurobiology of memory, two levels need to be considered: One is the cellular level; the other is the system level, that is, the synergistic interaction of nerve cells.

At the cellular level, we know that a variety of changes may occur in an individual neuron, including alterations in its membrane and synaptic physiology. Cutting-edge research recently published in *Nature* by Vardalaki, Chung, and Harnett (2022) demonstrates that an estimated 30% of all synapses in the brain's cortex are silent and become active to allow the adult brain to continually form new memories and leave existing conventional synapses untouched. Vardalaki and colleagues suggest that the flexibility of synapses is critical for acquiring new information, and stability is required to retain important information, enabling one to more easily adjust and change behaviors and habits as well as incorporate new information.

At the systems level, two critical regions mediate memory: the medial aspect of the temporal lobe (hippocampus and its connecting fibers, as with HM) and the midline structures of the diencephalon. Damage to either of these regions typically renders the individual impaired in establishing new memories (anterograde amnesia). An inability to recall past memories (retrograde amnesia) is commonly thought of as the definition of the term *amnesia*, and it can also be associated with hippocampal damage. Interestingly, the duration of posttraumatic amnesia (PTA) after a concussion or brain injury has greater prognostic value for predicting functional and cognitive outcomes (e.g., executive functioning, memory, and processing speed) than the severity of the injury (Li, Robinson, & Tam, 2019).

> **DON'T FORGET**
>
> Clients with damage to the brain, regardless of its hemispheric location, may be at risk for having diminished memory performance in and across a variety of functional domains.

Research also demonstrates that the brain as a whole participates in memory functioning. Thus, patients with damage to the brain, regardless of its hemispheric location, may be at risk for having diminished memory performance in and across a variety of functional domains (Takehara-Nishiuchi, 2021). Accordingly, there seems to be a nonspecific lowering of memory performance associated with neurological dysfunction in general. Because attention is a precursor to memory (e.g., see Riccio, Reynolds, & Lowe, 2001), it is not always clear whether decreased recall is attributable to affected memory systems or their related attention and concentration processes, so assessing both is necessary. Damage to temporal and temporolimbic structures will also disturb attention and concentration, as will frontal lobe damage, all masquerading as memory deficiencies. However, for intact brains, for new information entering the hippocampal circuit, long-term storage occurs as this structure seems to distribute the information via various neural pathways to the cerebral cortex, where memories have received the most extensive processing and are the least vulnerable to injury. Long-term memory, the recall of well-established information or events, tends to be one of the most robust of neural functions, while sustained attention, concentration, and the formation of new memories tend to be among the most fragile and, subsequently, the most sensitive to neural insult.

> ### PUTTING IT INTO PRACTICE
>
> Patients with damage to any region of the brain may be at risk for having diminished attention and memory performance, so assessing both is important.

> ### DON'T FORGET
>
> Memory can be fragile or robust! Old established memories are the last to be disturbed in most forms of trauma and even in degenerative neurological diseases, but the ability to form and acquire new memories can be disrupted sometimes by even mild head injuries. Accordingly, disruption in recent memory is often the first detected symptom of a degenerative central nervous system disease such as dementia of the Alzheimer's type.

Along with content-laden memory, a secondary emotional component is also stored with long-term memories. The amygdala and its surrounding structures are responsible for coloring informational memories with feeling. This emotional component has not been a focus of formal memory assessment or investigation, although it serves as an important cue when memories are retrieved. However, it is thought that the binding of emotion to informational aspects of memory is an ongoing part of memory that allows us to recognize whether positive, negative, or neutral affect is associated with past occurrences and to act accordingly. While not often recognized, this memory component is also a foundational ingredient of psychotherapy.

MEASURING MEMORY: FOUNDATIONS 31

Finally, along with the content of the memory as well as some emotional valence is a temporal marker that allows us to distinguish between memories of similar events that occurred at different times, such as accurately separating the recall of one year's holiday season from another.

IN THE PAGES THAT FOLLOW

With the foregoing background of both anatomical and memory testing evolution, this book is intended to introduce a variety of professionals to two widely used memory measurement instruments. The reader will initially be provided with a detailed but readable presentation of the WRAML3 followed by the EMS. For each, conveying clinical utility was a principal objective. You will find that each instrument's discussion reflects extensive clinical familiarity with the instrument, which is likely attributable to each discussion being written by a co-author of the respective instrument. For that reason, some bias undoubtedly has slipped into the narrative. However, we have tried to be objective and forthright in our treatment of the material, and it is hoped that the deep test familiarity will result in a good amount of timely, authoritative, and useful information for the reader. However, remember that all well-constructed and validated tests, despite their impressive sophistication, are only tools a well-trained clinician employs to form sound opinions. A misused tool can harm the object on which it is employed, even when there are the best of intentions. We hope you will find what follows of help in learning how to use these tools skillfully as you develop further proficiency in the clinical assessment of memory.

SOME CAUTIONS

Memory assessment is a particularly complex task requiring knowledge of lifespan developmental aspects, individual differences, psychometrics, individual assessment skills, clinical acumen and experience. Evaluation of the pediatric and senior populations, as well as individuals with central nervous system injury or illness, poses special challenges as well and requires far more than technical literacy with a test and its accurate administration. Memory is a complex phenomenon that, as we have just discussed, can be broken into numerous subcomponents, not all of which can be assessed with the WRAML3, the EMS, or any other lone scale of memory. Further, and as also mentioned earlier, many conditions other than memory deficits can mimic memory impairment. This is especially true for older patients whose medications may be taken improperly, younger adults who may be involved in recreational drug use, in youth with attention regulation problems, and in patients who are medically ill, such as those who have hypothyroidism or undiagnosed renal problems. Even something as common as poor eyesight or hearing loss can be overlooked and misinterpreted as a memory deficit. Consequently, a recently completed medical evaluation may be an important appointment for a high-risk patient prior to their assessment of memory functioning. Also, as mentioned earlier, motivation and effort can play an important role in memory performance, especially since tasks can seem less inherently interesting, tend to be fatiguing, and can engender elevated anxiety from concerns about what the test may uncover. Therefore, significant fatigue, psychiatric symptoms, or resentment from mandated testing can result in lower scores. Conversely, one also needs to be concerned about motivation to exaggerate impairment because of external factors such as a pending legal settlement. For these reasons, Performance Validity measures can be found on both the WRAML3 and EMS and serve as indicators of what degree of effort has been expended.

It is also important for those directly or indirectly using the scientific literature related to memory to humbly acknowledge and support the paradigm shift toward a more culturally sensitive science and practice within the field. Much of what is "known" may need modification or qualifiers as we work to embrace the best principles of science along with relevant aspects of inclusiveness, antiracism, justice, equality, access, and economic disparity.

Even though they will not be covered here, it deserves mention that many of the "basics" learned in introductory testing courses remain important to observe, such as the importance of establishing rapport,

MEASURING MEMORY: FOUNDATIONS 33

maintaining a comfortable and quiet testing environment, and insuring test security. These and many more areas related to good testing preparation are reviewed in subsections of Chapters 1 and 2 of the WRAML3 Administration manual, and despite hearing most of these guidelines before, regularly merit our attention.

By now it should be quite clear that quality memory test administration and interpretation are formidable tasks. It is hoped that the information on this and the coming chapters will make the completion of such tasks easier to perform and done at a high level of caring and professional sophistication.

> **DON'T FORGET**
>
> A thorough knowledge of the patient's history, current status, and physical state is crucial to memory test interpretation and for the generation of useful intervention recommendations.

🏹 TEST YOURSELF 🏹

Foundations

Decide if each of the statements below is True or False:

1. The major domains evaluated in most memory tests are short-term and long-term memory.
2. Among the most common complaints of individuals following mild head injury are difficulties with memory and attention.
3. The first Binet-Simon intelligence scale included a significant focus on memory skills.
4. Memory evaluation is nearly always included by psychiatrists and other physicians when conducting a mental status exam.
5. Hippocampal formations play a major role in distributing information into long-term storage.
6. Anterograde amnesia is a term related to difficulties in establishing new memories.

7. Poor performance on multiple sections of a comprehensive memory battery such as the WRAML3 provides strong proof that there is some kind of memory impairment in the person being evaluated.

8. Both the WRAML3 and the EMS can be used in the assessment of retrograde amnesia.

9. Alexander Luria was a principal force in the development of psychometrically sound memory assessment measures.

10. The case of HM provided support for the notion that recall of past events could often be erased when certain parts of the cortex are damaged.

11. The incidence of Alzheimer's and Lewy Body Dementia is about the same in those older than 65 years of age.

Answers: 1. = False; 2. = True; 3. = True; 4. = True; 5. = True; 6. = True; 7. = False; 8. = False; 9. = False; 10. = False; 11. = False

Three

OVERVIEW OF THE WRAML3

The WRAML3 is an individually administered test battery designed to assess memory ability in children and adults. The battery is intended for clinical evaluation of immediate, delayed, and recognition components of verbal and visual memory, and it provides global as well as more focused estimates of memory performance such as working memory and attention/concentration. The test remains appropriate for use in a wide variety of venues of clinical practice such as private practice, schools, hospitals, retirement centers, as well as research sectors.

The WRAML3 is not tied to any specific model of memory. Rather, the battery attempts to integrate widely accepted neuropsychological concepts with the aim of providing the most useful clinical information, given the typical time constraints observed for most evaluations. This chapter will provide an abbreviated overview of WRAML3's structure and rationale. The discussion is intended to lay the groundwork for the

---

Essentials of WRAML3 and EMS Assessment, First Edition.
Wayne V. Adams, David V. Sheslow, and Trevor A. Hall.
© 2024 John Wiley & Sons, Inc. Published 2024 by John Wiley & Sons, Inc.

36 ESSENTIALS OF WRAML3 AND EMS ASSESSMENT

next chapter that will explore each subtest and its process scores emphasizing their rationale and interpretation. In contrast, the following chapter will provide an overview that will aid in developing a better understanding of subtests that contribute to individual Indexes and prepare the reader for Chapters 5 and 7 which focus more on an integrated interpretation using all parts of WRAML3 and other commonly available findings.

We begin with a section provided especially for those transitioning from WRAML2 to WRAML3, but which nonetheless provides useful background that should also be helpful to those not familiar with prior editions of the test.

FROM WRAML2 TO WRAML3

Generally speaking, a clinician familiar with WRAML2 can learn to administer WRAML3 with relative ease because of considerable format and procedural similarity. Therefore, this section is written especially for those who are familiar with WRAML2 and are transitioning to WRAML3. As with many psychological tests in common use, periodically there is a need to restandardize these instruments in order to update norms to better represent demographic changes in the population. That process invites improvements in the structure, format, and content of the test that arise from new research findings as well as user and other stakeholder feedback. A new edition also allows for recalibration of item difficulties for test content that is retained. Lastly, revision affords an opportunity to update artwork and wording, so users and clients continue to find materials unbiased and appealing, having a contemporary feel. Each of these areas affording test improvement has been exploited in WRAML3's restandardization.

What has not changed in the new edition is the original goal of making a reasonably comprehensive test of memory pleasant for an examiner to administer, easy to score, appropriate across a wide age range, fun for an examinee to take, and diagnostically useful, all while providing data that rest on a strong psychometric foundation. Given that memory assessment can have tedious formats, it was no small task to incorporate enjoyment along with empirical rigor. WRAML2 users transitioning to "the 3" will be glad to know that a good portion of the battery's subtests and their formats will be familiar; in some cases, even the directions are nearly identical. The changes you will discover will hopefully elicit "ahs" reflecting feelings that each encountered modification improves the ease of administration and/or increases the worth of what the test's findings deliver.

The development of the WRAML3 was guided by several broad objectives:

1. Foremost, to provide a psychometrically sound measure of clinically relevant memory processes that would span a wide age range. To this end, the authors want to acknowledge the integrity of the Pearson staff in sampling, checking and rechecking data, orchestrating standardization, and carefully reviewing the necessary statistical analyses to insure WRAML3's high technical standard.

2. To provide a flexible but comprehensive test of memory that could respond to limitations engendered by a healthcare environment that tends to focus on the need for greater efficiency without negatively affecting outcomes. Time needed for evaluation is a key consideration and with it comes a variable interest for both quantitative and qualitative levels of analysis. To that end, three formats of the WRAML3 are now available that balance information obtainable with time available. Consequently, the different formats allow examiners the option to sample memory when a brief re-evaluation or screening is desired, or to conduct the traditional comprehensive assessment of memory as part of a larger psychoeducational or neuropsychological evaluation, or something in between.

3. To insure WRAML3 reflects important developments in neuropsychology over the past decade. This not only reflects increased emphasis on working memory but also the increased interest in dementia and other disorders affecting geriatric memory decay. To the last point, compared to WRAML2,

WRAML3 has an increased emphasis on the importance of "longer-term" recall. With the early memory tests discussed in the last chapter, there was a primary focus on immediate memory, indirectly defining it as the essence of memory. But we now know that examinees can sometimes perform reasonably well on immediate memory tasks but fail to retain that information minutes later, and so be misidentified as having no memory deficits without a re-examination after a delay interval. To this end, the WRAML3 provides a more complete array of longer-term memory tasks (Delayed and Recognition subtests) along with all the immediate "core" subtests found in WRAML2.

4. To enhance more nuanced memory assessment by adding additional "process" options designed to assist the examiner in better understanding how a given score might have been achieved, often contributing to enhanced diagnostic formulations.

5. To maintain enough similarity with WRAML2 that learning the new edition would be relatively straightforward and that encountered modifications were seen as improvements, not encumbrances.

Rapid Reference 3.1 lists the major changes made to the WRAML3. These include: (1) the addition of a Performance Validity Indicator (PVI) which will allow Examiners to evaluate whether reasonable client effort has been extended during battery administration; (2) the Design Memory subtest has been significantly revised so that it is now a parallel version of Verbal Learning, that is, four learning trials of a single stimulus card; the subtest is now known as Design Learning reflecting this new format; (3) similarly, a Visual Working Memory subtest has replaced the Symbolic Working Memory subtest, thereby also providing a visual counterpart to the Verbal Working Memory subtest; (4) a delayed memory component has been added for the Picture Memory and Design Learning subtests allowing a Delayed Visual Memory Index to join the lone Delayed Verbal Memory Index that appeared in WRAML2; (5) all Recognition subtests now have four-choice options

OVERVIEW OF THE WRAML3 39

≡ *Rapid Reference 3.1*

Major Changes to WRAML2 found in WRAML3

Modification	WRAML2	WRAML3
Performance Validity Measure	None	A two-component Performance Validity measure added
Immediate ("Core") Memory Subtests	Six "Core" subtests	Five of the six core subtests similar in format; Design Memory replaced with Design Learning, a visual counterpart to Verbal Learning. Finger Windows administration format greatly simplified.
Delay Memory Subtests	Two subtests	Four subtests (addition of Delayed memory versions of Picture Memory and Design Learning)
Recognition Memory Subtests	Four subtests, each with two-choice items	Four subtests, each with four choice items
Working Memory	Verbal Working and Symbolic Working Memory subtests	Addition of a Visual Working Memory subtest that is a parallel version of the Verbal Working Memory subtest (Symbolic Working Memory subtest dropped)
Abbreviated Versions	One four-subtest option (approx. 20 minutes)	One four-subtest option (approx. 25 minutes) A two-subtest option (approx. 13 minutes)
Qualitative Analyses Data	Multiple data sets on 5 subtests	Now called "Process Scores," 14 data sets exist nested within 4 core subtests

Modification	WRAML2	WRAML3
Age range	5–85+ years	5–90+ years
Age division within some subtest's administration	5–8 years old and 9 years and older	5–9 years old and 10 years and older
Administration sequence	Core subtests 1–6 interspersed with Delayed and Recognition subtests	The same 6 Core subtests (but starting with Picture Memory and then alternating visual, verbal, visual, etc.) interspersed with Delayed and Recognition subtests
Subjective rating of functional adult memory performance	None	While a separate measure, the *Everyday Memory Survey* (with *Self-Report* and *Observer* Versions) was normed for adults using a large portion of the WRAML3 standardization sample

(including a "none" choice) for each item rather than just the two options found on the second edition, greatly decreasing the potential for inflated recognition subtest scores from guessing; (6) a Brief (two-subtest) version of the WRAML3 has been added providing a second and yet more abbreviated (10–15 minutes) format allowing for a visual and verbal memory "sampling" when examiner time is restricted or when examinee stamina is limited; and (7) a much simplified administration and scoring format for the Finger Windows subtest was created. All these changes are thoroughly discussed either in this or the next chapter.

Another small but important alteration WRAML2 users should be aware of is the "age break" change found within subtests, other than Design Learning. These subtests continue to have somewhat different directions and content for younger and older examinees, but the age

OVERVIEW OF THE WRAML3 41

break comes between 9- and 10-years of age rather than 8- and 9-years. That is, WRAML has always provided different materials more appropriate to the younger age cohorts in order to achieve better developmental correspondence. With

> **DON'T FORGET**
>
> Subtest age "breaks" designed to achieve developmental correspondence between content and the examinee's age, all occur at age 10 years.

WRAML3, whenever those age-based format and content differences occur, the break is always at age 10 years. There are clear reminders in the *Administration* manual and on all Record Forms identifying where these breaks should be observed.

An additional minor change will be noticed in the Verbal Learning subtest. The difficulty of word "map" was found to have increased somewhat since the last standardization, so another easier "m-word," "moon," replaced it. That is the only change made with this subtest.

Additional aesthetic changes will be noticed throughout WRAML3 such as new artwork, as well as some minor changes in directions and procedures, and a Q-global scoring option. All subtest changes are described in detail in the next chapter. However, none will require much "re-tooling" for experienced WRAML2 examiners, other than for the two new subtests, Design Learning and Visual Working Memory.

PERFORMANCE VALIDITY

One of the important additions to WRAML3 was a PVI. Over the last decade, the importance of accurately assessing examinee effort has been stressed as a key element in test interpretation, especially on tests that are demanding sustained effort (Kirkwood, 2015; Larrabee, 2012). Obviously, a memory test is such a measure. Even before beginning the task of interpreting results, examiners must first determine if their examinee is giving a reasonable amount of effort (or if that effort is in the service of "faking bad") on the tasks being administered. In the past, it was common to note in test reports subjective statements like, "a reasonable amount of effort was expended by the client, and therefore the results reported below are considered valid." Unfortunately, many research studies have shown that examiners, even those with years of experience, are not accurate judging those expending genuine effort vs. those who are trying to "fool" the examiner by feigning deficits or just disengaging because of fatigue (Kirkwood, 2015; Larrabee, 2012; Schroeder & Martin, 2021). Consequently, measures of what has come to be known as "Performance Validity" have been developed. Typically, these were standalone measures and have demonstrated that they do a credible job determining when effort is suboptimal (e.g., the TOMM [Tombaugh, 1997] and the Word Memory Test [Green & Astner, 1995]). Because a standalone test makes an all-or-none determination, there has been a reasonable argument made that the cognitive tests themselves should also embed effort measures since it is possible that effort might be acceptable at the outset of an evaluation (when standalone measures are often administered) but flag thereafter. Accordingly, WRAML3 includes an effort measure. It is comprised of two components, termed "indicators": (1) the score of the Attention/Concentration Index (ACI) and (2) results from parts of each of the four Recognition subtests. Note that the ACI result would be obtained about halfway through the testing if the entire WRAML3 were administered, whereas the Recognition test data would be primarily obtained near the end of the evaluation. Using both performance indicators has been found to classify with 97% accuracy those known to be trying to "fool" the examiner (i.e., intentionally performing poorly) vs. matched controls in the standardization sample. Therefore, the examiner need not rely on subjective judgment about credible levels of effort, but can instead use the embedded effort measure for empirical verification.

> ### PUTTING IT INTO PRACTICE
>
> Clinicians have been shown to be poor judges of examinee effort. Instead, for estimating effort, rely on free-standing and embedded Performance Validity (PV) measures. WRAML3 provides an embedded PV measure for this purpose.

OVERVIEW OF THE WRAML3   43

Obtaining the PV measure is straight forward once the battery has been administered. As mentioned above, the first indicator is based on the ACI score, using a cut-off standard score of 70; scores above 70 earn a PV score of 0, and ACI scores 70 or below earn 1 point. Fewer than 3% of the standardization sample earned ACI scores of 70 or below, obviously a low probability event.

Explaining the use of the second indicator (Recognition scores) is a bit more involved. First, remember that recognition, as noted in Chapter 2, is known to be a very robust form of memory. Using that notion, all the items of each recognition subtest were ordered so that the least difficult items appear as the first 5 items, thereby creating a set of 20 items that more than 95% of the standardization sample obtained 17 or more correct (even the youngest and oldest cohorts); that is, scores below 17 across those 20 items is another low probability event. Therefore, the second indicator is based on the total score of those 20 recognition items. Scores of 17 or higher earn a PV indicator score of 0 points, and sums of 16 or lower receive a score of 1.

When the two indicator scores are used together, a PV score can range from 0 (the sum of 0 + 0) to 2 (1 + 1). Like golf, a low PV score is better than a high one. A PV score of 0 should be interpreted as evidence for reasonable effort having been expended and labeled on the WRAML3 Record Form as "Acceptable" performance. A score of 2 should be interpreted as "Questionable," that is, the examiner should be very cautious about using some or all the scores generated, especially low ones, unless there are other grounds to believe their veracity. For example, a examinee with a history of moderate intellectual disability might legitimately obtain PV score of 1 or 2; or an adult unable to make it to your office independently because of dementia could also earn a PV score of 1 or 2. However, without evidence of extreme deficits in their history and/or presentation, examinees with an indicator score of 2 are very unlikely to be giving reasonable effort, and so the test results are probably underestimating their memory ability.

Other suggestions of suboptimal effort might be communicated by an inconsistent or illogical pattern of performance within or across subtests, such as missing easy items while passing much harder items or doing well on Delayed Recall tasks but poorly on the corresponding Recognition tasks. History and observations also can be useful for spotting inconsistencies such as during the testing the examinee relates a content-laden conversation (later substantiated) they had with a landlord the day before, but demonstrates sparse recall of the content from both Story Memory narratives.

To return to the scores associated with the PVI, earning a PV score of 1 is a third option and is labeled "Indeterminate" on the Record Form. Obviously, this means there is inconsistent evidence pointing toward suboptimal effort, so a judgment must be tentative. In such cases, careful clinical judgment will be required noting the PV result is suggesting caution. The 1-point score could suggest inconsistent effort, or it could be caused by a marked deficit in a given domain, such as severe weakness in visual memory that results in poor visual immediate, delayed and recognition performance that, in turn, results in a low Recognition indicator while the ACI indicator might fall within the acceptable range. Alternatively, an indicator score of 1 could result when effort has been adequate for the first half of the battery, but because interest or energy fell mid-way, the PV indicators yield acceptable ACI performance but low recognition scores (those subtests administered in the latter half of the battery). Sometimes, a standalone effort measure will also have been administered, in which case that input may help determine how to interpret the inconsistent embedded PV finding.

It is not unusual for examiners to tell examinees before the testing begins that methods will be used to help the examiner know if the examinee is giving tasks a reasonable try. Methods for doing this, including scripts, have been developed suggesting how to phrase such comments so they do not come across as hostile or blaming, but instead will enlist reasonable effort from the examinee (see Lippa [2018] for more on how to go about this). Such scripts can also be adapted to include parents or others who have been shown can instruct a child not to do well in order to gain some objective. Note that it is now common for a PV alert to be presented in a consent form or during a pre-evaluation interview.

STRUCTURE OF THE WRAML3

The structure of what was called *core* subtests in WRAML2, remains the same in WRAML3, and is shown graphically in Figure 3.1; all boxes in that figure involve immediate memory subtests. As can be seen, the basic or core battery is comprised of six subtests that yield three indexes: a Visual Immediate Memory Index, a Verbal Immediate Memory Index, and an ACI. Combined, six subtests define three indexes which together make up the General Immediate Memory Index. The focus of WRAML3 exclusively on visual and verbal memory is because of the prominence that these two sensory systems have in effective functioning within our society. Discussion of each of the core subtests and their derivatives follows in the next chapter.

The Visual and Verbal Immediate Index graphic can be used again to understand how the Delayed and Recognition subtests are organized, as shown in Figures 3.2 and 3.3. Each of the Delayed memory subtests is administered 20–30 minutes following its immediate memory subtest counterpart. The time interval is, in part, based on Ebbinghaus' classic finding that there is about 45–50% loss of immediate rote information associated with that interval; as well, 20–30 minutes is an interval that can be reasonably accommodated in most testing settings. The Delayed and Recognition

> **DON'T FORGET**
>
> The greatest amount of memory loss occurs within the first 20–30 minutes following the information being learned, and so measuring that expected decrement is important, especially if greater than expected forgetting is found.

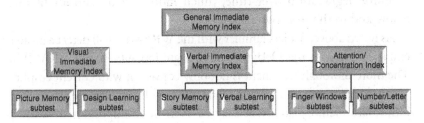

Figure 3.1 WRAML3 Immediate ("Core") Memory Subtests and Indexes.

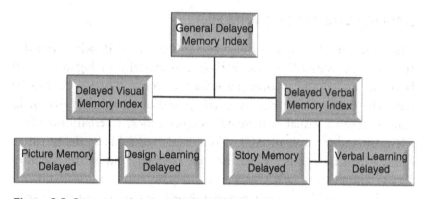

Figure 3.2 Structure for the WRAML3 Delayed Memory measures.

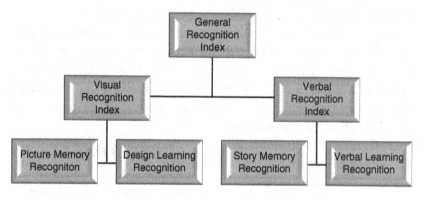

Figure 3.3 Structure for the WRAML3 recognition measures.

subtests are termed "supplemental" and various scenarios will call for or dispense with their use depending on the findings of the core (i.e., immediate) subtest findings. Given the importance of discrepant memory degradation over time, much more will be said about this below and in the next two chapters.

As noted above, readers familiar with the WRAML2 will detect a greater emphasis given to the Delayed and Recognition subtests in WRAML3. The more thorough treatment is not only consistent with current emphases on disorders of memory but, while it is useful to determine the level of immediate memory ability, it may be even more important to learn if memory is proportionately retained after 20–30 minutes. Adding the delayed components better reflects "real-world" aspects of functional memory. So, like with HM described in Chapter 2, while the ability to immediately recall a conversation or where one just placed important papers is important, it is even more important that each can be recalled a short time later. Some convincingly argue, in fact, that delayed memory performance should be *the* measure used when considering memory capacity rather than the traditional immediate memory result often reported.

The increased emphasis on Recognition tasks is also based, in part, on increasing awareness of the difference between memory retrieved and memory stored. For most of us, it is not unusual when trying to recall a piece of information, such as a person's name or an Internet password, to fail our attempt. However, without review, the information sometimes "percolates" to the surface seconds, minutes, or hours later. It would be difficult to logically argue that the word or concept had not been stored, otherwise how did it reappear? Instead, it seems more plausible to posit that there is a retrieval mechanism involved which sometimes may be faulty or inefficient, falsely giving the impression that the snippet of information had been forgotten. Cued recall, the process underlying recognition memory, often brings a "lost memory" into awareness, and that recognition component of recall has been shown to be rather robust well into old age. Therefore, in a memory battery, teasing apart the sub-processes of retrieval and storage is a useful and important test feature. Further, as will be mentioned later, the amount of testing time or examiner effort needed to obtain Delayed Recall results after having administered the immediate memory tasks, is relatively modest, so there is the potential for high yield with minimum investment. It should also be mentioned that memory performance on recognition tasks seems quite resistant to forgetting (compared to immediate and delayed processes), and so its measurement may be especially crucial when working

> **DON'T FORGET**
>
> Assessing recognition memory allows comparison between memory storage and retrieval. Clients in the early stages of dementia or who recently sustained a brain injury may especially struggle with retrieval of newly learned information that may nonetheless be stored but difficult to retrieve.

PUTTING IT INTO PRACTICE

Recognition memory is particularly robust. If there is no difference between Immediate and Delayed subtest scaled scores, it is rare that will there be a significant decline in performance observed on the corresponding Recognition subtests. However, for the PVI, the Recognition subtests are required.

with more impaired clients such as those in early recovery from a significant brain insult or in early stages of dementia.

In addition to the core Immediate, and optional supplemental Delayed and Recognition counterparts, there are several additional optional, but nonetheless important subtests that are available to further evaluate and parse various aspects of memory. Because of the importance of verbal memory in day-to-day functioning, the Sentence Memory subtest has been retained in WRAML3. Sentence Memory likely captures the short-term verbal memory demands made when trying to follow oral directions or convey a message just received to another. As will be discussed in the next chapter, Sentence Memory can also be part of useful comparisons with performance on other verbal subtests that make greater (e.g., Story Memory) and lesser (e.g., Number Letter) verbal demands.

In recent years, there has been a marked interest in phenomena associated with working memory. Working Memory is often defined as the ability to briefly hold onto information while organizing or manipulating that information in short-term memory (Baddeley, 1992; Dehn, 2015). While the Verbal Working memory subtest was included on the WRAML2, the new edition also provides a visual working memory analogue allowing visual/verbal comparisons. Since many everyday recall tasks utilize working memory, providing this coordinated and co-normed "package" when desired by the examiner was an important addition. Much more will be said of the working memory subtests in the next two chapters.

Timing Details

There are no time limits imposed on examinees for responding to any subtests in the battery; however, there are four subtests for which the examiner must carefully observe exact stimulus presentation times to

OVERVIEW OF THE WRAML3 49

achieve a standardized administration: Picture Memory, Design Learning, Finger Windows, and Visual Working Memory. In addition, all Delayed Memory subtests must be administered

> **DON'T FORGET**
>
> Nowhere within subtests of the WRAML3 are there response time limits imposed on examinees.

within an interval of 20–30 minutes following the administration of their immediate memory counterparts. This applies as well when the examiner chooses to use a Delayed subtest as part of either of the two abbreviated formats.

While, as stated above, there are no time limits on how long an examinee has to respond, elapsed time is an enemy of memory performance. Accordingly, examinees are appropriately urged to gently intervene when an examinee fails to respond in a reasonable time using prompts like, "It is okay to guess," or "just try your best," and "is it okay to move on as no one gets all the items." There are no "bonus points" or other scoring adjustments based upon examinee performance times anywhere in the battery.

The administration of the six core subtests by an experienced examiner typically takes less than 40 minutes. That varies somewhat by examinee age, with older adult examinees requiring a bit more time. While some perfectionistic, anxious, or compulsive clients (and examiners!) will need encouragement to move along, most clients will perform within the administration time intervals just stated and found below. These time approximations may be especially useful in estimating appropriate elapsed time intervals to use before administering Delayed Memory subtests when planning a partial administration of WRAML3.

The additional time needed for administration of the four supplemental Delayed Memory subtests is about 10 minutes; the four supplemental Recognition subtests take about 18 minutes more. There are also two supplemental Working Memory subtests, which together generally require about 20 minutes to administer. The final supplemental subtest already mentioned is Sentence Memory which takes about 3 to 4 minutes. A summary of time estimates for each WRAML3 testing format is found in Rapid Reference 3.2. Specific averages for each subtest and format for each age cohort can be found

50 ESSENTIALS OF WRAML3 AND EMS ASSESSMENT

≡ Rapid Reference 3.2

Time Estimates for Administering Different WRAML3 Formats (Minutes)

WRAML3 Formats				
Core (Immediate Memory)	Entire Battery	Screener	Brief (Core)	Brief (Delayed and Recognition)
30–35	77–89	24–28	12–14	25–29

in Table 2.2 of the *WRAML3 Administration* Manual. In that same table are also times for special clinical groups; it will be noted that those times do not vary much from those obtained for the standardization sample.

As will be noted in Rapid Reference 3.2, the two abbreviated versions of the test, Screener and Brief formats, require about 24 and 13 minutes, respectively. While there are 17 subtests in the total battery, the examiner has some flexibility in how those can be put together by choosing different formats. How that can be done will be the topic of Chapter 7. Subtests with sequential items observe the customary test progression from easy to gradually harder items, and basal and ceiling discontinue rules are often employed to speed along subtest administration.

Scores Available

The scores that most psychologists using tests have come to expect are provided by WRAML3; a listing is found in Rapid Reference 3.3. Tables for Indexes for all formats (Standard, Screener, and Brief) include standard scores (M = 100, SD = 15), standard errors of measurement, confidence intervals, and percentiles; similar tables are also provided for all subtests and allow conversion of raw scores to scaled scores (M = 10, SD = 3).

OVERVIEW OF THE WRAML3 51

≡ Rapid Reference 3.3

Scores Available in WRAML3

- Performance Validity Indicator (cut-off scores)
- Standard (Scaled) Scores, Confidence Intervals, Standard Errors of Measurement, and Percentiles for:
  - General Indexes (Immediate, Delayed, Recognition)
  - Visual Indexes (Immediate, Delayed, Recognition)
  - Verbal Indexes (Immediate, Delayed, Recognition)
  - Attention/Concentration Index
  - Working Memory Index (Visual and Verbal subtests)
- Discrepancy Scores (Critical p values and Base Rates)
- Process Scores (14 of these optional scores are available with standard scores and/or cut-off scores)
- Age Equivalents (ages 5–22 years)

It is usual to find differences among the scores mentioned in the above paragraph. To assist the examiner in determining whether a difference merits attention, WRAML3 provides a conventional "two factor" decision-making model. Typically, to decide if any finding is clinically important, the finding must be both statistically significant and relatively rare. Statistical significance for discrepancy analyses is provided for both the .05 and .10 levels. Typically, the $p \leq .05$ level is used by most examiners to be reasonably certain that a given finding is not the result of chance. However, on occasion, clinicians may choose to use the .10 significance level when they want to be sure they are not dismissing something that may have diagnostic importance, especially if findings elsewhere in the history or evaluation support that suspicion. The second component that helps with deciding if a result deserves attention is "Base Rate." Base rates tell the examiner the frequency a given finding occurred in the standardization sample, and are provided from the $\leq 2\%$

52 ESSENTIALS OF WRAML3 AND EMS ASSESSMENT

occurrence rate up to the ≤ 25% of occurrence. It is left to the examiner to decide how stringent to be in deciding how rare a finding must be to merit interpretive attention. Remember that it is possible for a finding to be statistically significant but nonetheless somewhat common, in which case, the clinician may want to consider it within normal limits and not warrant further clinical consideration. Thus, statistical significance provides the clinician evidence that a finding is unlikely to be the result of chance, and the base rate communicates how rare the finding is in the general population. Both metrics are important aids in test interpretation. Tables for significance levels and base rates are included for obtained discrepancies found between Indexes or subtests; most Process scores (discussed below) also have base rates provided. Discrepancy tables for subtests and indexes can be found in Appendices 18–21 of the *Administration* Manual.

It should be noted that all possible comparisons between indexes and subtests are not included in the manual (there would be hundreds), but readers should know that on the Pearson website, additional discrepancy comparisons have been computed and posted as users make a case for the importance of their inclusion. So, if a comparison is not found in the *Administration* manual, check the following website for WRAML3 *Technical Reports*: (https://www.pearsonassessments.com/content/dam/school/global/clinical/us/assets/wraml3/wraml3-technical-report-visual-and-verbal-index-comparisons.pdf). Alternatively, you can compute your own critical values using the SEM data provided in the *Technical* Manual (Table 3.4).

Age equivalents (Table A.28, *Administration* manual) are also available for clients, but only up to age 22 years, since, as descriptors, age equivalent scores, which are psychometrically weak to begin with, become increasingly less meaningful after childhood. That is, while there may be some heuristic value for age equivalents when consulting with teachers or parents, examiners should not believe or communicate that a 15-year-old with a GIMI age equivalent of a 10-year-old "remembers like a 10-year-old." Technically, the subtest raw scores earned by the 15-year-old and then converted into scaled scores, are equivalent to the summed scaled scores earned by an average 10-year-old. Interpretation beyond that is likely speculative.

Also available for clinical investigative use are more than a dozen "Process Scores" which are provided for aiding diagnostic precision. These will be especially welcome for those who embrace the "detective" role in assessment, looking for clues on how a given examinee may approach a memory task. These were called Qualitative Analyses in WRAML2, but while the name has changed, Process Scores still serve a similar function of mining already collected subtest data to focus on the "how" in addition to the "what" of test results. More will also be said about Process Scores and their use in the chapters that follow. Scaled scores and base rates are also provided for most Process scores.

Qualitative descriptors for performance levels appear in Table 4.1 of the *Administration* manual; an abbreviated version of that table is found in this chapter (Rapid Reference 3.4). Like with age equivalents, descriptors should prove helpful when discussing findings with those unfamiliar with more technical concepts such as standard scores or

≋ Rapid Reference 3.4

Score Descriptors Corresponding to Standard and Scaled Scores, and Percentiles

Qualitative Score Descriptor	Number of SDs from the Mean	Index Standard Score	Subtest Scaled Score	Percentile Rank
Extremely High	≥ +2.0	≥ 130	≥ 16	≥ 98th
Very High	+1.3	120	14	91st
High Average	+1.0	110	13	84th
Average	0	100	10	50th
Low Average	−1.0	85	7	16th
Very Low	−2.0	70	4	2nd
Extremely Low	< −2.0	< 70	< 4	< 2nd

percentiles. Be aware, though, that these descriptors are arbitrary terms with cut-offs based on standard deviation "distances" from the mean. As such, the descriptors may or may not be exactly consistent with the terminology or derivations used by other test instruments.

Psychometric Integrity

Extensive information related to development, standardization, reliability, and validity of the WRAML3 is found in its *Technical* manual. While no attempt will be made to summarize that detailed narrative here, several aspects are highlighted so that users can see at a glance that WRAML3 easily meets and often exceeds the high standards psychologists have rightly come to expect in the standardized tests made available to them in recent times. Details beyond what are mentioned below can be found in Chapters 2–4 of the *Technical* Manual.

Standardization. Well before standardization, many efforts were made to insure items and directions were understandable and free of obvious gender and ethnic bias. Items deemed acceptable were then administered to several small samples of child and adult volunteers to assess breath of difficulty and ease of comprehension for new content or procedures being considered for inclusion in the revision. Thereafter, a pilot sample of almost 200 volunteers representing young children, adolescents, young adults, and older adults, as well as others from several special groups (e.g., Intellectual Disability and Alzheimer's disease) were administered an initial "mock-up" draft version of the evolving subtests. The resulting data were then examined for psychometric qualities, adequacy of developmental coverage, again, apparent bias, as well as input from both examiners and examinees. Upon being satisfied with the results after this input and some additional modifications, standardization was planned. The normative sample consisted of 1,270 persons divided into 14 age bands representative of the US 2017 Census data with respect to gender, race/ethnicity, education level, and geographic location. Start points and Discontinue rules were eventually determined using these standardization data.

Reliability

A sample of reliability data is found in Rapid Reference 3.5 and shows that there is strong internal consistency across the subtests and indexes of the instrument. All coefficients there and appearing in the *Technical manual* exceed levels normally considered acceptable for cognitive tests. Examining test–retest reliability for a memory test is a bit of a dilemma since embedded within that traditional measurement procedure is the confound of the construct being measured—memory! That is, testing at Time 1 and then again at Time 2 some days later assumes the construct being measured is the same at both times, or said differently, it assumes short and longer-term memory abilities are comparable in those being tested. But we know that is not the case, especially in clinical

---

≋ Rapid Reference 3.5

WRAML3: Sample Reliability Data (Coefficient α)

Core Subtests ($N \geq 1,270$) (Immediate Memory)	Internal Consistency Reliability Coefficients
Picture Memory	.71
Story Memory	.89
Design Learning	.92
Verbal Learning	.90
Finger Windows	.78
Number Letter	.81

Indexes				
Visual Immediate Memory Index	Verbal Immediate Memory Index	Attention/ Concent- Ration Index	General Immediate Memory Index	General Delayed Memory Index
.87	.93	.84	.93	.91

populations. Even so, correlations are at respectable levels (*r*s ranging from .59 to .77 for subtests and .72 to .83 for indexes). Of greater clinical relevance, for subtests using meaningful material (e.g., Story Memory), scores differed across testings by 2.6 points, whereas with rote tasks (e.g., Number/Letter), the scores differed by 0.5 points. That is, as expected, meaningful memory tended to be stored and remembered better than rote, even with the 49-day average interval used in the WRAML3 test–retest study. Complete data sets for all subtests and indexes are found in Table 3.6 of the *Technical* manual.

Validity

Regarding validity, it is likely useful to mention that there are inter-correlation data of WRAML3 performance with several other test batteries often used in cognitive assessments found in the Validity chapter of the *Technical* manual (Chapter 4); Rapid Reference 3.6 lists the six tests included. Such comparison of results is of interest. For

≡ Rapid Reference 3.6

Tests Administered with the WRAML3. (Inter-correlation Data are Provided in the Validity Chapter of the WRAML3 *Technical* Manual)

Wide Range Assessment of Memory and Learning, Second Edition (WRAML2) (Sheslow & Adams, 2003)

Wechsler Memory Scale – Fourth Edition (WMS-IV) (Wechsler, 2009)

Wechsler Intelligence Scale for Children, Fifth Edition (WISC-V) (Wechsler, 2014)

Wechsler Adult Intelligence Scale, Fourth Edition (WAIS-IV) (Wechsler, 2008)

Wide Range Achievement Test, Fifth Edition (WRAT5) (Wilkinson & Robertson, 2017)

Wechsler Individual Achievement Test, Fourth Edition (WIAT-IV) (Wechsler, 2020)

OVERVIEW OF THE WRAML3   57

example, achieved performance between the WRAML2 and WRAML3 is surprisingly similar, typically less than two points per Index, making one wonder if the Flynn Effect exists or is as strong with memory testing as is typically found with intelligence testing. A sampling comparing WRAML3 with academic measures shows correlations between the two domains tend to be in the low moderate range, with the surprising result that the Number Letter subtest tends to be the most highly correlated core memory subtest across most academic domains, including reading, spelling, and math. Correlations between IQ and WRAML3 indexes and subtests generally show moderate correlations as well with the counterintuitive finding that correlations with adult IQ performance are noticeably higher than those with children. These IQ findings were similar to WRAML2.

Clinical Groups Findings

Also found in the chapter discussing validity are results from seven clinical groups, which are listed in Rapid Reference 3.7. Here is a sampling of some of those findings which may be of special interest and

---

≋ Rapid Reference 3.7

Clinical Diagnoses of Special Groups for Whom WRAML3 Findings are Included in the Technical Manual

- Attention-Deficit Hyperactivity Disorder
- Intellectual Disability—Mild
- Learning Disability in Reading and/or Written Expression
- Amnestic Mild Cognitive Impairment and Dementia of the Alzheimer's type, mild severity
- Mild Depressive Disorder
- Pediatric Brain Injury
- Simulated Head Injury

merit follow-up study since the sample size of each group tends to be 35 or fewer. More details related to the diagnosis and composition of each group are provided in the validity chapter of the *Technical manual*.

ADHD

As expected, the only significant differences found comparing index scores of this group with matched controls were on the Attention/Concentration (primarily from Finger Windows) and Working Memory Indexes (primarily from Visual Working Memory), suggesting that visual rote information is especially challenging to this clinical group. Also, performance on the Design Learning subtest was somewhat (but significantly) lower than the controls, possibly due to perceptual-motor inefficiencies commonly reported in this clinical population (e.g., Kleeren et al., 2023). But stated more positively, no significant differences were found with the non-clinical group's performance for 13 of the 17 WRAML3 subtests, and among indexes, only the Attention/Concentration and Working Memory Indexes were found lower.

Intellectual Disability—Mild

This clinical group had a mean IQ of 65, ranging from 54 to 72; a large majority of this group's WRAML3 Memory Indexes also fell within this range. Interestingly, the exception to this finding was Visual Immediate, Delayed and Recognition Index results, all of which were found in the mid 70s. One wonders if, generally, visual memory tends to be somewhat better preserved in this population, which if true, has academic and vocational training implications.

Learning Disability in Reading and/or Written Expression

While a mixed diagnostic group, it is of interest to note that 14 of 15 Index comparisons with a matched sample were statistically significant with respectable effect sizes, strongly implying that memory deficits are commonly found in this clinical population. These results are consistent with the study mentioned in Chapter 1 (Weniger & Adams, 2006).

Recognition, while significantly lower than controls, was nonetheless consistently higher than Delayed performance, suggesting both encoding and retrieval problems may be challenging those with reading/writing disorders.

Mild Cognitive Impairment and Mild Alzheimer's Dementia

While all subtest and index scores were significantly lower than those of matched controls, as might be expected, recall on immediate memory tasks was better than that demonstrated on delayed or recognition tasks. So, for this group, initial impressions of their memory ability will likely be overestimates of actual storage and functional recall. Accordingly, Number Letter was the subtest that stood out with the highest scaled score (=9.0), compared to other subtests that generally ranged from 5 to 7.

Major Depressive Disorder

There is inconsistency in the literature related to the degree depression affects test performance. In this sample, scores tended to be about .35 SD lower than matched controls, with no index falling below the average range. Even though about a third of the group was not taking anti-depressant medication, it is still reasonable to conclude that older adults with this disorder can be differentiated from those with mild cognitive impairment, an important finding in the differential diagnosis of mild dementia and depression. Also, testing depressed patients taking medication, and possibly those who are not, as well as testing patients with dysthymia versus major depression disorder would provide important clinical information.

Pediatric Traumatic Brain Injury

Results from this clinical group were surprising. While about half of the brain injuries sustained would be considered more serious than "mild" (e.g., "simple concussion"), there were no differences between a set of matched controls and those in this group which was evaluated 6 to 36 months post-injury. There are studies not showing such positive outcomes (e.g., Babikian et al., 2015). While there are several explanations for this unexpected benign finding, two that are overlapping and seem reasonable include the neuroplasticity of the nervous system at younger ages, and more immediate as well as sophisticated medical attention extended to these clients from the outset compared to even a decade ago.

Head Injury Simulator Group

This group was comprised of 48 volunteers who were asked to convince a "blind" examiner that they had sustained a head injury (basic background was furnished on the nature of head injury). However, in order to do that the volunteers were aware to not perform so badly that the examiner would suspect they were exaggerating their symptoms. This basic design is often used to determine if a standalone PV test is able to distinguish between feigning vs. real memory disturbance. Accordingly, using this common procedure, a validity study was designed including both the WRAML3 and a well-known PV measure (the Test of Memory Malingering [Tombaugh, 1997]). Results showed that the WRAML3 correctly classified 97% of the combined sample (those attempting to simulate injury vs. those not doing so). It was 99% accurate in picking out those who were not simulators, and there was a .52 probability of accurately identifying those not putting forth adequate effort. There was good agreement with the TOMM, but of interest, using both (free-standing and an embedded measure) increased the classification accuracy, supporting the use of both varieties of PV measures in "high-stakes" testing. It was clear that the WRAML3 subtests that contributed most to correctly discerning between the groups included the Recognition subtests as well as the two Attention/Concentration subtests (Finger Windows and Number Letter) leading to their selection as PV indicators.

Test Forms

There are three different forms associated with the WRAML3 Standard administration: Record Form, Picture Memory/Design Memory Immediate/Delayed Recall Response Booklet, and Picture Memory/Design Memory Recognition Response Booklet. The 28-page Record

OVERVIEW OF THE WRAML3   61

Form is designed to assist the examiner in administering and scoring the test in a manner that promotes accuracy and efficiency. Reminders of important procedural rules associated with each subtest's administration are provided. The content of each verbal subtest appears on the Examiner Form, eliminating the need to look in the manual for this material. The two Response Booklets provide a permanent record of the client's responses for the Immediate, Delayed, and Recognition components of the Picture Memory and Design Learning subtests, allowing them to be scored and re-examined later.

In addition to the forms associated with the Standard version of test administration, there is also an additional pair of forms for the Brief administration version of the test: the 12-page Brief Record Form and the Brief Response Booklet, the latter of which provides the forms necessary for administration and scoring of Immediate, Delayed, and Recognition components of the two subtests comprising this abbreviated format, avoiding undue waste and inconvenience using the much longer Standard Record Form and its two Response Booklets. Chapter 6 fully describes the content along with when and how to best utilize the Brief version of WRAML3.

It should be noted that special care is needed when using the subtest stimuli and the record forms related to all visual subtests. If test stimuli or prior examiner responses to them are ever seen outside of what is prescribed by the standardized procedures, that constitutes another "teaching" exposure, likely contaminating related administrations for delayed or recognition components. Consequently, it is important for the examiner to develop a system that is convenient yet that keeps test stimuli and examinee output out of sight when not the direct focus of the test administration. Rapid Reference 3.8 lists the contents of a complete WRAML3 testing kit. Rapid Reference 3.9 lists relevant publication information related to the WRAML3.

On-line Assists

WRAML3's publisher, Pearson, has provided on-line means to input WRAML3 raw scores and receive a completed "Score Report," saving examiners precious time. The report is delivered using a Pearson system

62 ESSENTIALS OF WRAML3 AND EMS ASSESSMENT

≣ Rapid Reference 3.8

WRAML3 Test Kit Components

The WRAML3 Test Kit includes the following materials:
- Administration and Technical Manuals
- 25 Record Forms (Standard administration)
- 25 Picture Memory/Design Memory Immediate/Delayed Memory Response Booklets (Standard administration)
- 25 Picture Memory/Design Memory Recognition Response Booklets
- 5 Record Forms (Brief administration)
- 5 Response Booklets (Brief administration)
- Complete set (7) of Picture Memory Stimulus cards
- Design Learning Stimulus Card
- Complete set (20) of Finger Windows Stimulus Cards
- Complete set (29) of Visual Working Memory Stimulus Cards
- Custom carry bag
- Digital Administration and Technical Manuals along with 1-year Q-global scoring and interpretive report subscription; includes unlimited scoring per user within an account. The digital asset is accessible by logging into Q-global and visiting the Q-global Resource Library. It is a view-only digital file.

known as Q-global, and converts the raw score input supplied by the examiner into all the tabled values found on the Record Form, including Discrepancy and Process Score analyses. In addition, Pearson also makes available a Q-global Interpretive Report that includes everything provided by the Q-global Score Report, but in addition, suggests ideas the examiner may wish to consider when formulating their own interpretation of a specific set of test results. More information pertaining to the Score and Interpretive Reports can be found on the Pearson website.

OVERVIEW OF THE WRAML3   63

☰ Rapid Reference 3.9

Publication Information for the WRAML3

Authors: Wayne Adams and David Sheslow
Publication Date: June 2021
Age Range: 5–90+
Administration Times:
  Core subtests: 30–40 minutes
  Screener subtests: 24 minutes
  Brief Version subtests: 13 minutes
Scoring and Interpretive software available
Publisher:
  NCS Pearson, Inc.
  5601 Green Valley Drive
  Bloomington, MN 55437
  +1 (800) 627-7271
  www.pearsonassessments.com

DIVERSITY ISSUES

Pearson test publishing company and the authors are proud of extending with WRAML3 the excellent record on diversity issues established with prior versions of the test. For WRAML3, this was achieved by multiple steps, starting with the early discussions related to revisions of the new edition. Preliminary picture stimuli, wording of items and instructions underwent internal and external reviews related to diversity issues. Planning for standardization made sure that the normative sample obtained appropriately reflected race/ethnicity proportions by using the most recent (2017) census data on five ethnic groups: African American, Asian, Hispanic White, and Other. The Other option encompassed race/ethnicities not included in the first four options including non-Hispanic multiracial, Native American, and Pacific Islander. As the battery neared standardization, internal statistical analyses were again completed for item bias. Then, stimuli were sent to a nationally recognized researcher on bias and diversity issues at the University of Chicago, who along with her class, reviewed all stimuli to "flag" any concerns. Appropriate modifications were made based upon the few concerns that were expressed.

Lastly, prior to standardization, all test items were analyzed for differential success/failure rates across all groups used in pilot testing, with special focus on gender and race (White, Black, and Hispanic). No consistent bias was detected. Sensitivity to gender and ethnic differences are injunctions found in the *Administration* and *Technical* manuals as well as this volume as illustrated in the section that follows.

USER QUALIFICATIONS, RESPONSIBILITIES, AND CAUTIONS

This and succeeding chapters are not intended as a substitute for the information found in the WRAML3 *Administration* manual. That and the *Technical* manual must be used to learn step-by-step instructions, rationale, guidelines, and content for all WRAML3 procedures. As indicated in the *Administration* manual, the WRAML3 should only be used by trained clinicians and/or researchers experienced in the administration of psychological tests, knowledgeable in the academic domain of memory, and having received supervised experience working with a variety of age groups and differing cultural and ethnic backgrounds as it relates to testing. Although a teacher or certified technician can learn with supervised practice how to administer and score the battery appropriately, the interpretation of the results should be restricted to those with graduate professional training and supervised clinical experience in the area of cognitive assessment, including memory. In addition, examiners should be familiar with *Standards for Educational and Psychological Testing* (American Educational Research Association, et al., 2014), and its subsequent periodic updates. Licensed or certified psychologists, speech and language pathologists, and learning specialists, including educational diagnosticians, are among those who traditionally have such training and may find the battery especially useful.

Training in assessment typically also includes an understanding of the importance of preparing the testing setting and the examinee so that

OVERVIEW OF THE WRAML3 65

the transition into and through the evaluation will go smoothly and be remembered as a positive experience. The many steps mentioned in most testing texts will not be reiterated here despite their importance to obtaining a representative sample of results. Some of those important aspects are included in a checklist (Rapid Reference 3.10) that can be used for training (or review) purposes. Space is left to add items unique to the testing setting in which you work.

≡ Rapid Reference 3.10

General Test Administration Rubric

	Yes	No
1. Room well lit		
2. Furniture comfortable and size-appropriate		
3. Room relatively free from distractions		
4. Participant seated and positioned appropriately at the table		
5. Examiner sits at a proper distance across table from participant		
6. Attempts to establish/maintain rapport evident		
7. Participant told breaks are okay		
8. Avoids use of words "test" and "pass/fail"		
9. All test forms are easily available but not visible to client		
10. Test materials available (e.g., test materials, pencils, timer)		
11. Any preliminary questions asked by participants answered		
12. Sequence of subtests followed accurately		
13. Examiner speaks loudly and clearly		
14. Responses encouraged if hesitant or unsure		
15. Responses recorded immediately and accurately		
16. Efforts to maintain motivation evident and appropriate		

	Yes	No
Add below those additional considerations unique to your setting.		
17.		
18.		
19		
20.		

Those trained in the use of psychological tests know to take precautions to preserve the security of test materials. These materials should, at all times, be considered similar to other clinical information and treated in a confidential and protected manner. For example, test kits, forms or reports should not be left or stored in unsecured areas, nor should test materials or the test manuals be made available to nonprofessionals or others with inappropriate training or questionable motives. While review of test results is appropriate and encouraged when working with clients, parents, and fellow professionals (such as teachers and therapists), consistent with HIPAA and FERPA guidelines (and updates) (FERPA, 1974; HIPPA, 1996), such activities never should include disclosure or copying of test items, record forms, or other test content that would compromise the security or validity of the test imperiling its usability as a measurement tool. This is an especially germane and sensitive topic in the era of misuse of social media and Internet blogging.

> **DON'T FORGET**
>
> Test kits and forms should never be left in unsecured physical or digital "areas." Likewise, leaving test forms open for "casual viewing" by an examinee or colleagues is also a serious breach of test protocol.

As noted in the *Administration* Manual, since the WRAML3 was normed using the traditional in-person format, it is unknown how its use in telepractice (administration by digital means) may affect performance. Studies may be underway to explore this question, but until those data are available, it is advised not to deviate from the standardization (in-person) format.

When evaluating those with special needs, one may be tempted to implement various alterations in test administration. At times, such modification may be necessary. Guidelines and various considerations when working with special populations are detailed in sections subtitled **Modifications** and **Accommodations** found near the end of the first chapter of the WRAML3 *Administration* Manual.

Finally, the WRAML3 is not intended as an exhaustive assessment of memory abilities, or even an instrument exclusively assessing memory abilities. As already discussed, memory processes are complex and intertwined with other cognitive, emotional, and environmental contributors that can impact memory performance during test administration. So, even if both WRAML3 manuals and record forms imply this is a test of memory, it more accurately should say, "is a test primarily of memory but including other cognitive and emotional processes." That is, cognitive testing is somewhat like using fitness machines. A given machine says it is designed to strengthen the trapezius, rhomboid and posterior deltoid muscles. And it does when used as directed. But obviously, the machine engages core, biceps, and numerous other muscle groups necessary for the targeted muscle groups to receive the specified attention. So, it is with any psychological test; the WRAML3 certainly evaluates memory processes, but in so doing it also activates attentional processes, executive functioning, personality traits, etc. Ultimately, the test is a tool that is intended to aid in professional decision-making, not an omniscient device honed to faultlessly appraise memory functioning and nothing else.

Rarely mentioned is another source of testing interference, namely the professionally integrative role of the examiner, the caring individual responsible for empathetically questioning, supporting, and emotionally connecting with the examinee on the one hand, while also being the data-driven detective well-versed in psychometrics and an expansive memory literature, striving to be rigid in testing procedures yet innovative in diagnostic formulation and remediation planning. Can new or even seasoned examiners be competent in all these disparate areas? While each examinee brings their unique background, competencies, and cognitive skills to the testing session, a similar aggregation of varying qualities is also true for the examiner. Like golf, psychological assessment can be easy to learn but hard to play well.

While the WRAML3 was standardized assuming all subtests would be administered, because of examiner time pressures and limited stamina in clients, it is not uncommon for clinicians to administer only portions of this and other tests. While clinically there does not seem to be any noticeable difference when this is done with the WRAML3, the reader is reminded that empirically, it is unknown how a partial administration or a subtest order alteration may impact an examinee's scores. For example, the core subtests alternate between visual and verbal memory demands; a change in this sequence could conceivably increase client fatigue by confronting them with multiple tasks that make extended memory demands of one sensory modality. Therefore, clinician should always be reluctant to deviate from a standardized administration, but when that occurs, they should approach findings with greater caution.

> ### CAUTION
>
> The clinician should always be reluctant to deviate from the standardized subtest sequence, but if that occurs, examiners should approach findings with greater caution.

With the background, rationale, guidelines, and injunctions of these first three chapters, let us proceed to the next two that will use much of this information as we turn to consider how to use the WRAML3 as a diagnostic instrument.

TEST YOURSELF

WRAML3 Overview

1. Which of the following WRAML3 subtests is thought to be the hardest for examiners to learn to administer and score properly?
   (a) Design Learning
   (b) Story Memory
   (c) Picture Memory Recognition
   (d) Finger Windows
   (e) Visual Working Memory

OVERVIEW OF THE WRAML3   69

2. **The age range for the WRAML3 is**
   - (a) 5 to 17 years.
   - (b) 6 to 22 years.
   - (c) 16 to 79 years.
   - (d) 18 to 85 years.
   - (e) 5 to 90 years.

3. **When comparing the Standard WRAML3 format to the abbreviated versions,**
   - (a) standard scores on the Standard version tend to be 5 to 10 points lower likely because of its greater length
   - (b) the Memory Index of both abbreviated versions tends to be less than 2 points different from the General Memory Index of the Standard version
   - (c) the correlations between the Standard and the two abbreviated versions mostly range from .50 to .75.
   - (d) the abbreviated versions primarily provide a quick measure of rote learning
   - (e) the abbreviated versions require the examiner to decide if they want to measure visual or verbal memory

4. **General Immediate Memory Index subtests are to Screener Index subtests as**
   - (a) 2:1
   - (b) 4:2
   - (c) 6:4
   - (d) 8:4
   - (e) 9:6

5. **Which statement is correct about WRAML3?**
   - (a) administering specified parts of the test has been approved to be done by telepractice means
   - (b) the test now provides norms for 1-, 2-, as well as 3-subtest abbreviated versions
   - (c) there is an increased emphasis on delayed and recognition memory assessment
   - (d) the full 8-subtest Standard administration requires about an hour
   - (e) each of the subtests assesses new learning over trials

70 ESSENTIALS OF WRAML3 AND EMS ASSESSMENT

6. **The WRAML3 Performance Validity Index helps examiners**
   (a) estimate if reasonable examinee effort has been demonstrated
   (b) assess whether validity quotients are being properly used
   (c) determine the degree of bias demonstrated for a given gender or ethnicity
   (d) determine if all intended parts of the test were administered properly
   (e) know if a given test administration fits the 3-component model of the factor analysis

7. **Which is correct with respect to findings from WRAML3 validity studies reported in the test's *Technical* Manual?**
   (a) A sample of those with ADHD demonstrated uniformly lower memory scores compared to matched controls.
   (b) A sample of those with Reading Disorders and/or Disorders of Written Expression demonstrated uniformly lower memory scores compared to matched controls.
   (c) A sample of those with Mild Cognitive Impairment and early stages of Alzheimer's Disease were largely free of memory problems compared to those later in the progression of these conditions.
   (d) Memory scores show very modest correlations with academic performance in the early grades.

Depressed individuals should not be administered the test because depression has been shown to significantly lower memory performance.

Answers: 1e, 2e, 3b, 4c, 5c, 6a, 7b

Four

INTERPRETING WRAML3 SUBTESTS, INDEXES, AND PROCESS SCORES

This chapter walks readers through the subtests comprising the WRAML3. While test Indexes will also be discussed, the emphasis will be on understanding subtests and how they fit together conceptually to comprise their respective Indexes, as well as how their results might be useful clinically. For each subtest, the several components listed below are provided to help examiners familiarize themselves with the various aspects of the battery's content, and better understand how various diagnostic formulations emerge from subtest findings. Rather than using the standardization sequence of subtest administration to guide the order of this chapter's narrative, you will find a conceptual organization with Visual, Verbal, Attention/ Concentration, and Working Memory Index groupings discussed separately. Further, individual subtest "families" (Immediate, Delayed,

---

Essentials of WRAML3 and EMS Assessment, First Edition.
Wayne V. Adams, David V. Sheslow, and Trevor A. Hall.
© 2024 John Wiley & Sons, Inc. Published 2024 by John Wiley & Sons, Inc.

and Recognition components) are discussed together as conceptual units. For each subtest discussion, the following components will receive attention:

1. Subtest rationale, basic procedural content, and reasonable diagnostic hypotheses to be entertained when atypical performance is found.
2. How Process Scores related to a subtest can enhance the examiner's understanding of how an examinee approached the task demands, thereby further enriching diagnostic understanding.
3. The value-optional subtests may provide for a deeper understanding of an examinee's recall ability.
4. Interesting observations that could enhance qualitative insights into how the examinee may have approached the task requirements and associated diagnostic possibilities. Most examiners are aware of potentially important observations while conducting any assessment, such as consistency of examinee response, cooperation, quality of speech and language, frustration tolerance, persistence when encouraged, distractibility, body language, and so on. These important domains of observation are not mentioned in the *Interesting Observations* sections of this chapter because it is assumed that examiners are familiar with their importance. Instead, what is listed are those specific to the subtest or, in some cases, unique to the WRAML3 overall.
5. Common errors made in a subtest's administration, information that could be especially helpful to professionals new to the test as well as to supervisors. Similar to the Observation sections, in the *Common Administration Errors* sections, generic examiner mistakes are not included (e.g., not following standardized procedures, using a noisy or poorly lit room, etc.) since basic examiner test competencies are assumed and Rapid Reference 3.10 has already included examples. Instead, highlighted are

those most frequent subtest administration errors uncovered from: (1) training held for examiners involved in the battery's standardization, (2) the authors' teaching the WRAML3 to psychology graduate students, interns and post-docs, and (3) those commonly encountered during professional workshop presentations.

A subtest Administration Rubric ends each discussion of a subtest grouping and is there to help new learners administer the battery accurately. The rubric takes the form of a checklist, including the most important subtasks required to demonstrate competency in a given subtest's administration. We recommend those learning a subtest to video practice administrations and then use the checklist soon thereafter as they (and supervisors) review the videoed performance to empirically determine if more practice is indicated. This procedure is consistent with the increasing emphasis of many professional organizations on objective methods to determine competency in practice.

VISUAL IMMEDIATE, DELAYED, AND RECOGNITION MEMORY INDEXES

As the name suggests, the Visual Immediate Memory Index (VisIMI) provides an estimate of short-term visual memory and is comprised of two subtests, Picture Memory and Design Learning. Across all age groups, the two subtests show a .48 correlation, which suggests they are measuring the same domain but with limited redundancy. The subtests intentionally differ considerably in content and task demand. For example, the Picture Memory subtest requires more visual search strategies using meaningful scenes, whereas the Design Learning subtest uses relatively meaningless simple arrays of familiar shapes. The Design Learning subtest also allows the examiner to observe growing recall of the same content over four learning trials, whereas the content is varied across isolated trials with Picture Memory. Used together, the two

VisIMI subtests provide a varied sampling of visual memory. When performance on both these subtests is comparable, it is reasonable to conclude that the summary score (i.e., the VisIMI) is a usable estimate of overall immediate visual memory. Discrepancy between the scores, however, can have varied meanings, and that variability is discussed in this and the next chapter.

Visual Memory demands are found in many tasks within our culture and vary widely. Those demands are apparent in tasks such as a toddler initially learning their way around a residence, a kindergartener remembering b/d and p/q differences, a 10-year-old taking a geography map test or remembering visual details in a book or digital illustration, the teenage driver remembering how to return home the shortest way to meet curfew, or an adult professional exercising those skills on the job (e.g., reading blueprints) or during leisure time (learning new lines of musical notation or remembering where the hammer was left).

However, it is also important to recognize that the brain seldom uses one cognitive subsystem alone to solve a problem, so the examinee using verbal memory to assist with VisIMI subtests will increase the diagnostic challenge for the examiner. Nevertheless, some tasks naturally make more visual demands and are less aided by compensatory subsystems, and it is in these tasks that visual memory strengths or weaknesses will be most apparent. Using other findings within the WRAML3, as well as other measures, and history help bring clarity to what can be a confusing intertwining of visual and verbal memory systems, and this also is illustrated within this and the following interpretation chapter.

Picture Memory (PM)

PM is the first subtest to be administered for the standard WRAML3 administration. It is a good task to start with since it demands no verbal response so examinees who may be shy, anxious, or slow to "warm up" are not intimidated by verbal demands at the outset of the battery. Instead, the subtest starts with a simple explanation of the task, accompanied by an initial demonstration for which additional instruction is permitted should the examinee still seem puzzled. The artwork is engaging, and the format appears game-like; plus the examinee's required response is simple (any kind of a pencil or pen mark) using a Response Form which provides a permanent record, thereby allowing the examiner to devote full attention to establishing rapport and recording first impressions. Following the first item, there are three different additional scenes that repeat the same procedure. The subtest's scenes are designed to be developmentally appropriate, so, following a common training item, there is a different set of scenes for younger (ages 5 to 9 years) and older (>9 years) examinees. Like all WRAML3 visual and verbal subtests, PM initially is a short-term memory task that can be followed a short time later by optional delayed and recognition recall components related to the immediate memory task.

Administration Procedure

The examinee is asked to scan a laminated picture of a colorful everyday scene for exactly 10 seconds at which point it is removed and immediately replaced with a similar but not identical picture found in the Recall Response Booklet. The examinee is asked to mark elements in the facsimile that were "changed, added, or moved." The first scene presented is a training stimulus card with relatively few elements. This teaching scene is used with all ages. When the examinee is finished responding to this first scene, the original picture is re-introduced, and the examiner interacts with the examinee noting all the correct responses and pointing out any errors or omissions. No changes to the Response Booklet are allowed since only initially correct responses are credited. The subtest proceeds as with the teaching item except after each scene the examinee now is allowed 20 seconds to compare the original picture stimulus to the one just marked in the Response Booklet (without any narrative) in order to notice anything that may have been missed or erroneously marked. After completing each scene, the examiner should quickly look over the response page to be sure it is clear what items were intended to be marked since sometimes the examinee's response may be ambiguous. When that happens, directions are provided to help the examiner know what was intended to be marked so scoring can be done accurately and expeditiously. The total number of correctly marked alterations on all four scenes constitute the subtest's total raw score. For those new to the subtest, the correct choices for each scene are graphically identified in Appendix B of the *Administration* Manual. Since the Response Booklet provides a permanent record of the examinee's responses, it allows for subsequent scoring and response/pattern analysis.

Optional Related Subtests

Picture Memory Delayed

Following a 20–30-minute delay, the PM Delayed subtest may be administered. Without additional exposure to any of the laminated scenes or already completed response pages, the examinee is again asked to mark items that were "changed, added, or moved" in the originally administered four scenes. The same facsimile pages are used as with the immediate condition and are also found in the Recall Response Booklet. Again, the total number of correctly identified alterations across all four scenes constitutes the PM Delayed subtest raw score.

Picture Memory Recognition

After the PM Delayed subtest, the PM Recognition subtest may be administered. It is found within the Recognition Response Booklet. Each of the 35 items of this subtest includes four choices, one picture segment taken from the original scene, two segments that are facsimiles, and an "X" ("none of these") option. The examinee marks which of each item's four choices is correct, and guessing is encouraged if the examinee is not sure. The raw score for this Recognition subtest is the total number of correct responses on the 35 items comprising the subtest. Since the original PM scenes differ for the two age groupings, Recognition items for 5- to 9-year-olds are different from those for those 10 years and older. Therefore, the examiner should be careful to give only items 1–35 or 36–70 depending on the examinee's age.

Process Score

There is one process score associated with the PM subtest, namely Commission Errors. This process score is associated only with the immediate recall portion of this subtest. Commission Errors are misidentified picture elements that were marked as altered but were not changed, added, or moved. Since mistakes are not penalized, an examinee who impulsively or carelessly over-responds on this subtest could achieve an inflated raw score. However, knowing the number of Commission Errors made can alert the examiner when to be cautious in interpreting the immediate PM score. To assist with that determination, age-related means, medians, SDs, and base rate cut-offs for the standardization sample are provided in Table A.25 in the *Administration* manual. It becomes clear, as one scans over the age bands, that Commission Errors are relatively rare occurrences, with 3–4 errors found for 5- to 9-year-olds (i.e., roughly one Commission Error per scene), and a total of about two errors thereafter until age 75, at which point it again edges up to about three errors over the four cards. Therefore, finding an examinee with, for example, 10 Commission Errors (base rate of ≤5% for all but 5-year-olds) should capture the examiner's attention given its likely impact on the raw score achieved and its possible behavioral importance. Lack of effort, impulsivity, and oppositional-defiant behaviors are among several diagnostic options that should be considered. Also, the examiner should be sensitive to the impact the confounded higher PM score might have on the Immediate Visual Memory Index and also adjust interpretation of it accordingly.

Interesting Observations
- Consistently ignored sections of the Response Form's PM pages (i.e., no marks are placed) might suggest a visual field cut (resulting from impairment of the retina, optic nerve, or occipital lobe regions) or visual neglect. Compare with results from the Design Learning subtest to confirm the suspicion.
- While behavioral dysregulation should be considered, the client marking numerous incorrect elements (i.e., a large number of

Commission Errors) may signal misunderstanding of the task (usually apparent during the Teaching item), cognitive impairment, poor visual acuity, or a significant visual memory deficit.

- Observe eye movements as the examinee scans the stimuli to evaluate visual search strategies, noting if the examinee is looking at most parts of the scene in an organized manner during both the 10- and 20-second exposures; perseveration or inconsistent searching may be important observations. Developmental allowances should be made before drawing conclusions, but most examinees older than 6 tend to show left-to-right, top-to-bottom scanning while gazing at much or all of a scene.
- While impulsivity can also create what looks like excessive responding, children with ADHD have not been shown (as a group) to perform differently from matched controls on this subtest with WRAML2 (Weniger & Adams, 2006) and this finding was replicated for WRAML3 in the ADHD clinical group reported on in the *Technical* Manual.
- Note if the client is nonresponsive when asked to respond. Over-analyzing, being unsure as to how to begin, or behaving as "it will come to me if I just think about it" are all ineffective strategies for a short-term memory task. It is appropriate to prompt responding and encourage "just do your best." A delayed response to task might lead the examiner to wonder about perseverative tendencies, excessive performance anxiety, deficient executive functioning, and/or a significant visual memory deficit. Alternatively, the examinee's attention may be arrested or overly engaged by only a portion of the scene (e.g., familiarity with or some emotionality the scene elicits). Querying associations to the scene at the end of the battery may be indicated in such instances.
- Note examinees squinting or moving their faces noticeably closer to the initial scenes and subsequent Response Form alternatives since this may indicate visual acuity problems. Is the client wearing his/her glasses, or unaware of a need for glasses?
- Note if the client does not seem to understand the task even with the prescribed teaching component associated with the first

scene. With an older child or adult, this may suggest low intellectual ability, advancing dementia, and/or poor executive functioning (intuiting the nature of the task). Alternatively, severe hearing loss could also create examinee confusion.

- If the PM immediate subtest score is higher than other core subtest scores (especially when compared to Design Learning and Visual Working Memory), consider the "inflationary" effect of random guessing by consulting the Commission Errors Process score.

Common Administration Errors

- Giving the wrong age-appropriate scenes to the examinee is the most common error made when administering this subtest.
- Since there was no re-exposure component on WRAML2, those familiar with the prior test version might be more prone to skip this new component of the subtest. The re-exposure aspect adds a bit more interest and game-like feel to the subtest, and more importantly, allows an additional exposure to each scene generating more psychometrically robust levels of performance when the Delayed Recall and Recognition portions of the subtest are administered.
- Making mistakes in timing is another somewhat common error. That is, the examiner is not exact in observing the initial 10-second exposure while giving the directions and placing the materials needed during that interval. Similarly, not accurately observing the 20-second re-exposure (inspection) interval is another error examiners can make with timing. In addition, a timing error can also be made when administering the Delayed portion of the subtest (i.e., administering it before or after the prescribed 20–30-minute interval).
- Should the examiner not retrieve the pencil (or pen) after each marking response (as stated in the Directions), the pencil may become a distraction during the 10-second viewing of the next scene, and/or make it possible for the examinee to respond during the re-exposure segment. Also, obtaining the pencil/pen following the initial marking of Response Booklet prevents

80 ESSENTIALS OF WRAML3 AND EMS ASSESSMENT

PUTTING IT INTO PRACTICE

Across all age cohorts, Commission Errors are relatively rare responses for an examinee, and so should receive clinical attention when several are found.

premature starting when presenting the Response Form. Returning the pencil to the examinee as the Response Booklet is placed also provides a nonverbal signal to the examinee to start in addition to the accompanying oral direction.

- By not watching the performance of the examinee or not quickly examining the Response Booklet after each marking interval, the examiner may miss ambiguous responses and therefore not make the prescribed follow-up queries that allow accurate scoring.

≋ Rapid Reference 4.1

Subtest Administration Rubric: Picture Memory

Immediate PM Subtest	Yes	No
1. Table area needed for drawing cleared for examinee		
2. All instructions included, read verbatim and clearly		
3. Scenes exposed for exactly 10 seconds and then removed		
4. Response Form scenes immediately presented with oral directions		
5. Marker provided each scene along with marking directions		
6. Correct and incorrect responses in Scene 1 (Teaching) pointed out during re-exposure, using directions		
7. No additional teaching done for re-exposure component beyond the first (Teaching) scene		
8. Age-appropriate four scenes administered, and in proper order		

INTERPRETING WRAML3 SUBTESTS, INDEXES 81

Immediate PM Subtest	Yes	No
9. Exactly 20 seconds allowed for original scene to be re-examined starting with second scene		
10. Inquiry made when marking(s) ambiguous		
11. Scoring for teaching scene correct		
12. Scoring for second scene correct		
13. Scoring for third scene correct		
14. Scoring for fourth scene correct		
15. Subtest total raw score across all four scenes computed accurately		
16. Scaled score accurately obtained		
17. Commission errors accurately detected and recorded		
18. Stimulus (laminated card) scenes as well as marked scenes in Response Booklet never subsequently visible following teaching item		
Optional Delayed and Recognition PM Subtests	Yes	No
19. Instructions included, read verbatim, and clearly		
20. No re-exposure of original laminated scenes or marked facsimile pages in Response Booklet		
21. Age-appropriate Response Booklet items used for Delayed PM subtest		
22. Scoring completed correctly across the four Delayed scenes		
23. Delayed Recall raw score accurate		
24. Delayed Recall scaled score accurately obtained		
25. Age-appropriate items used for Recognition subtest		
26. Guessing encouraged when examinee hesitant to make Recognition choices		
27. Scoring completed correctly for Recognition items		
28. Accurate total raw score and corresponding standard score obtained		

Design Learning (DL)

This subtest somewhat resembles the Design Memory subtest from WRAML2, but its content and procedures are substantially different. Of all the retained subtests, DL has undergone the greatest modification in the transition to the third edition.

This subtest and its Delayed and Recognition components evaluate short- and longer-term retention of quasi-meaningful visual information through repeated learning trials of a complex, novel array of familiar shapes. The subtest now is a visual analogue to the Verbal Learning subtest which is similar in format, that is, repeated learning trials using quasi-meaningful verbal stimuli (isolated words). Consequently, comparison between visual vs. verbal learning across trials is easily performed by viewing their respective learning curves found on adjacent pages of the Record Form.

DL evaluates a client's ability to learn and remember new, relatively unrelated visual information, such as might be tapped by a first grader copying unfamiliar letters or a design from the board, computer screen, or a workbook, or an adult trying to immediately recreate a portion of a diagram or map just seen in a computer attachment or set of blueprints. In academic areas, DL tends to be more related to mathematics than reading or spelling areas. On WISC-V, of the six core subtests (immediate recall subtests), DL has the highest correlations with the FSIQ and the Nonverbal Index ($r = .53$ for both).

DL has the highest reliability amongst the battery's immediate subtests: alpha = .91 for those 5 to 9 years of age, and .92 for those 10 and older; similar high reliabilities are found for the Delayed subtest as well; these high reliabilities are also found for the clinical groups. In part, the subtest's high reliability is attributable to the many points typically earned across the four trials since each of the many geometric shapes can earn 0–2 points for accuracy and 0–2 points for placement, with a maximum of 288 points possible across the 4 trials.

It is appropriate to note that DL shows the greatest increase in raw score performance across the 5- to 9-year age range. Also, it is the subtest to show the most noticeable decline in adulthood and begins that decline around 25 to 30 years of age. (More is said about developmental trends in the final chapter of this book.) It is sobering to observe that most 65-year-olds earn the same total raw score as that of 8-year-olds on the DL subtest! Since Picture Memory is in the number two spot for most decay with age, a case can be made that like intelligence, visual/spatial tasks tend to show decline faster than verbal tasks. This trend was also found with the WRAML2 and WMS-IV. It may be that the greater demand for age-sensitive spatial skills found in DL is the basis for the greater decline observed in this task. Because of its strong reliability with both clinical and nonclinical populations, its broad performance range, and its demonstrated rate of decline, DL is probably a very good measure to use to monitor older populations to determine if a suspected rate of decline is at an age-appropriate rate or greater.

Administration Procedure

Differing from the prior version of this subtest, the WRAML3 employs a single card with an array of 18 simple geometric shapes. The stimulus card is presented for exactly 10 seconds followed immediately by a 10-second delay after which the client attempts to draw a reproduction of the card. This procedure is repeated three more times allowing a learning curve to be created of performance over the four trials. Examiners will note that the *Administration* manual directs that the drawing instructions should be given during the 10-second delay while the card is removed and the Response Booklet placed before the examiner; when read properly, the directions and booklet placement should take exactly 10 seconds. Similar to Picture Memory, it is suggested that the pencil be removed and then returned to the examinee at the end of the 10-second delay interval to prevent drawing before the end of the enforced delay. Performance is scored based upon accurate retention of content as well as accurate location placement. Unlike Picture Memory, there is no teaching component, and all ages follow the same procedure using the same stimulus material. Abbreviated scoring guidelines are provided on the Examiner Record Form, but a detailed set of scoring criteria is found immediately following the Directions section for the subtest in the *Administration* manual (Table 3.3).

Because fine-motor difficulties are sometimes experienced by the WRAML3's youngest and oldest participants, as well as others with motor issues between those age extremes (e.g., those with cerebral palsy or tremors), an optional, brief "warm-up" copy task (called the Practice Item in the *Administration* manual) may be administered before the actual subtest is begun. Using the Practice Item, most of the shapes found on the stimulus card will be copied, providing the examiner with a "general standard" that can be used to judge the "accuracy" criteria. This copy procedure allows deficits in fine-motor or perceptual-motor ability to play a minimal role in performance on this visual memory subtest. The Practice Item may be omitted if you have reason to believe drawing the various shapes will be performed well enough that scoring their accuracy later will not be difficult. This evidence might be obtained from other perceptual-motor tasks completed during the evaluation (like writing their name or drawings done in the waiting area), from history (e.g., art as a hobby), or from materials already supplied by teachers or family members. Since the Practice Item generally takes less than a minute, when in doubt, administer it. If unneeded, it may nonetheless bolster examinee confidence! Generally, we recommend most 5- and 6-year-olds routinely complete the Practice Item, as well as older adults and those with any fine-motor compromise, such as those whose handwriting shows obvious tremor, or stroke or injury victims who must use their nondominant hand.

Since the drawn response for each trial is made on a separate page of the Recall Response Booklet, a permanent record of performance over trials is created, and can be scored later (like Picture Memory). This subtest has the most subjective and involved scoring procedure of the battery; yet, as the test's *Technical* manual reports, inter-rater correlation for scoring consistency is .98, suggesting that the specific scoring guidelines are sufficiently clear that consistent scoring across conscientious examiners is realistic. There is a steep learning curve for examiner scoring so that time to score improves quickly with practice.

OPTIONAL RELATED SUBTESTS

Design Learning Delayed

Following a 20–30-minute delay, the DL Delayed subtest may be administered. Without additional exposure to the stimulus card used for the immediate learning component of the subtest, examinees are again asked to draw a reproduction of the card. By using the same Recall Record Form, all five trials (four immediate and one delayed) are in one place for easy inspection and comparison. For example, does a recalled grouping continue to appear in subsequent trials? On average, the DL Delayed procedure takes less than 2 minutes, so the potential yield-per-unit-time is considerable; therefore, administering it makes good clinical sense unless the examiner has other evidence that longer-term visual memory performance is commensurate with that of short-term. The scoring system used for the immediate component is again employed for scoring the delayed administration; that is, both shape accuracy and correct placement contribute to the total Delayed raw score.

Design Learning Recognition

Following the DL Delayed subtest, the Picture Memory Recognition subtest may be administered. As with Picture Memory Recognition, the DL Recognition subtest is found in the Recognition Response Booklet and again uses the four-option multiple-choice format generally consisting of small segments of the stimulus card, two facsimiles, and a none-of-these option. For each item, the examinee marks which of the four choices is correct, and guessing is encouraged if the examinee is not sure. Unlike Picture Memory, there is one set of Recognition items for all ages. The raw score for this Recognition subtest is the total number of correct responses on the 30 items comprising the subtest.

Process Scores

There are three Process scores associated with the DL subtest. All Process Score data related to the DL subtest are found in Table A.26 of the Administration manual.

Learning Trials Performance

The Trials Process score offers an analysis of learning over the five learning trials of the subtest (four Immediate and one Delayed). The initial four individual learning trial scores provide a "learning curve" for the subtest. For each age band, normative means, medians, SDs, and base rates are provided for each trial, and those statistics can be used for age-based comparison purposes when evaluating the examinee's learning trajectory. Figure 4.1 illustrates an example using a fictitious client we will call Sam who is 9 years, 3 months old. The line with black diamonds shows the mean total raw score results for those from Sam's standardization age cohort; the line with open circles marks Sam's performance. Note that his visual learning starts rather slowly (base rates show his performance on Trials 1 and 2 lower than 5% of the standardization sample), but by the last two trials, the base rates suggest that he is performing within age expectations. This learning curve would suggest that with select visual memory demands, Sam seemingly

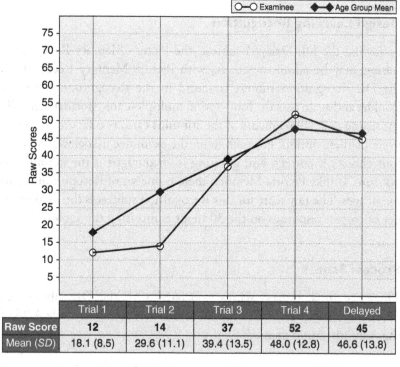

Figure 4.1 **Design Learning Performance of Sam, compared to his 9-year-old cohort, as it appears on a WRAML3 Record Form.** Copyright © 2021 NCS Pearson, Inc. Reproduced with permission. All rights reserved.

struggles initially, but with repetition, seems to "catch up" to age-mates. Further, he seems to retain what he learned given his age-appropriate performance in the Delayed segment of the subtest. If these findings are accurate (i.e., replicable), then one would expect that on tasks with significant visual memory demands (such as learning the map locations of the original 13 US colonies), extra review will likely be necessary, but despite the slower start, Sam eventually will likely demonstrate age-appropriate competency because of extra practice. That is, practice, as might be expected, makes for improvement for Sam. However, notice that while the total raw score is within the average range, that sum masks the fact that the learning trajectory is different from that of many age mates. Without the Trials breakdown, one would be unaware of the initial struggle this child likely experiences with at least some visual memory tasks. This Process component helps the examiner understand that Sam seems to go about learning new visual information somewhat differently than many of his same-aged peers. While additional data are needed for confirmation, the Trials Process Score does generate a hypothesis that leads to a useful and empirically based intervention strategy (e.g., extra classroom review or subsequent tutoring will probably help recall visual content).

In contrast, the learning curve for "Ted" is different, demonstrated by the open-circle line in Figure 4.2. Ted's learning also starts lower than peers and while there is some gain, it is negligible over all four trials. This pattern would suggest that while practice brings about some learning, clear recall limitations are operating. Further, the Delayed trial suggests that what Ted manages to learn over trials is mostly forgotten with the passage of time. The Recognition Memory task for this subtest would be helpful in substantiating that conjecture. Based just on the findings of this one subtest, one would predict that mastery of new tasks making heavy demands of visual memory would be especially challenging for Ted, and that practice will result

in only limited improvement. In fact, given that repetition is rather frustrating for Ted and his teachers, review may be counterproductive, and the recommendation may be to avoid repetition whenever frustration accompanies review. In addition, an alternate remediation

88 ESSENTIALS OF WRAML3 AND EMS ASSESSMENT

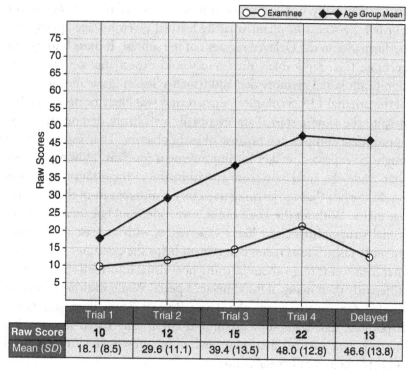

Figure 4.2 Design Learning Performance of "Ted," compared to his 9-year-old cohort, as it appears on a WRAML3 Record Form. (Used by Permission. Copyright © 2021 NCS Pearson, Inc. All rights reserved.)

strategy would likely be more fruitful, such as emphasizing a verbal instructional component to help guide the acquisition and retention phases (assuming Ted has stronger verbal memory performance). For example, helping Ted create a mnemonic acronym for the north-south order of the colonies might decrease the visual memory demands and may lead to greater success. Again, this is just one subtest, so one needs to be careful not to get too attached to the hypothesis that was just generated, but such hypotheses are important to examine and evaluate further as other subtest findings are gathered. Also recommended would be reviewing Ted's educational and leisure time histories; corresponding weaknesses reflected in hobbies avoided (e.g., art) or everyday demands reflecting undue struggle (e.g., getting lost easily) may have been underappreciated on the first read and can become valuable in supporting or refuting the hypothesis and remediation option mentioned above.

Slope Analysis

Another DL Process score is Learning Slope Analysis, and is related to the learning curve just described. The Slope Analysis score is derived from a quantitative comparison of performance between Trials 4 and 1, and so yields a quick estimate of the overall learning achieved across trials. The arithmetic differences between raw scores of the two trials can be compared with age-mates' performance, and base rates are again provided for interpretive purposes. Using the examples of Sam and Ted, the difference between the total raw scores earned for the first and last trials was about 30 for Sam and 12 for Ted. The table in the Manual shows the average difference for this age group to be about 30, and a difference of 11 or more is found in 5% or less of the standardization sample. Consequently, Sam's learning slope (Trial 4 vs. Trial 1) is found well within normal limits, whereas Ted's stands out as atypical compared to age-mates.

Quadrant Analysis

The third DL Process Score is new to WRAML3, and is called Quadrant Analysis; it allows the examiner to determine if the distribution of points earned across quadrants is atypical. Remember that the stimulus card is divided into four equal quadrants by dotted lines. There are four scored details contained within each quadrant (4 details × 2 points for accuracy + 2 points for placement) allowing 16 possible points per quadrant per trial. Using those metrics, the Quadrant Analysis allows the examiner to compare total quadrant performance. Using both accuracy and placement scoring criteria, total raw scores for each quadrant can be compared with that of age-mates with relative ease since examinee data are being generated anyway when scoring the subtest. A place on the Record Form allows quadrant data to be simply separated should the examiner wish to examine quadrant performance. This would normally happen if there is a differential number of correct responses across

90 ESSENTIALS OF WRAML3 AND EMS ASSESSMENT

quadrants such as might occur with an examinee with a visual field cut, visual neglect, extreme perseveration, or unusual visual scanning skills. Total mean and median raw scores per quadrant with base rates are provided in Table A.26 in the *Administration* manual.

Interesting Observations

- Be aware of the visual scanning strategies utilized by examinees during the stimulus card presentation. By at least the third trial, you should notice that all quadrants are being scanned and attention is not restricted to only one or two. Scanning strategies can be taught which might make a useful recommendation if deficits are noted across the four trials. Check also Picture Memory performance as if its scenes had quadrants and see if a similar weakness appears on that subtest. As with Picture Memory, examinees 7 years and older generally scan left to right, top to bottom on DL. Quadrant norms suggest that the upper right quadrant tends to earn slightly fewer points across all age bands, even though each quadrant has the same number of potential points that can be earned. It is possible that the scoring criteria for that upper right quadrant are a bit more rigorous than those of other quadrants, or examinees find the shapes and their configurations a bit more challenging to recall or reproduce.
- Is there a noticeable difference between points earned for accuracy and placement? More earned for accuracy may suggest spatial weaknesses; that is, an examinee remembers the "what" of the card but is confused with the "where" component. Obviously, the reverse is possible too.
- It is common for examinees to appear "overwhelmed" with the task demands on the first trial. Comments such as "I'll never remember all that" may signal a need for examiner encouragement in order for the examinee to start responding. Note the calming words of encouragement provided within the subtest's optional directions in the manual. Examinee concern about task difficulty generally dissipates by the second or third trial as confidence builds through improved performance from

repeated exposure, and more of a game-like nature of the task is felt. Given that trend, notice if the client "recovers" after the first (or maybe second) exposure, that is, does self-confidence increase or is actual improvement even noticed? A hypothesis for supportive counseling may start to be raised at this point in the battery and again trigger the need for the examiner to consult examinee history.

- Notice if the client waits before beginning to respond, seemingly expecting that "a solution will come to me." This is an ineffective strategy for a short-term memory task and should not be used, or if initially tried, quickly abandoned. Otherwise, one would wonder about perseverative tendencies and/or deficient executive functioning. Of course, a poor visual memory can cause such behavior too.

- Squinting or moving his/her face noticeably close to the stimulus card or off to one side may indicate visual acuity problems. Be sure to always ask if the client wears glasses at the outset of the evaluation, and uses them if glasses are typically worn for reading or other close-up work.

Common Administration Errors

- The most frequent examiner error made on the WRAML3 is made on this subtest, with the examiner reversing the orientation of the stimulus card. The *Administration* manual clearly shows the correct orientation of the card (see Figure 3.1 in the *Administration* manual), and proper placement is aided by arrows on the back of the card (pointing to "Examiner" and to "Examinee"), obviously indicating which orientation of the card is correct.

- Another common examiner mistake is not strictly adhering to the 10-second stimulus card exposure, and/or the 10-second delay imposed once the stimulus card is removed. As noted above, the required 10-second delay can be made to feel "natural" if the examiner appropriately paces what should be done following stimulus card removal – that is, with a bit of practice, supplying the Response Form, saying the directions, and then providing a pencil can be completed to comfortably fill the requisite 10-second delay interval.

- Inadvertently displaying the stimulus card other than during its 10-second exposure for each trial is another common error when first learning the subtest because of the necessary "juggling" of materials while conforming to the correct timing requirements. Obviously, additional exposure of the stimulus card should be avoided even at the end of the core subtest (immediate) in case Delayed and/or Recognition components are administered. Plus, leaving the stimulus card within sight after the subtest is finished may have some impact should the battery be subsequently administered for a re-evaluation. Some examiners use an opaque 5 × 7 envelope in which to store the card during and after the subtest administration, thereby eliminating any possibility of its being accidentally viewed. Examiners should also note that there is a copy of the card on the Record Form, and so exposure to that page (and most any other pages of that form) should be avoided.
- In a similar vein, avoid re-exposing any page having an examinee's drawing (in the Recall Response Booklet) following the completion of any learning trial.
- After an initial careful review of them, the scoring guidelines (found in the *Administration* manual's Table 3.3) should be periodically consulted by all examiners otherwise tempted to depend upon their recollection of the criteria. Using the complete guidelines whenever in doubt or periodically just to verify your accurate use of the guidelines tends to prevent "scoring drift" over time. Obviously, new users must initially familiarize themselves with the scoring details associated with each of the 18 items on the stimulus card. Having an experienced user also score the first several administrations for comparison is highly recommended. Of all the WRAML3 subtests, this one makes the greatest scoring demands.
- Not awarding points to an examinee's item because of the client's inability to draw will sometimes occur because the examinee

skipped the preliminary Practice Item copy procedure used to define correctness. This is especially true when testing those with various forms of motor disability. Should the examiner realize once the subtest has stated that they should have utilized the Practice Item, one alternative is to administer it at the conclusion of the subtest. While this violates standardized procedure, it does provide a means to score the subtest more appropriately. Notation in the report of this relatively minor violation of procedure should also be made.

⇒ Rapid Reference 4.2

Subtest Administration Rubric: Design Learning

Immediate DL	Yes	No
1. Drawing area of table cleared for participant		
2. Optional Practice Item (preliminary copy task) completed if appropriate		
3. All instructions are included being read verbatim and clearly		
4. Stimulus card placed about 18 inches from edge of table, correctly oriented to client		
5. Stimulus card exposed exactly 10 seconds for each trial		
6. Exactly 10-second delay imposed while saying directions		
7. Examiner points to record form area when saying directions during enforced 10-second delay		
8. Recall Response Booklet and pencil (without erasure) are immediately available after 10-second delay		
9. Pencil and Response Booklet removed after each drawing trial is completed		

Immediate DL	Yes	No
10. Participant prompted to respond following 10 seconds of nonresponsiveness, as necessary		
11. Scoring criteria consulted when appropriate		
12. Erasure not allowed if attempted but "drawing over" is allowed for correcting a response		
13. Stimulus card hidden from sight before and immediately after each 10-second card exposure		
14. Completed Recall Response Booklet drawing page hidden from sight following each completed trial		
15. Scoring for trial 1 drawing correct		
16. Scoring for trial 2 drawing correct		
17. Scoring for trial 3 drawing correct		
18. Scoring for trial 4 drawing correct		
19. Total raw score computed accurately		
20. Scaled Score accurately obtained		

Delayed and Recognition DL Subtests	Yes	No
21. Directions for Delayed trial read correctly		
22. Card not re-exposed for the one delayed DL trial		
23. Drawing pages of the Response Booklet already used never seen by examinee		
24. Raw score accurately computed for Delayed DL trial		
25. DL Delayed scaled score accurately obtained		
26. Directions for Recognition trial read correctly		
27. Total raw score accurately computed for the Recognition trial		
28. Recognition scaled score accurately obtained		

TEST YOURSELF

Visual Memory Index Subtests

1. **Which statement is correct regarding the immediate PM subtest?**
   (a) Scenes following the teaching item should be initially exposed for 10 seconds followed by a 20-second "review" interval.
   (b) Scenes following the teaching item should be initially exposed for 20 seconds followed by a 10-second "review" interval.
   (c) A high Commission Errors score invalidates this subtest.
   (d) Children with ADHD tend to have high number of Commission Errors.
   (e) All examinees are shown the same scenes other than the teaching item.

2. **The Picture Memory Recognition subtest**
   (a) Requires marking the original scenes with a different colored marker.
   (b) Has items each of which offers examinees two-choice (right or wrong) options
   (c) Should be administered after the Delayed PM subtest
   (d) Uses the same item set for all ages
   (e) Uses one set of items for 5–8-year-olds and another for those 9 years and older

3. **True or False?** The PM subtest is significantly correlated with the other subtest comprising the Immediate Visual Memory Index, namely Visual Working Memory.

4. **True or False?** Those with fine-motor handicaps should probably not be administered the DL subtest since their impaired drawing skills will lead to lower memory scores.

5. **Which procedure reflects a proper administration of the DL subtest?**
   (a) Using a 10-second card exposure followed by an enforced 10-second delayed latency before allowing drawn recall to start.
   (b) At the end of each trial, providing a 10-second interval for the examinee to compare what they drew with the content on the card

96 ESSENTIALS OF WRAML3 AND EMS ASSESSMENT

> (c) Presenting the stimulus card for exactly 10 seconds for each learning trial as well as the Delayed trial
>
> (d) Orientation of the stimulus card is determined based on examinee preference
>
> (e) Orientation of the stimulus card is determined based on examiner preference
>
> **6. T or F?** An examinee earns a scaled score of 10 on the immediate phase of the DL subtest. It would be reasonable to assume that their learning curve (raw scores over trials) will resemble that of the examinee's age cohort.
>
> *Answers:* 1a, 2c, 3F, 4F, 5a, 6F

VERBAL IMMEDIATE, DELAYED, AND RECOGNITION MEMORY INDEXES AND SUBTESTS

The Verbal Immediate Memory Index (VerIMI) measures short-term verbal memory using one meaningful, narrative task and one less meaningful list learning task. Similar to the two subtests of the VisIMI, the two immediate recall subtests comprising the VerIMI (Story Memory and Verbal Learning) are related but not redundant; for 5- to 9-year-olds, a correlation of .32 between the two subtests was obtained, and for those 10 and older, .47. Thus, when sampling the area of verbal memory, administering both subtests provides examiners with a broader understanding of recall abilities in this domain than using either subtest alone. Comparable correlations are found between the Delayed and Recognition subtest pairs as found with Immediate.

Story Memory (SM)

Because learning in Western and many Eastern cultures is so heavily verbally dependent, results of verbal memory subtests can have great ecological importance. The SM subtest taps skills needed, for example, to remember a classroom discussion or podcast presentation, recall relevant content from information read on a computer or in a book, follow the flow during a conference call, or remember details of a backyard conversation with a friend. The SM subtest was selected as the second subtest to be administered in the standardized sequence as most examinees find stories interesting and nonthreatening. In fact, because of the commonality of story engagement, a lack of interest in the stories may be clinically relevant and could suggest a language disorder, dimmed alertness, significantly impaired intelligence, or opposition to testing. Like several other WRAML3 subtests, the SM subtest has immediate, delayed, and recognition memory components. Again, this subtest family starts with core or immediate recall component.

Administration Procedure

The Immediate SM subtest is comprised of two stories that are individually read to the examinee. Stories A and B (for 5- to 9-year-olds) differ from Stories C and D (for those 10 years and older) in developmental content, complexity of the storyline, and semantics. To maintain attention and familiarity with the younger examinee, it is especially important to adjust rate and intonation to mimic the tone of a story read by an interested parent or classroom teacher. On the other end of the developmental spectrum, it is important to read to older adults with sufficient loudness and rate so that information is not unintentionally missed as a result of hearing loss. After each story, the examinee is asked to recall as much of that story as can be remembered. Encouragement and praise are appropriate in this process to maintain rapport. If it seems that the examinee is hesitant, the examiner might say something like, "What else comes to mind?" or "It's okay to guess." It is appropriate to ask an examinee to "slow down" or "say that again" if the story is being recalled too rapidly for accurate scoring.

There is room on the Record Form to note atypical or ambiguous responses for later scoring. Recording the examinee's responses exactly as recalled may allow identification of such phenomena as confabulation or disordered language processing, and allows capture of examples that can be incorporated in a report or used in a reporting conference. The details of the stories are arranged sequentially on the Record Form to facilitate scoring. Familiarity with the story content

98 ESSENTIALS OF WRAML3 AND EMS ASSESSMENT

allows the examiner to number the examinee's responses sequentially as they are being recalled. Being able to subsequently examine the recall pattern is frequently revealing but the examiner's only checking correct responses on the Record Form will not allow for this useful result. For example, recalled story details that are seemingly ordered randomly may constitute an important clinical finding, possibly suggesting phenomena such as erratic retrieval, poor organizational functioning, or dysregulated attention. Narrative recall typically follows a story's logical progression such that the beginning precedes the middle and the middle precedes the end and there are logical transitions between those segments. Numbering responses sequentially will also help confirm that pattern, and also help determine consistency of performance since most examinees perform similarly across the two stories. Likewise, a detailed comparison between immediate and delayed recall performance is possible. In the same vein, examiners may rightly expect to find the "typical" recall phenomenon of primacy and recency in the recall of each story. Generally, more content is remembered from the end of the story, followed by the beginning of the story, with least information normally recalled from the middle; violation of this traditional distribution signals an unusual manner of recall, but can only be detected when the examiner numbers responses in the order they are recalled, not marked just right and wrong.

With the client's (or guardian's) permission, it is permitted to electronically record the examinee's telling of the stories, particularly when accent, speech, or language disorder, or excessively fast reporting might hamper scoring or recalling important qualitative findings. Again, the written or recorded record not only allows for subsequent accurate scoring but may also provide useful examples for the test report. The pattern of recall on SM can be effectively contrasted with WRAML3 subtests that make different recall demands, like Sentence Memory or Number Letter (discussed further below).

Raw scores for Immediate SM are calculated by awarding one point for each story detail accurately recalled and zero points for information omitted or not properly recalled. Order of story content reported does not affect scoring. The raw score for the subtest is the total number of correct details recalled from *both* stories.

Remember that SM casts a wide net into the sea of cognitive processing. A low score may mean there are verbal memory deficits but other compromised processes may also be contributing to lower SM performance, such as intelligence, social awareness, language proficiency, and behavioral wellness.

Optional Related Subtests

SM Delayed

Following a 20–30-minute delay, the SM Delayed subtest may be administered. Without any additional exposure to the stories, examinees are again asked to recall their content. Responses for the delayed condition are scored (and recorded) directly on the Record Form next to those from the Immediate trial, making comparison of items from both conditions easy. The raw score is calculated in the same manner as the immediate condition, and the administration and scoring suggestions given for the immediate condition apply to the Delayed SM condition as well.

While assessing verbal memory abilities, it is important to include the delay conditions to obtain a more ecologically valid assessment of verbal retention since there are neurological conditions for which immediate recall can show considerable decay over time so that only assessing immediate recall may lead to an overestimate of memory for meaningful verbal content. Plus the Delayed component of the subtest takes only a few minutes.

Inspection of the norms for performance on the immediate and delayed components of this subtest will show that generally there is little difference between average performance for the two conditions except for the youngest and oldest age cohorts. But even then, the differences are relatively small: there is about a 10% decline in raw scores with the delayed condition for 5- and 6-year-olds, and about 20% for those 70 years and older. As expected, verbal recall for meaningful verbal narratives is relatively robust. Thus, marked differences between immediate and delayed conditions are likely clinically important as are changes in the pattern of memory recall between conditions.

Further, it may be of interest to learn that there is evidence that shows that when the Delayed trial was administered to adults one to two days later rather than using the standardized delay interval of 20–30 minutes, the amount of recall was sufficient to maintain the subtest's reasonable psychometric integrity despite a somewhat reduced overall recall raw score, suggesting the subtest could actually be used as a "long-term" memory measure (Frise & Adams, 2010; Burkhart & Adams, 2011). Again, it is shown that meaningfulness is a very strong enabler of recall.

SM Recognition

Following the Story Memory Delayed subtest, the SM Recognition subtest may be administered. The examiner reads each item which is a question about the story, followed by four possible answers, one of which is a "none of these" option. The examinee orally identifies the choice deemed correct. It is permissible to repeat items or to briefly clarify the meaning of the "none" response if the examinee appears puzzled. Also, guessing is encouraged. You will remember that one purpose of the Recognition subtest is to investigate memory retrieval vs. storage of previous content.

As would be expected because of different developmentally sensitive stories being used, Story Recognition items for 5–9-year-olds are different from those for those 10 years and older. The raw score for the SM Recognition subtest is the number of correct responses earned from *two* stories. Correct items are found in equal proportion in each of the possible four positions, so perseverating on one position throughout would result in about 25% success.

As noted in the last chapter's broader discussion of Delayed vs. Recognition recall tasks when the SM Delayed subtest shows little decay in performance from the immediate recall condition, it is unlikely that the SM Recognition subtest will yield important clinical information as recognition memory is considered considerably more robust than free recall. This would be true of the visual recognition procedures too, as well as the Verbal Learning subtest whose discussion soon follows. Yet, there may be other reasons to administer a Recognition subtest, such as to calculate a Performance Validity score.

Process Scores

There are two sets of Process scores associated with the SM subtest, and each pertains only to the immediate recall component of the subtest. All Process Score data related to the SM subtest are found in Table A.2 of the *Administration* manual.

Verbatim and Gist

Examinees are credited for recalling content items of each story. However, for additional examination, all responses are also subcategorized as demonstrating greater competency in recalling verbatim or gist information. Verbatim responses, indicated with an upper case font within the subtest's scoring area of the Response Form, earn credit only when they exactly match the word used in the story. Gist responses, in lowercase font, earn credit whenever they conform to the general storyline and do not have to exactly match the word or words used in the story. Scoring criteria and examples for Verbatim and Gist responses are provided in Table 3.2 of the *Administration* Manual. Since responses should be recorded on the Record Form, ambiguous gist responses can subsequently be considered for later scoring. (As elsewhere in the battery, the general principle for scoring items for SM is that a response which, in the examiner's opinion after careful consideration could go either way, is awarded credit.) An example of scoring these items appears in Figure 4.3. Notice that this examiner numbered the order of response rather than simply scoring correct and incorrect, and recorded the actual responses when errors or ambiguous responses were given so that subsequent scoring decisions and qualitative analysis were possible. The total raw score for the Verbatim as well as the Gist measure is the total number of correct responses within the

102 ESSENTIALS OF WRAML3 AND EMS ASSESSMENT

	Story Details		Immediate		
			V	G	Score
18.	SEEDS	_seeds in the ground_	1 1		1
19.	Annie planted	A put		12	1
20.	straight row				0
21.	seeds covered	dirt over		1 4	1
22.	with dirt	ʺ ʺ		1 3	1
23.	YELLOW		←		0
24.	WATERING CAN	. can	0		0

Figure 4.3 Illustration of scoring using Story B as it might appear on the WRAML3 Record Form. (Used by Permission. Copyright © 2021 NCS Pearson, Inc. All rights reserved.)

respective category. Corresponding Verbatim and Gist scaled scores for each age cohort are found in Table A.2 in the *Administration* Manual. You will notice in that Table that, not surprisingly, the raw score totals show that examinees tend to favor somewhat the Gist responses, especially for the youngest and oldest age cohorts.

When there is a marked difference between Verbatim and Gist recall, diagnostic suspicions are raised about possible conditions such as language, autism spectrum, or selective memory disorders. For example, those with language delays or disorders may report a distorted meaning of portions of the story, sometimes changing the ending to conform to a language misunderstanding earlier in the story. Some individuals with autism spectrum disorders may be adept at recalling exact story details but fail giving the information as a sequential story narrative. Alternately, some individuals presenting with dysregulated or divided attention may correctly recall much of the overall narrative but fail specific rote story components such as a name, color, or a test score embedded in a story. When extreme differences between Verbatim and Gist scores are obtained (generally more than 3 scaled score points) and a similar finding can be corroborated elsewhere in the battery and/or in history,

INTERPRETING WRAML3 SUBTESTS, INDEXES 103

recommendations about intervention strategies related to where to focus tutoring for listening/reading are appropriate, as may be a school referral to an LD specialist and/or speech and language pathologist.

Story 1 vs. Story 2 Comparison

Individual scaled scores are available for each of the two stories administered and are found in Table A.2 of the *Administration* manual. These separate scaled scores allow for comparison of performance between both stories. Since the two stories are individually normed in Table A.2, consistent performance (i.e., approximately similar scaled scores) should be observed. When there is an atypical discrepancy (generally more than 3 scaled score points), attention, motivation, language, and/or fatigue may be among the influences operating. Also, highly variable performance between stories suggests a degree of caution in applying the subtest score as a meaningful summary measure of verbal memory for narrative memory. If the inconsistent result is replicated in the "real world" (e.g., from teacher report), then the examinee may be experiencing what one of our clients with ADHD reported as "It's like someone changes the channel of the TV, and when the channel returns, I know I've missed stuff." Such dysregulated attention has profound social as well as academic implications.

Interesting Observations

- While scaled score comparisons between stories are useful, examining the pattern of successful responses within each story may be an additional source of important data. For example, an examinee who remembers almost all the last sections of each story is likely using a different memory system than an examinee who has sketchy recall of one story and adequate recall of the second story, or another examinee who randomly recalls comparable snatches of information throughout each story. Internal analysis of story recall patterns is often profitably compared with performance on the Sentence Memory and Verbal Working Memory subtests.

- Blending portions of the story content of the first story with the second is highly unusual and may be suggestive of significant information processing deficit or thought disorder.
- Expect somewhat better performance when there is a meaningful match between story content and the examinee's life experience. So, for example, a soccer player or dog lover may devote greater attention to WRAML3's *Lost and Found* story.
- The SM subtest is a valuable source for detecting language processing difficulties. For example, in the *Lost and Found* story, an examinee with a language disorder might make some of the following distortions: saying "dinner" rather than "breakfast," "lock" rather than "key," "over" rather than "under the flower pot," "Buddy" is a person rather than a "dog," and the last sentence is not reported (extra petting given) because of the increased language subtlety of that concluding portion of the story. Other atypical examples of language disorder may include unusual ordering of a sentence in addition to distorted meaning. During a reporting conference to unaware parents, spouses, teachers, or associates, examples from those recorded by the examiner while administering or scoring the subtest can be very helpful in illustrating the nature of language disorder.
- It is not unusual for teens to roll their eyes or challenge the idea in Story D that technology might not be as fun as other things!

Common Administration Errors

- Administering the incorrect stories to the examinee given their age is the most common error committed, and it is a "fatal error." There are no norms for recalled stories that are inappropriate for the examinee's age. Further, this kind of mistake would also spoil SM Delayed and Recognition.
- A common oversight involves underestimating the angst that may be associated with oral narrative. SM requires the most listening and speaking of the core subtests; therefore, anxiety and frustration may be noted during its administration. For this reason, taking time to provide encouragement and support when

INTERPRETING WRAML3 SUBTESTS, INDEXES 105

these demands could become upsetting is always appropriate (e.g., I know it's hard, but just do the best you can," or "No one gets all the story, but see if some more parts pop into your head.").

- Care should be exercised not to give directions or read the story too quickly, and/or to read the story lacking "story-time" inflection.
- It is important to make sure that the examinee is attending when the examiner starts each story.
- Cultural sensitivity is required when recording and scoring examinee responses from those with different language norms or language experiences from those of the examiner. The goal of the subtest is "story memory" so that when an examiner believes a "culturally different" but seemingly correct response from those provided in the guidelines has been given, generally mark the gist response as correct. The authors recognize that slang or culturally acceptable equivalents to the scoring guidelines provided in the manual are always changing, so if you are unfamiliar with a term, you may ask the examinee to clarify at the end of the subtest.

⩵ Rapid Reference 4.3

Subtest Administration Rubric: Story Memory

Immediate SM	Yes	No
1. Correct two stories used given examinee's age		
2. Instructions read verbatim		
3. Instructions and stories read clearly and at appropriate pace		
4. Stories read with inflection, tone, and loudness to match developmental level		
5. Story recall requested after each story		

Immediate SM	Yes	No
6. Prompted examinee to slow down, speak up, guess or query when appropriate		
7. Both stories scored consistent with criteria provided		
8. Total raw score accurate		
9. Correct scaled score obtained		
10. Correct scaled scores obtained for Gist and Verbatim		

SM Delayed and Recognition	Yes	No
11. Delayed SM subtest administered 20–30 minutes following Immediate		
12. Appropriate pair of stories re-administered		
13. Instructions read verbatim, and Stories not read again		
14. Stories not read again		
15. Raw score total for SM Delayed accurate		
16. Scaled score for SM Delayed accurately obtained		
17. Recognition subtest items appropriate given the examinee's age		
18. Recognition instructions and items read verbatim		
19. Recognition four-choice format clarified if needed		
20. Recognition items repeated if requested or needed		
21. Raw score for Recognition computed accurately		
22. Scaled score for Recognition accurate		

Verbal Learning (VL)

The Immediate VL subtest is the other subtest of the two comprising the Immediate Verbal Memory Index. This subtest assesses short-term memory for less meaningful verbal information. It has its roots in psychology's long tradition of studying memory phenomena using a list learning format. Unlike the meaningful narrative of the Story Memory subtest, the VL subtest requires learning a list of common nouns across four learning trials, generating the classic learning curve. The VL subtest provides an interesting comparison with the visual stimuli of the Design Learning subtest that shares a similar format of learning over trials. In addition, contrasting performance between VL and the Number/Letter subtest (discussed later in the chapter) can generate interesting clinical hypotheses since the latter task uses relatively meaningless stimuli (isolated numbers and letters) and, perhaps less obvious, the VL format "dumps" a large amount of information at once, whereas the Number/Letter subtest starts off with minimal memory demand that gradually increases as the task proceeds. Also, the sequential demands of the Number/Letter subtest may provide yet another interesting contrast. Lastly, by Trial 4, many examinees engage in a subjective organization strategy (i.e., words of related meaning recalled together such as "wood" and "door") that is not possible with the Number/Letter subtest. More will be said of the possible clinical implications of these kinds of comparisons in the next chapter.

The VL subtest taps varied everyday skills. The first learning trial of the subtest might reflect competency on tasks like remembering the verbatim details when immediately relating a phone message, or recalling the ingredients to obtain from the pantry after having just scanned a new recipe. For children, VL performance should be related to hearing and writing/typing a reminder from memory of a teacher's requested set of items needed for the next class. Of interest, the subtask of Trial 1 performance is somewhat different from remembering that content after additional exposures. Trial 1 may allow a more "head-to-head" comparison with Number/Letter or a digit recall task.

Like the Story Memory subtest, the VL subtest has immediate, delayed, and recognition memory components. It is worth noting that, as might be predicted, examinees in the Reading Disorder and/or Disorder of Written Expression clinical group, showed their lowest performance on both Verbal Memory subtests in the Immediate condition, and showed even worse Story Memory scores in the Delayed and Recognition conditions.

108 ESSENTIALS OF WRAML3 AND EMS ASSESSMENT

Administration Procedure

For each of the four trials of the VL subtest, a list of common nouns is read to the examinee who is then asked to recall as many as possible. For 5–9-year-olds, the list consists of thirteen words while for those 10 years and older, the list contains 16.

The word list is to be presented with neutral inflection with a pause of one second in between words. Care should be taken to pronounce words with adequate volume and clear articulation for final consonants, especially for older examinees who might be experiencing some hearing loss. Like with Story Memory, it is important to initially confirm young examinee's attention before the list is begun. Encouragement and praise are appropriate after each recall trial to maintain motivation. No feedback is permitted as to how many words were recalled or comprise the list. Should the examinee ask if a word is on the list, simply say something like, "Do the best you can, or "Keep going so you don't forget." Sometimes an examinee will say, "Not again!" by Trial 3 or 4, or the recall Trial. Simply say something like, "You're doing fine and we'll be done soon," or "Keep trying your best."

It is intended that all words (correct and incorrect) be recorded on the lines provided on the Record Form; words not on the list should be written out phonetically for subsequent analysis. It is interesting to see whether detected errors are self-corrected over trials (an encouraging sign) or if the distortions remain despite repeated exposures to the correct stimuli. This kind of information would be gladly received by the speech and language pathologist receiving a referral on a given examinee.

If the examiner is unable to record responses because they are given too fast, it is appropriate to ask the examinee to "slow down" or "say that again" to clarify. A helpful hint for recording responses quickly is to record just the first letter of a list word since each word begins with a unique letter.

Prompting the examinee to guess or repeating the direction that words "can be recalled in any order" is acceptable if the examinee seems hesitant. Alternatively, saying something like "How did the list begin/end?" or "What others pop into your head" is acceptable to encourage

INTERPRETING WRAML3 SUBTESTS, INDEXES   109

effort. If the examinee appears frustrated by the length of the word list, it is appropriate to reiterate the direction that "Most people don't remember all of the words; just do the best you can." On the other hand, extended waiting at the end of a trial after the examinee stops reporting words following such a prompt, seldom adds much to the examinee's trial performance.

One point is awarded for each correct word recalled. Plurals of the target words are counted as correct. The subtest raw score consists of the total number of correct words reported (across Trials 1–4). In the Record Form, space is available to sketch the examinee's performance across trials and appears immediately adjacent to the learning curve of the Design Learning subtest for ease of comparison. The size of each space also allows for the trial recall data from the examinee's age cohort to be added for additional comparison.

OPTIONAL RELATED SUBTESTS

VL Delayed

Similar to the other Delayed subtests, following a 20–30-minute interval, examinees are again asked to recall as many of the words they can remember from the list that was read "over and over." The list is not read again for the Delayed condition. Similar to the Immediate condition, record all words for the Delayed trial in the space provided on the Record Form making comparison of items across both conditions easy.

The raw score for the Delayed VL subtest is the number of words correctly recalled in that single trial. Note that there is a restricted range for the Delayed VL subtest (13 data points for the younger and 16 for the older examinees) so the basal and ceiling levels will offer less precision psychometrically since there are not enough raw score points to cover a scaled score range from 1 to 19. Consequently, for example, a raw score of 0 for a young 7-year-old will earn a scaled score of 2; nonetheless, that scaled score would still be interpreted as a significant weakness and a rare event. Accordingly, the examiner should realize that for this subtest, it is possible that lowest and highest earned scaled scores

ESSENTIALS OF WRAML3 AND EMS ASSESSMENT

may be relative underestimates of "true" weakness and strength, respectively. Using the Immediate memory scaled score (made up of many more raw score points) may be a way of reasonably estimating the degree of over- or underestimation. The norms found in Table A.27 of the *Administration* manual indicate that the median difference in performance between Trial 4 and the Delayed trial is generally a loss of about one to three words except for the youngest age group (5-year-olds). Therefore, the loss of many recalled words in the Delayed condition is unusual and likely of clinical importance, particularly if this pattern of memory decay is also found for the Story Memory subtest.

VL Recognition

Following the VL Delayed subtest, the VL Recognition subtest may be administered. Like Story Memory Recognition, the examiner reads each item that includes three choices (words) and a "none of these" option. Also as with Story Memory, it is permissible to repeat a Recognition item as well as briefly clarify the meaning of the "none" response if the examinee appears confused. Corresponding to the Immediate and Delayed conditions, there are three fewer items for 5- to 9-year-olds than for those 10 years and older with Recognition; that division is clearly marked on the Record Form. The raw score for the VL Recognition subtest is the number of correct responses earned.

As noted in other discussions of Delayed vs. Recognition subtests, when the VL Delayed subtest shows little or no forgetting, it is unlikely that the Recognition component will yield important clinical information as recognition memory is typically more robust than free recall. Yet, there may be reasons to administer the subtest, such as to calculate the Index Score for Recognition Memory or to obtain a Performance Validity indicator.

Process Scores

The VL subtest has the most Process Scores associated with it. Raw score norms for all VL Process Scores are found in Table A.27 of the *Administration* manual.

Individual Learning Trial Performance

As already noted, the VL subtest is an intentional analogue with the Design Learning subtest providing another "real time" novel learning and memory experience that can be observed in "real time" by the examiner. Immediate, Delayed, and Recognition performance from both subtests provides an easy comparison of visual vs. verbal acquisition, longer-term recall and retrieval. Accordingly, both subtests employ some Process Score analyses in common such as the learning acquisition curve. Using the VL trial-by-trial results clinically has already been described above as well as in Chapter 3.

Learning Slope Analysis

Analogous to the Design Learning subtest, the VL Slope Analysis is simply the difference between the number of words recalled on Trials 4 and 1, and so yields a quick estimate of the overall learning achieved. The derived difference can be evaluated using a significance-based comparison with age-mates' performance, and/or by using an age-related base rate frequency. Over the course of the learning trials, an increasing number of words are typically recalled yielding a positive Learning Slope. Little change in Slope suggests that repetition and perhaps prompting may have limited positive effect on learning less meaningful verbal information, such as reviewing facts for a history test. A negative Learning Slope result would be highly unusual and would call into question the examinee's effort, marked fatigue, or severe disability.

As with Design Learning, the Learning Slope statistic of VL is a summary statistic and so atypical variability on the intervening trials (i.e., Trials 2 and 3) will not be taken into account. Noting normative performances for all four trials can be helpful here, and its clinical usefulness was illustrated in the case of Sam in Chapter 3.

Semantic and Phonetic Errors

Semantic errors occur when the examinee recalls a word that is related in meaning to a target word (e.g., "pond" for "lake"). Phonetic errors occur when the examinee recalls a word that sounds like the target word (e.g., "late" for "lake"). These kinds of recall errors are examined in the procedure used with the VL Recognition subtest. Each item of that subtest includes four alternatives, three words and a "none" option. When the word grouping includes the correct list word (e.g., boat), the two incorrect alternatives will include one with phonological "facsimile" (e.g., coat) and the other with a semantic "facsimile" (e.g., ship). Such errors, while not creditable, may be clinically relevant. Word finding difficulties or language processing confusions may underlie semantic errors and may be evidence of language processing issues. Phonetic errors may have similar diagnostic roots but also could be indicators of poor auditory discrimination or compromised hearing acuity. Both Phonetic and Semantic errors are often found with left temporal lobe neurological deficits, such as seizures, focal brain injury, etc. While such errors can point to language deficits, they can as well imply memory difficulties, or both conditions.

Intrusion Errors

An intrusion error occurs when an examinee "recalls" a word that is not on the target list. Intrusion errors are tallied only for the immediate recall trial. However, while there are no data for intrusion errors for the Delayed trial, documenting the same intrusion errors after a time delay may further support suspicions of memory difficulties, difficulty profiting from feedback and possibly a tendency toward perseveration. Interestingly, among the standardization sample, there is little change in the tendency to make Intrusion errors with age. Over the four VL Immediate trials, younger examinees average one to one-and-a-half intrusions while examinees over 65 years average about 2. Since they are a relatively rare event, multiple intrusions should capture clinical attention.

It is important to note that when words are presented over and over, there is the opportunity for "corrective feedback" from more exposure from additional trials. Therefore, one would expect spontaneous removal of intrusion errors made on an earlier trial. Comparing the acquisition pattern on the VL with that on the analogous Design Learning subtest or with Story Memory might provide some clinical clues as to how pervasive strengths or weaknesses are in new learning and recall.

Repetition Errors

A list word (or an intrusion) repeated would be considered a repetition. Multiple repeats of the same word within a trial constitute additional Repetition errors. However, examinees who, for example, are talking to themselves while looking up at the ceiling, should not be charged with a repetition error. On occasion, it may be difficult to determine if a repetition is a "true" repetition as examinees can sometimes "self-cue" to help themselves remember what was just reported. At that point, it is permissible to ask if the examinee thinks the response was already said for that trial (e.g., "Did you say that one before?"). If the examinee does not recall saying the word previously, it is recorded as a repetition error. The rule of thumb for the examiner is that when the list word is thought to be repeated as an examinee's test response (*vs.* a self-prompt) it is considered a Repetition error. Repetitions may represent an absence of self-monitoring, a tendency toward perseveration, divided attention, or a severe memory problem. It should also be noted that an Intrusion error is recorded as such the first time a word is recalled but if repeated during a trial, then it is then considered a Repetition error even though the word was not on the list. The total number of Repetition Errors across the four Immediate trials is the Raw Score for this process variable. Repetition Errors are a bit more frequent than Intrusions, but still are relatively rare responses across all age cohorts and hence, often of clinical interest.

Primacy and Recency

From the early days of research by Ebbinghaus (1885), a Primacy/Recency recall effect has been an enduring finding of memory research. Accordingly, examinees typically recall the first (primacy) and last (recency) words most efficiently on this subtest. Failure to do so raises concerns about whether the examinee's memory system operates in a "typical" fashion and whether that atypicality shown in a verbal Immediate memory task may extend into other aspects of verbal memory performance, such as with Delayed or long-term memory. Random recall could suggest difficulty with organizational abilities which naturally will affect overall recall. If found, it should be corroborated with other subtest results such as those of Story Memory and Verbal Working Memory both of which have strong organizational components related to executive functioning. Theoretically, primacy and recency should be most obviously observed with the first and maybe the second learning trial. Thereafter, executive functions start organizing words so more can be remembered (e.g., combining "door" and "wood"), so early trials probably merit a closer look qualitatively for primacy/recency effects. For those examinees primarily recalling mostly the last few words presented, even on Trials 3 and 4, raises serious concerns about a "short memory loop" as might be seen in dementia.

It is of academic interest that comparing median performance on this subtest across age cohorts, a developmental shift seems to occur. Specifically, there is a slightly higher percentage of Recency words reported over the four trials for those 5 to 7 years of age. At 8 and 9 years, the percentages are fairly equal, and then primacy becomes slightly higher from ages 10 to 69 years, at which age recency regains the advantage. The differences are never more than a few percentage points, but even so, the trends are sufficiently consistent that there may be some credence to the finding. It is unclear if this recall phenomenon is unique to WRAML3 or list learning generally since developmental trends in primacy and recency have apparently not been investigated given the existing literature.

Primacy

The Primacy score is differentially calculated depending on the age of the examinee. For 5- to 9-year-olds, sum the number of initial times the examinee says each of the *first three* words on each of the four immediate trials (i.e., "sand," "game," "hat"). For the 10–90 age group, because of the longer word list, sum the number of initial times the examinee says each of the *first four words* (i.e., "sand," "game," "hat," "tree"). Repetitions are not included in the calculation. The Primacy Score is divided by the VL subtest total raw score, rounded to the nearest whole number, and multiplied by 100. This calculation represents the percentage of Primacy words of the total words recalled.

Recency

The Recency score calculation is obtained in a similar manner as for the Primacy score. For the younger group, sum the number of times the *last three* words on each immediate trial are recalled (i.e., "nail," "ice," "boat") while for the older group, sum the number of times the examinee recalls the *last four words* summed over the four trials (i.e., "boat," "page," "ant," "lake"). For both age groups, the Recency Total Score is then divided by the VL Total Raw score, rounded to the nearest whole number, and multiplied by 100. This calculation yields the percentage of Recency words recalled out of the total words recalled.

Interesting Observations

- If total responses on Trial 1 are atypical compared to Trial 3 and 4 (compared to the examinee's age cohort), consider anxiety as a possible cause when the examinee is confronted with a long list of random words they fear they cannot learn adequately.
- Subsequently numbering words in order of recall is recommended. It allows corroboration of atypical verbal sequencing findings as well as consistency of responses over trials. This is especially useful if the expected primacy/recency findings are not obtained.
- For those who would like to create a visual representation of primacy and recency, draw a straight line from the first primacy word recalled from the first Trial (column 1) to the position of that same word on the second, third and fourth Trials. Repeat this procedure for the remaining primacy words recalled. Do this again for the set recency words. The resulting graph should show basically a top and a bottom grouping of lines across the four trials. Many mid-list intersecting lines or dis-connecting lines across trials suggest an atypical pattern of recall. This procedure could be extended to include the Delayed trial as well.
- The maintenance of intrusion errors in subsequent trials may suggest hypotheses like language disorder, limited ability to learn from mistakes, perseverative tendencies, cognitive disinhibition, difficulty with self-monitoring, hearing difficulties, or intellectual disability.
- At the end of the battery, it is permissible to ask how the examinee remembered the words (or patterns with Design Learning). Especially with older children and adults, asking might provide a window into the examinee's metamemory ability.

- Generating phonetically similar words like "free" for "tree" might suggest hearing or auditory discrimination problems, as might "leaning in," cupping an ear with a hand, or requesting repetition of instructions or the actual words.
- For older children and adults, it is common to observe associational patterns that aid recall such as a "tree-wood-door" sequence to emerge by Trials 3 or 4. Such subjective organizational strategies imply a good use of executive functions to aid rote recall.

Common Administration Errors

- Inappropriately using the wrong length VL word list given the examinee's age.
- Reading the words too slowly or too quickly. (When learning the test, record your administration of the subtest, and then check its accuracy, especially pacing.)
- Not enunciating words clearly (e.g., Is "beau" an intrusion error, or the correct recall of what the examiner said when they omitted the ending consonant sound in "boat?").
- Incomplete recording of the examinee's performance because of their fast recall pace. This is a common problem for examiners new to the test. Solutions: (1) record the subtest (with guardian or examinee's permission, if needed) and score it later, or (2) write only the first letter of each correct word recalled since each word on the list starts with a unique letter; that way, the list can subsequently be recreated and scored, and the order of word recall can be examined.
- Not noticing that most words given on Trial X are not also provided in Trial X + 1. When this initially occurs, be sure to use the prompt found in the WRAML3 *Administration* manual, "Be sure to tell me all the words you remember – the words you told me last time as well as any new words you remember."
- Telling the client how many words make up the list.
- Reading the word list in the VL Delayed administration.
- Age-inappropriate list of items used with VL Recognition.

Rapid Reference 4.4

Subtest Administration Rubric: Verbal Learning

Immediate VL	Yes	No
1. Administered correct word list for client's age		
2. Instructions are read verbatim and clearly; all instructions included		
3. Encouragement given if examinee seems overwhelmed by the task		
4. One-second pause between words		
5. Neutral intonation used for each word other than last word (voice drops)		
6. Prompts after examinee stops to ensure they are finished with Trial		
7. Prompt of "both old and new" words given if needed, Trials 2–4		
8. Four trials administered		
9. All responses of examinee accurately recorded		
10. Raw score computed accurately		
11. Intrusions accurately recorded		
12. Repetitions accurately recorded		
13. Accurate scaled score obtained		
VL Delayed and Recognition	**Yes**	**No**
14. Directions for Delayed trial read correctly		
15. Delayed trial raw score correct		
16. Delayed scaled score correct		
17. Age-appropriate item set used for Recognition		
18. Recognition directions read correctly		
19. Recognition choices read at proper speed and with clear articulation		
20. "None of these" option explained as needed		

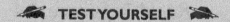

TEST YOURSELF

Verbal Memory Index Subtests

1. **Comparing Immediate to Delayed Story Memory raw score performance**
   (a) there is a decline of about 20% in Delayed Memory scores for young teens.
   (b) males decline more than females in Delayed scores.
   (c) a decline of about 20% is observed for those 70 years and older.
   (d) there is little decline regardless of age.
   (e) there is so much variability that age or gender generalizations are difficult to make.

2. **Some individuals with Autism Spectrum Disorder might be adept at recalling specific story details but struggle with the meaning of the narrative. To investigate this possibility, which Process Score might help confirm that diagnosis with a given examinee?**
   (a) Primacy and Recency
   (b) Quadrant Analysis
   (c) Gist vs. Verbatim
   (d) Story A vs. Story B comparison
   (e) Story Comprehension

3. **A 9-year-old was referred for academic difficulties. The examinee's WRAML3 raw score performance on Verbal Learning trials 1–4 was as follows: 4, 5, 6, 5; Delayed 4. Which hypothesis seems supported from just these results?**
   (a) Speech and Language therapy is indicated.
   (b) Additional homework in reading is indicated.
   (c) The teacher's instructional sessions should be recorded so this student could listen again.
   (d) Exploring visual learning approaches is indicated.
   (e) Efforts teaching a phonetic approach should be redoubled.

INTERPRETING WRAML3 SUBTESTS, INDEXES 119

4. **What should be an examiner's expectation for Intrusion errors when administering the Verbal Learning subtest?**
   (a) they are heard more often in teens than 30- to 40-year-olds.
   (b) those older than 65 show the most intrusion errors.
   (c) intrusion errors noticeably decrease with age until age 70.
   (d) intrusion errors noticeably increase with age until age 70.
   (e) intrusion errors average fewer than 1 per learning trial for all age ranges.

5. **For the Story Memory subtest, it is clinically appropriate to**
   (a) repeat the first story if it is poorly recalled.
   (b) number the examinee's responses sequentially as they are being recalled.
   (c) administer Story A and B if an adult examinee does poorly on C and D.
   (d) start with the recognition component before delayed recall.
   (e) omit the subtest with examinees known to have language disorders.

Answers: 1d, 2c, 3d, 4e, 5b

Attention Concentration Index (ACI)

Many of you have viewed the classic video that asks the viewer to count the number of times a basketball is bounced. Meanwhile, a seven-foot gorilla leisurely walks across the screen amidst the players. It is common for most first-time viewers to come up with a correct number of bounces but be totally oblivious of the gorilla. (To find the video simply search online for "gorilla basketball video.") This video was cleverly developed to demonstrate that focused attention essentially blocks out competing sensory stimuli from being put on the processing "conveyor belt" leading to memory encoding and storage. Because attention is so central to memory acquisition, it is not surprising that most "memory modelers" believe that it is the preliminary component in the recall sequence (Angelopoulou & Drigas, 2021; Atkinson & Shiffrin, 1968). Therefore, given the importance of attention, it is not surprising that providing an estimate of attention within a memory battery would be considered important.

The WRAML3's ACI measures immediate memory using attentionally demanding, relatively rote, sequential information using two subtests; one of these makes rote visual processing demands and the other rote verbal demands. Across all age groups, the two subtests show a correlation at the low-moderate end of around .26 which suggests they are assessing related but distinct content. As the ACI subtests appear later in the battery, they may also yield important observations about how an examinee's attention may be affected by cognitive fatigue. Given the variability of attention as it interacts with different stimulus arrays, having two different measures of attention has utility.

With time pressures, particularly when similar data are compiled from other test procedures, the examiner may want to skip administering the ACI subtests and for those situations, the WRAML3 Screener Index format has been provided (more will be said of it in Chapter 6). However, when time permits, it is strongly recommended that the ACI subtests be administered. There are several reasons for this recommendation. First, the subtests may not be duplications of other short-term memory measures already obtained. For example, one of those ACI subtests, Number Letter, is not, as with several other tests, contaminated with a backward recall procedure which involves additional cognitive subprocesses (such as working memory) than digits forward by itself. The other ACI subtest, Finger Windows, does not employ symbols per se, and provides an estimate of visual, rote sequential memory which might, for example, provide an interesting finding for youngsters with reading or language disorders. Results from Number Letter and Finger Windows not only provide a good estimate of attention but also provide diagnostically meaningful standardized comparisons with other WRAML3 measures. For example, comparing performance on Number Letter with that from Story Memory allows comparison of a memory task making heavy semantic demands with one making minimal such demands. Adding the Sentence Memory subtest (discussed below) allows yet a further comparison with a task making verbal memory demands that conceptually fall somewhere between Number Letter and Story Memory.

Also, as both ACI subtests tend to be heavily dependent on the ability to concentrate, it is good to include both verbal and nonverbal measures of rote recall for clinical utilization. It should also be noted that rote memory measures such as the ACI subtests are highly related to ecologically important tasks, such as academic skills. For example, the ACI is generally more highly correlated with reading, spelling, and math achievement than are the more content-heavy Visual and Verbal Indexes for both Immediate, Delayed, and Recognition formats. Having such differing measures, therefore, can be very useful in diagnostic formulation as well as for generating and meeting remedial goals.

From a practical perspective, the ACI measures are relatively quick to administer. As such, they provide an efficiently obtained estimate of attention, but since the ACI is one of the Performance Validity indicators, its utilization serves an important additional purpose as well, boosting its value of clinical return given the minimal investment of time.

ACI subtests obviously do not have Delayed or Recognition counterparts since they intentionally focus on attending only to short-term memory demands. There are no process scores associated with its two subtests, in part, because of test length as well as reasonable redundancy with some Process Scores already found as part of the Visual and Verbal Memory Index subtests.

Finger Windows (FW)

Prior to the beginning of the WRAML3 re-standardization effort, the authors asked for user feedback about needed changes for the next edition. One consistent response was a request to make the longer items of the FW subtest easier to administer. As a result, the single card of the WRAML2 was replaced with multiple FW cards each showing one or more of the correct "paths" for FW items. For all items, the examiner now sees numbers and arrows leading from a starting "window" to an ending "window" shown on the back of the new stimulus cards; directions also appear with the illustrated sequence(s) to ease administration. Multiple cards are used to prevent confusion with overlapping sequences when combining several items. Obviously, the examinee never sees the side of the cards with the pathway numbers and arrows; those are viewed exclusively by the examiner. While the administration of the FW subtest has been greatly simplified using the new cards, the downside is that there are more parts for the examiner to manage and keep out of examinee view.

As the analogue to Number Letter, the FW subtest evaluates immediate memory for relatively rote visual sequential information. A young child trying to reproduce a motor sequence right after watching a friend's efforts (e.g., shoe tying or playing Simon Says) is likely using similar memory skills; adults may be using FW recall skills when making turns in a new neighborhood immediately after viewing a route map.

Administration Procedures
While the subtest is named Finger Windows, as the directions state, the examiner uses the eraser side of a pencil to demonstrate the path of the window sequence, but the examinee is asked to use a finger to replicate it. Some younger examinees playfully use more than one finger to point out the visual sequence, which can add to scoring confusion. A request like "point with just one finger" usually suffices.

Present the FW Stimulus Card perpendicular to the table about 12 inches from the examinee. Make sure not to block any "windows" with your hand or fingers when holding the edge of the card. Also, since smaller children can often see directly through the "windows" while seated, it may be appropriate to wear a smock or apron should the examiner be wearing clothing or jewelry that could be distracting. The examiner should maintain a uniform pace in demonstrating sequences, and one second should elapse between the examiner's removal of the pencil's eraser from a "window" and its insertion through the next. Typically, the subtest's game-like format is attention-getting and easily elicits involvement. All cards can withstand sanitizing wipes.

With respect to scoring, it is recommended that the numbered response sequence produced by the examinee always be recorded so the execution of the task can be subsequently analyzed. This is especially important when recording errors. For example, missing a 7-element item and making one mistake connotes a different level of "weakness" than if most of the sequence is forgotten or full of mistakes. One point is awarded for each completely correct sequence and correct items are summed for the total raw score.

Interesting Observations

- Individuals with a high level of impulsivity may begin pointing before the examiner gives the required prompt, "Begin." If this persists after a reminder, this behavior may be relevant to concerns around oppositional or disinhibited tendencies.
- It is not unusual for some examinees to simply indicate that they do not think they can do a harder item. At least for the first and second time this happens, it is worthwhile to urge the examinee to "Just give it a try. You might surprise yourself." It is not uncommon for performance on this (and the Design Learning subtest) to be better than the examinee expects.
- It is typical for examinees to do better with "windows" near the corners and less well in the middle (a visual equivalent to primacy and recency?). This normally holds unless a client has a field cut or attentional dysregulation such as with visual agnosia.
- Performance on FW can be compared to the spatial placement on the Design Learning subtest if the examiner records the examinee's numbered sequence rather than simply marking the item correct or incorrect.
- Diagnostically, the FW subtest may provide a useful comparison with Picture Memory performance and that of the first and maybe second trials of Design Learning.
- The directions indicate that the examiner should be sure the examinee is focused on the card before each sequence is administered. This is especially true for younger examinees. The fact that the examiner must frequently orient the child to the task before beginning an item is a noteworthy observation.

124 ESSENTIALS OF WRAML3 AND EMS ASSESSMENT

Common Administration Errors

- Start places (dependent on age), a reverse rule, and a discontinue rule are all parts of this subtest and may be neglected by examiners.
- New examiners often need additional work to achieve a smooth "cadence" of presentation, including maintaining the one-second latency between window exits and entrances.
- Avoid withholding an FW card at an angle; it seems to make the task a bit harder.
- Allowing the examinee to see the back of one or more FW cards likely contaminates the subtest.
- By not having the subtest materials well-organized at the outset, fumbling and administration errors are more likely to occur with this subtest.

≡ *Rapid Reference 4.5*

Subtest Administration Rubric: Finger Windows

	Yes	No
1. Work area clear for administration		
2. Instructions appropriate for examinee's age, and read verbatim and clearly		
3. Correct starting item selected, based on age.		
4. All cards sequenced accurately, and each placed about 12 inches from examinee		
5. Cards held perpendicular to the table in front of client		
6. Examiner's hand or fingers not blocking any windows when holding cards		
7. Printed side of card never seen by participant.		
8. Examiner is sure examinee is looking before starting pointing sequence throughout		
9. Eraser end of a pencil used by examiner to pass through windows		

	Yes	No
10. Each sequence done accurately		
11. Pencil latency between removal and next insertion lasts 1 second per window		
12. "Begin" direction immediately follows examiner's demonstration throughout		
13. If a 10-year-old or older examinee fails the first item (#5), reverse rule to item 1 followed after training		
14. Discontinue rule observed (2 consecutive 0 responses)		
15. Raw score computed accurately		
16. Scaled score accurately obtained.		

Number Letter (NL)

The NL subtest assesses the examinee's ability to recall rote, sequential auditory information using a digit-span forward paradigm. This short-term ability is likely utilized in such tasks as immediately recording a dictated phone number or birthdate. Difficulty with the NL subtest is likely reflected in weaknesses with other rote memory demands of everyday life such as a warehouse supervisor orally telling an employee on which numbered shelves desired items may be found; or a student's recalling the verbatim content upon hearing the teacher say "Turn to page 44 in your math book, and do problems 1–4, and 10–14." Similarly, correctly recording specifics of a desired recipe mentioned on a cooking show (tablespoon vs. teaspoon) would likely be challenging for those with poor NL results.

Some consider the NL subtest a bit more difficult than a digit recall task as two symbol systems are employed (numbers and letters). This may be especially evident with examinees with auditory processing deficits, some forms of learning disability, or those with marked deficits with sustained focus. Because of the two symbol systems, the NL subtest

Administrative Procedures

As with the Finger Windows subtest, examinee age determines one of two start points. The subtest's administration is straightforward: read a group of random numbers and letters one per second, dropping one's voice slightly at the end of the string to signal the end of the item, and inviting the examinee's response. Because there are no semantic clues to help with processing, it is important that examiners speak loudly and clearly. This is especially important with older examinees who may be experiencing hearing loss (particularly when enunciating sound-alikes such as "3," "B," and "D"), as well as for examinees who may be culturally different from the examiner. Examinees with speech impairment or a strong accent may present a particular challenge to the examiner as well. If, after listening closely to the examinee, the examiner is unsure of a response, it can be flagged, and at the end of the subtest ask the examinee to repeat the ambiguous elements separately for scoring purposes. For example, the examiner may ask the examinee at the end of the subtest: "Say T. Now say 3," and then appropriately score the item.

One point is awarded for each totally correct item sequence. No feedback is permitted (but reasonable encouragement is always appropriate) and examinee questions or extraneous comments should be responded to by a quick reminder to respond to the task at hand ("Let's talk about that later; here's the next one. Ready?").

Interesting Observations
- An atypical recall pattern that suggests divided or inconsistent attention skills is one in which erratic successes are interposed with intermittent misses so that failure on easy items is followed by success on more difficult items. This sometimes leads to a "ceiling" that is achieved much later than the examiner anticipated.
- Listen for sound discrimination errors, examinees leaning in to hear, or asking for items to be repeated (which is not allowed).

INTERPRETING WRAML3 SUBTESTS, INDEXES   127

Such observations may suggest compromised hearing and/or auditory discrimination, possibly leading to an audiology referral. Alternatively, these observations may suggest that the examiner is not speaking loudly or clearly enough.

- If the examiner has access to the scores from a traditional digit span task, comparing NL performance with "digits forward" is probably worthwhile in order to assess comparability. Longest length of correct items and subtest scaled score results should be roughly similar between measures, although those who struggle more with symbol processing (e.g., those with reading disability) may show somewhat lower NL performance because of greater symbol manipulation demands. Along that vein, comparing NL with Verbal Working Memory may provide an approximate way to separate rote recall and executive function components.

- A comparison between the Number Letter and the Finger Windows subtests allows for hypotheses around rote visual-verbal recall discrepancies if supported by the discrepancy analysis for these two subtests.

- Comparing the first trial of the Verbal Learning subtest with the NL subtest may serve as a consistency check. For those 10 years and older, the maximum number of elements consistently recalled on NL often corresponds to the number of words recalled.

- Examine whether an item is failed because most of the elements are wrong, or only one or two is/are incorrect. A series of "close failures" may temper one's interpretation of a mediocre scaled score.

- With incorrect items, note whether item elements are typically missing, transposed, or wrong. Transpositions may signal sequencing problems, whereas missing or incorrect elements often connote memory weaknesses. Note that this will require recording what the examinee says rather than just marking an item right or wrong.

- Note if an item is failed because elements from the previous item or two are incorporated into the subsequent item. "Leaky" rote verbal memory skills have clinical implications (e.g., confusing which details are associated with which steps in a set of directions).

- It is always appropriate to examine academic functioning when suboptimal NL performances are observed given the demand for

128 ESSENTIALS OF WRAML3 AND EMS ASSESSMENT

rote sequential memory with reading and spelling, particularly in the early grades.

Common Administration Errors

- Start places (dependent on age), a reverse rule, and a discontinue rule are all parts of the procedures associated with this subtest and are sometimes neglected by examiners.
- Numbers/letters read too quickly or too slowly (versus one per second) can negatively influence performance. Examiners can sometimes unconsciously "speed up" item presentation (especially near the end of a test), or chunk a lengthy item into a "telephone number" cadence.
- Performance can be negatively impacted when elements are not enunciated well or not loudly enough by the examiner (e.g., possibly signaled when the client says "two" when the examiner says "Q").
- The examiner fails to drop their voice at the end of a sequence leaving the examinee waiting for the end of the item.
- Not evaluating poor examinee articulation sufficiently when scoring an item can result in a questionable score.

≡ Rapid Reference 4.6

Subtest Administration Rubric: Number Letter

	Yes	No
1. All instructions read verbatim, clearly, and chosen correctly for examinee's age.		
2. Correct starting item used, based on examinee's age.		
3. Letters and numbers read clearly at a rate of one per second.		
4. Voice drops at end of item string.		

	Yes	No
5. Items read with equal inflection (other than final items) at a steady rate (one per second).		
6. For those 10 years or older, if a score of 0 is obtained on item 5, reversing to item #1 followed.		
7. Discontinue rule observed (2 consecutive failed items).		
8. Correct Raw score computed.		
9. Correct Scaled score obtained		

TEST YOURSELF

Attention/Concentration Index Subtests

1. **Which is an incorrect statement for the Finger Windows subtest?**
   (a) The subtest uses a "discontinue" rule.
   (b) The subtest uses a "reverse" rule.
   (c) The subtest uses age to determine the starting item.
   (d) The subtest is timed.
   (e) All the above statements are correct.

2. **A referred student does poorly on the Number Letter subtest. Which statement would be most reasonable to expect to be reported in teachers' or parents' comments if the test finding is valid?**
   (a) The student refuses to do chores at home.
   (b) The student struggles with math.
   (c) The student has trouble with verbatim parts of oral directions.
   (d) The student forgets to bring their homework to school.
   (e) All these comments are related to poor performance on the subtest.

130 ESSENTIALS OF WRAML3 AND EMS ASSESSMENT

3. Which is true of the Finger Windows subtest?

(a) Multiple plastic cards are used to aid the examiner's sequencing of windows.

(b) Both examiners and examinees demonstrate the window sequence using their index finger.

(c) No teaching is allowed for failed items.

(d) The subtest's total raw score should be close to that of the first trial of Design Learning.

(e) Forward and backward sequences are included in the subtest's administration.

4. Administering both Attention Concentration subtests is worthwhile

(a) only if no other measure of rote memory has been used.

(b) when attention on other parts of WRAML3 seems problematic.

(c) mostly when stimulant medication doses are being evaluated.

(d) when testing time is limited.

(e) when a Performance Validity measure is desired.

5. The Attention Concentration Index

(a) has the lowest reliability among WRAML3 Indexes.

(b) consists of subtests that are fairly time-consuming for examiners to administer.

(c) consists of subtests that are highly correlated with each other.

(d) is more correlated with academic achievement than the Immediate Visual or Immediate Verbal Index.

(e) measures attention rather than memory.

Answers: 1d, 2c, 3a, 4e, 5d

Sentence Memory (SenM)

Because of the importance of like-content in our culture, the Sentence Memory subtest was retained on WRAML3. This optional subtest demands a short amount of verbal recall providing an important intermediate comparison between the Story Memory subtest's extensive demands and the Number Letter's nonsemantic auditory recall. Note that the content of SenM is akin to the bulk of verbal directions or requests heard in the real world, making the subtest an ecologically relevant recall measure. Comparison with Story Memory performance essentially provides insight into what happens to an examinee's verbal memory when the linguistic load significantly increases. When Story Memory performance plummets compared to SenM, hypotheses about verbal memory capacity might be entertained along with possible language processing difficulties. Often evidence for language difficulties can be detected in simpler tasks once content reaches a certain "language load" and then performance drops precipitously. Language disorder may present early on as distortions (e.g., "Scott really likes to watch basketball" is recalled as "Scotch really likes to TV basketballs.") more than omitting a part of the sentence. (Incidentally, the example just provided contains evidence for considering auditory discrimination difficulties as well.) Regardless of the reason, it is understandable that if there are struggles with recall of five- or six-word sentences, then performance on Story Memory would be expected to be especially challenging. Language problems can be confused as memory problems and trigger referrals for memory assessment.

For examinees with specific language processing weaknesses, this subtest may be of particular interest. Since the sentences to be recalled increase in length and complexity, they can provide a window into the nature of the examinee's language disorder. Limitations in the length of connected word recall, semantic confusions, and issues with grammar may be observed on this subtest. For examinees with significant temporal lobe insult, the SenM subtest may be "acceptable" to the examinee whereas the Story Memory subtest might be frustrating after the first few sentences.

It can be useful to note the sentence length when memory errors begin to appear on this subtest, and when overall performance is poor compared to age-mates, the examiner can recommend that the length of novel classroom or home-based verbal directions (or instructions) generally not exceed that sentence length. In addition, looking at Number Letter performance will provide an expectation of whether specifics within the directions may not be encoded efficiently. For example, the direction, "Turn to page 81 in your math books, and let's look at problem 5," has about 14 words and about three important verbatim elements. The examiner can reasonably estimate how much of that sentence will be successfully encoded (barring context) by checking verbal recall capacity using SenM, as well as verbatim capability using Number Letter and easier portions of Story Memory. Comparison with Verbatim and Gist measures on Story Memory should also be examined to ensure a consistent diagnostic message is being obtained.

Administration Procedure

Only an immediate memory condition is used for SM. All sentences are provided on the Record Form, and begin with items of a few words and gradually become longer. It is a simple subtest to administer. Each sentence is read verbatim using both rate and tone appropriate for storytelling. The subtest's starting point is determined by age, and Discontinue and Reverse Rules are to be observed.

It is important to record examinee responses precisely using the space just above each sentence in the Record Form; record additions above the sentence segment using a caret, cross out words that were omitted, and write over the words that were altered. This information is often useful to address questions arising as diagnostic formulations are being worked on. For examinees who speak too quickly or with speech issues, recording subtest responses for later scoring is encouraged with the appropriate permissions. Normally, however, prompting the examinee to "slow down," "speak louder," or "say as much as you can remember" is sufficient to encourage acceptable responding.

For scoring, additions, omissions, or substitutions are counted as errors, and strict scoring applies (e.g., "you are" recalled as "you're" is an error) with exceptions for local accent or colloquialisms; the *Administration* manual gives examples of these. Two points are awarded for a correctly recalled sentence with 1 point awarded if one error is made; two or more errors earn 0 points. The subtest is discontinued once 0 is earned on two consecutive sentences.

INTERPRETING WRAML3 SUBTESTS, INDEXES 133

Interesting Observations

- An examinee who makes a few minor errors on failed items likely has a different verbal memory than an examinee who forgets whole segments of the sentence but earns the same score. Performance that preserves most of the sentence's meaning but still earns 0 point is worth noting for diagnostic and prescriptive purposes. Thus, recording examinee errors verbatim is important.
- Encourage guessing so that qualitative information can be captured.
- Compare consistency of common SenM errors with those found in Story Memory (e.g., semantic and phonological errors). Noting sentence length in SenM may be of interest in determining why certain Story Memory content was or was not retained.
- Once examinees begin to earn 0 points for items, a ceiling is typically near. The exception to this might be examinees who are poorly attentive and specific sentence content re-establishes focus so a variable pattern of success-failure occurs near the end of the subtest.

Common Administration Errors

- Incorrect starting place for age of examinee.
- Failing to employ the reverse rule for those 10 years and older who perform poorly on item 6.
- Sentences are read too quickly or slowly, rather than with a "story-like" reading rate, rhythm, and inflection.
- Sentences are read too quietly or with slushy articulation.
- The examiner's voice fails to drop at the end of a sentence leaving the examinee waiting for more.
- Not speaking loud enough or clear enough especially for older examinees.
- Scoring items too leniently, such as overlooking changes in tense, adding a word, or changing nouns from singular to plural; conversely, scoring too strictly without accounting for cultural differences.

134 ESSENTIALS OF WRAML3 AND EMS ASSESSMENT

≡ Rapid Reference 4.7

Subtest Administration Rubric: Sentence Memory

	Yes	No
1. Correct starting item used (based on age)		
2. Reads instructions verbatim and clearly		
3. If items 1 and/or 2 failed, teaching extended		
4. Reverse rule accurately followed, if needed		
5. Relaxed "story reading" rate and tone used		
6. Examiner's voice drops slightly at end of each sentence.		
7. Scoring follows 2, 1, 0 criteria applied strictly		
8. Discontinue rule appropriately applied		
9. Accurate raw score computed		
10. Accurate scaled score obtained		

Working Memory Index (WMI)

A discussion of the nature of working memory is found in Chapter 3. Consistent with the WRAML3 domain format, the WMI provides estimates of both visual as well as verbal working memory. Reflecting the nature of working memory, each domain requires that certain executive functions be coordinated with the short-term memory demands involved with the subtests. Consequently, the subtest scores reflect an integration of short-term memory and selective frontal lobe processes. Therefore, it should not be surprising that the WMI has a relatively high correlation with both WISC-V and WAIS-IV Full Scale IQ scores (.65 and .62, respectively), which are among the highest correlations of any of the WRAML3 indexes. Accordingly, it is not surprising that Visual and Verbal Working Memory performance is impressively correlated with academic achievement as well. For example,

INTERPRETING WRAML3 SUBTESTS, INDEXES 135

the WRAML3 working memory subtests consistently yield the highest correlations with Wide Range Achievement Test (WRAT5) performance for individual word and sentence reading as well as math calculation (ranging from .48 to .61). As would then be expected, the composite WMI shows the highest correlation with WRAT5 scores compared to all other WRAML3 Indexes. Similar results are found for correlations with the WIAT-4. Clearly, working memory is a critical component of academic achievement.

Like Verbal and Design Learning subtests, the two working memory subtests have parallel formats so the examiner can compare visual vs. verbal working memory performance using tasks that have similar demands and yield scores derived from a common norm group. Since both working memory subtests are administered near the end of the entire battery, the examiner should be especially sensitive to fatigue; a brief break before starting these two subtests may be appropriate. Nevertheless, nearly all the standardization sample was able to complete the entire battery in one sitting which should give confidence to examiners to push on unless an examinee has a known or suspected condition (e.g., dementia, traumatic brain injury, etc.) that would suggest an extended break or rescheduling to complete the evaluation.

Perhaps to state the obvious, the working memory subtests do not have Delayed or Recognition counterparts since working memory, by definition, is a memory phenomenon related to short-term memory. Also, there are no process scores associated with either working memory subtest, in part, because of considerable redundancy with those processes associated with the other related immediate visual and verbal memory subtests of the WRAML3.

Visual Working Memory (VisWM)

For many examiners, the VisWM subtest is found to be one of the battery's most challenging to administer. In part, that is due to the need to coordinate the numerous stimulus pages while following the extensive guidelines and directions in the Manual and recording the examinee's responses accurately. Several practice sessions will likely be needed to master the procedures for a smooth administration; administering this subtest "cold" is ill advised. The stimulus pages themselves provide starting directions and scoring helps which should ease the pointing and recording requirements. Beyond practice, probably the best thing the examiner can do to ensure a successful subtest administration is to create ample space to place used and yet-to-be-used subtest materials out of the examinee's sight; folders or envelopes for this will prove useful. Also, examiners need to keep the Record Form handy but also out of sight. Benefiting the examiner is the subtest's game-like format, and therefore, the examinee typically finds the task enjoyable so that maintaining motivation is not typically an additional challenge.

Since this is a visual subtest, it is especially important that the examiner not ad-lib additional verbalizations for clarification, but follows the directions verbatim, especially those procedures related to instances when the examinee fails training items. Also, reading the directions relatively slowly (e.g., pauses between sentences) should minimize the verbal content demands of directions on this visual subtest. Despite the need for practice and the challenge of coordinating materials, learning the VisWM is well worth the investment as the subtest provides a useful comparison with its analogous VerWM counterpart.

As has been mentioned, working memory can be thought of as a task with both short-term memory and certain executive functions operating. That is, information must remain in the short-term memory buffer while it is "operated on" or reorganized before recall. Examining the performance of the ADHD clinical sample, it can be seen that those with the disorder tended to do more poorly on visual than verbal working memory. Looking more closely (see Table 4.15 in the *Technical Manual*), it seems that the rote visual memory aspect of the task (as assessed using the Finger Windows subtest) may have a greater negative impact than the executive component since the VisWM standard score is not lower than that of Finger Windows.

Visual working memory is less apparent in Western culture given our hyper-verbal societies. However, it can nonetheless be noted in many situations such as "reading" piano music (trying to stay a measure ahead of what it is one is playing), using visual clues of a video game while developing tactics for what is happening on the screen at the moment, and not getting lost while hiking in nonfamiliar territory that does not have clear trail markings after referring to a trail map. However, as already mentioned, exclusively visual or verbal working memory tasks in the real world may be hard to identify since brains defy the single-factor assumptions test authors like to make when developing subtests! Most brains will simultaneously use memories from multiple sensory systems to try to solve any problem at hand.

Administration Procedure

Procedurally, two item sets are administered to all examinees, the second set being a bit more demanding of working memory. As with other subtests, materials used with 5- to 9-year-olds are not the same as those for 10 years and older. The younger group is administered Sets A and B, whereas the older group gets B and C. The A set has a number of teaching items intended to help guide the young examinee to understand that the examiner will be pointing at common pictures that appear on the stimulus page, and the examinee will need to repeat what was touched but according to a rule provided by the examiner. Roughly half the pictures on a stimulus card belong to one "family" (such as birds) and the remaining pictures belong to a different but related "family" (such as nests). For Set A, the examiner's pointing intermingles some of the items from the two families. The examinee, however, must first point to all that were touched belonging to one family before pointing to those touched and belonging to the other family. Items are arranged in order of increasing difficulty. Following Set A, Set B alters the directions a bit, now asking the examinee to again first point to one family's selected pictures, but in order of *increasing size* before pointing to the indicated pictures from the other family *in any order*. For the older age group (10 years and older), the starting set is Set B. Set C asks the examinee to first point to the designated elements from the initial family grouping *from smallest to largest*, and then *do likewise* with the related family grouping.

Unlike its Verbal Working Memory counterpart on which each item can earn a maximum of 2 points, VisWM items can earn a maximum

138 ESSENTIALS OF WRAML3 AND EMS ASSESSMENT

of 3 points. The difference in scoring exists because, with VisWM, an additional point is awarded when the examinee gets all the items of each grouping correct and also remembers to report the correct grouping first. So, for example, for Set C, Item 3, if the examinee points to all the designated squirrels in the correct size order, and touches all the designated acorns in the correct size order, and touches all the squirrel family elements first (before acorns), then the examinee would earn 2 points for the Group Score and an additional point for the Order Score. Since the Verbal Working Memory directions state that the examiner asks the examinee which "family" to report first and second, no additional point for remembering in which order to report the groupings is awarded for that working memory subtest.

Interesting Observations
- Notice if the client earns credit for recalling the animal or nonanimal grouping, but is seldom successful with both. That would suggest the examinee is trying, but the task taxes their working memory. If one watches only for animals or nonanimals, that removes much of the "working" demand and changes the task into one that is more like a short-term visual memory task. Comparison with Design Learning and Finger Windows results may help in making this determination. Examinees who use this "single family" approach will earn partial credit for items, but the total score may somewhat exaggerate their real visual working memory capability.
- Take note if errors within harder items are "close successes" or full of major omissions or commissions. That is, there are "good errors" and "bad errors." Examinees making "good errors" (missing only one or two elements across both families) as they near the discontinue rule cut-off, probably have better working memory skills than those whose responses to the relatively harder items consist of mostly errors. Such a nuance may be important in the overall interpretation.
- If the subtest is part of a standard administration, look for signs of fatigue given the preceding hour of attention and memory

demands. If the examinee continues to "hang in there" you have strong evidence supporting perseverance, frustration tolerance, and perhaps a strong work ethic, which may merit mention in the Observations section of the report.

- Note if the examinee shows excessive dependence on the teaching items in order to understand the nature of the task. Most clients who are not markedly fatigued will succeed with almost all the teaching items unless there is intellectual disability or oppositional tendencies (both of which should be apparent well before this part of the evaluation).
- Be cautious about very low raw scores on this subtest. Note that the working memory subtests' norms do not show a full range of low-scaled scores in the 5-year-old and 80+-year-old cohorts. For a "good floor" to be had for these groups, considerably more easy stimuli would be needed, potentially lengthening the subtest further. The psychometric precision that would be achieved were these items added would be of minimal clinical value since the performance would be interpreted as poor, regardless; having the psychometric basis for adding "very" in front of "weak performance" has minimal value. Nevertheless, be aware that raw scores of 0–3 in these age cohorts can yield scaled scores of 3 or 4, potentially leading the examiner to somewhat underestimate the examinee's working memory deficit.

Common Administration Errors
- Administering the wrong age-related sets to the examinee is the most common error committed with this subtest; be sure to administer A and B to the younger group and B and C to the older group.
- Mixing up the order of the stimulus pages can contribute to a nonstandardized administration including an incorrect discontinue decision. Mixing up the order of the transparent pages most often occurs when "cleaning up" after completing subtest administration, so extra care will be needed to avoid problems with the subtest's next use.

- Failing to discontinue after two *consecutive* item scores of 0 is another common mistake made by those with less experience with this subtest, as is failing to administer the second set once the first set was discontinued.
- Wearing distracting jewelry or clothing by the examiner can interfere with performance when visible through the transparency.
- Be sure not to expose the back of the transparent stimulus pages to the examinee, possibly suggesting a performance strategy.
- As appropriate, be sure the examinee is wearing their glasses during this subtest given the small size of some of the stimuli being shown.
- Unlike the Verbal Working Memory subtest, there is an additional point awarded whenever both groupings are entirely correct and the groupings are reported in the requested order. Sometimes examiners forget this feature and score VisWM like its verbal counterpart.

CAUTION

The Visual Working Memory subtest is considered by many as the most challenging WRAML3 subtest to learn to administer.

Rapid Reference 4.8

Subtest Administration Rubric: Visual Working Memory

	Yes	No
1. Both correct item sets are used given the examinee's age		
2. Instructions are read verbatim and clearly; all instructions included		
3. Task clarified if the participant has questions (teaching items only)		

	Yes	No
4. Examiner's distracting clothing or jewelry not visible through transparent cards		
5. Examiner fingers holding card do not block any items		
6. Card-side with numbers and letter on back of pictures always face examiner		
7. Examiner checks to see examinee is visually attending before beginning pointing sequence		
8. Pointing done with one second between picture "touches"		
9. Sequence of client responses correctly recorded for both groupings for all items		
10. Discontinue rule using item scores is appropriately applied within each set		
11. For all teaching items answered incorrectly, examiner uses teaching sequence appropriately		
12. Scoring includes both groupings		
13. Bonus "Order Score" point awarded to items when both groupings correct and groupings given in correct order		
14. Total item raw score calculated correctly		
15. Accurate scaled score obtained		

Verbal Working Memory (VerWM)

Verbal working memory is found in numerous tasks of daily life. For example, when hearing last night's sports scores on a morning broadcast, the announcer might say something like "While it was a close game between 49-ers and the Steelers with the score tied at halftime, the Steelers pulled ahead with a touchdown only seconds before the end of the fourth quarter, for a 27–20 final score." To fully understand what is being said, rote information such as team names and scores need to be held in short-term memory, while processing additional incoming verbal concepts such as "tied score," time frames, and winning. And this needs to be done quickly since the announcer is quickly moving on to report the results of yet other games played.

In school, by third or fourth grade, reading assignments tend to have multiple paragraphs and storylines that build from the opening introduction. Working memory comes into play when reading comprehension is dependent upon not just remembering the content of a sentence or paragraph from its start to its end, but added to that is the demand to process meaning from paragraph to paragraph so that comprehension can be cumulative, and contexts established for discerning ambiguities that language often contains. Likewise, reading poetry meaningfully makes heavy demands on working memory (e.g., processing metaphor while recalling the words which can change meaning and offer surprise during reading or listening). Correctly following more involved oral directions (e.g., "if-then" format) in a school or work setting also requires strong verbal working memory. Probably, the most demanding verbal working memory task would be simultaneous translation such as that performed daily by UN interpreters.

It is worthwhile to note that among all the subtests found on WRAML3, it is the VerWM subtest that has the highest correlations with academic achievement as measured by the WRAT5. For example, the VerWM subtest is shown to have a correlation of .61 with reading recognition and .53 in Sentence Reading. These correlations rival or exceed correlations of reading with intelligence (Ghabanchi & Rastegar, 2014). Therefore, a credible measure of verbal working memory is an important tool for examiners involved in psychoeducational assessment.

Administration Procedure

The VerWM parallels the Visual Working Memory subtest in terms of overall format and cognitive demands. Accordingly, the VerWM subtest has two different difficulty levels based on age. Item sets are made up of common nouns, some of which are animals and others nonanimals. Sets A and B are administered to 5- to 9-year-olds. Akin to the Visual Working Memory subtest, for Set A, the examinee is asked to repeat the randomly

INTERPRETING WRAML3 SUBTESTS, INDEXES 143

arranged words read by the examiner always first reporting the animals before reciting the nonanimal words. Items of Set B are also comprised of animal and nonanimal nouns, but like its VerWM counterpart, the examinee is asked to first recall the animals in order of size (smallest to largest) and then the nonanimal words in any order. For examinees 10 years and older, Sets B and C are administered. Set C, with an additional level of complexity, requires both the animal words and the nonanimal words to be recalled in order of size. Thus, the examinee must hold relatively rote oral information (animal and nonanimal nouns) in a short-term memory buffer while manipulating that information conceptually (family grouping and size determination) prior to responding.

Scoring this subtest has changed somewhat from WRAML2; specifically, correct recall of animals earns 1 point, and of nonanimals earns 1 point. As mentioned earlier, no Order Score point is earned by reciting the animal grouping first (as was the scoring procedure with WRAML2) because the examiner now asks for the animals and then the nonanimals, so there is no opportunity for the examinee to earn points for correct reporting order.

All the stimuli for Sets A, B, and C appear in the Record Form as do Start points, indicators for where teaching is allowed for initially failed items, as well as Discontinue rules. The subtest raw score consists of the total item score using the two sets administered.

Interesting Observations

- Does the client earn credit for recalling the animal or nonanimal grouping, but is seldom successful with both? That would suggest the examinee is motivated, but the task may be too taxing on working memory. If an examinee listens for only a nonsize ordered category (e.g., nonanimals), much of the "working" demand is removed, and changes the task into one that is akin to a short-term memory task. Comparison with Number Letter or Trial 1 of Verbal Learning may help in confirming this hypothesis.
- If the subtest is part of a standard administration, look for signs of marked fatigue given the preceding hour of attention and

memory demands; a brief break may be appreciated. Regardless, if the examinee continues to "hang in there," you have strong evidence supporting motivation, perseverance, and a strong work ethic.

- Does the examinee show excessive dependence on the teaching items in order to understand the nature of the task? Most clients who are not markedly fatigued, showing attention dysregulation, or cognitively compromised will initially succeed with almost all the teaching items.
- The battery's norms do show that the 5-year-old and 80+-year-old cohorts found working memory tasks sufficiently difficult that the lowest basal scores were sometimes not obtained in the (nonclinical) standardization sample. For example, raw scores of 0–3 can yield scaled scores of 3 or 4, leading to an underestimate the examinee's working memory deficit. Nevertheless, the obtained scaled score clearly connotes significant weakness. It may well be that low raw scores result from different sources. For example, the youngest groups may not yet have well-developed executive's skills while the oldest groups may have experienced decline in their executive abilities.
- Occasionally, an examinee will ask about the relative size of a given word (such as "How big a pizza? I saw one on TV that was a city block long!"). In such cases, it is appropriate to say, "Think of the usual size of things." Repeated querying is atypical and should be noted.

Common Administration Errors
- Administering the wrong age-related sets to the examinee is the most common error committed with this subtest.
- Another common error, especially among examiners new to the subtest, is to stop after finishing the first set of items, neglecting to give the required second set level as well.
- Be careful to maintain a consistent cadence, reading the words with a 1-second pause between finishing one word

and beginning the next. As elsewhere in the battery, the examiner's voice should drop slightly with the last word of each item.

- Examiner articulation, pace, and loudness should be carefully monitored, particularly for younger and older patients.

≡ Rapid Reference 4.9

Subtest Administration Rubric: Verbal Working Memory

	Yes	No
1. Age-appropriate item Sets administered		
2. Both item Sets administered		
3. Instructions read verbatim and clearly; all instructions included		
4. Clarifies task if the participant has questions (teaching items only)		
5. One-second pause between words		
6. Same intonation for each word of items other than last word (voice drops)		
7. Sequence of client responses recorded for both groupings for all items		
8. Discontinue rule is appropriately applied for both Sets		
9. Before the discontinue rule is reached, all incorrect answers for teaching items are followed by proper directions and procedural repetition		
10. "Intrusion responses" recorded		
11. Items scored correctly based only on two Group Scores (no Order Scores awarded)		
12. Total raw score accurately computed		
13. Accurate scaled score obtained		

TEST YOURSELF

Working Memory Subtests

1. **An examinee earns a scaled score of 7 on Number Letter, Sentence Memory, and Verbal Working Memory subtests. Which is the most reasonable diagnostic hypothesis the examiner might entertain from just this result?**
   (a) Language disorder
   (b) Oppositional disorder
   (c) Executive Functioning weakness
   (d) Verbal short-term memory weakness
   (e) Pervasive Developmental disorder

2. **Which immediate subtest performance is most influenced by working memory?**
   (a) Picture Memory
   (b) Story Memory
   (c) Design Learning
   (d) Verbal Learning
   (e) Number Letter

3. **In a school-wide math competition, arithmetic word problems are asked orally to eighth-grade contestants. Which memory system is going to be most utilized by most contestants?**
   (a) General Immediate memory
   (b) Short-term memory
   (c) Verbal working memory
   (d) Long-term memory
   (e) Visual working memory

4. **Which is true about the Working Memory subtests found on WRAML3?**
   (a) These subtests are not administered to 5- to 8-year-olds because working memory does not mature until older ages
   (b) Two different item sets must always be administered, and one set is more difficult than the other

(c) Visual and Verbal Working Memory subtests are of comparable difficulty to administer

(d) Scoring for the working memory subtests is the same across subtests

(e) None of the above statements is true

Answers: 1d, 2b, 3c, 4b

Five

WRAML3 INTERPRETATION: LEVELS OF ANALYSIS

This chapter builds on the discussion of interpretation started in Chapters 3 and 4. The focus there was mostly at the subtest level with the goal of mastering the content of each subtest and Index, as well as how each interrelates. This chapter employs a wider lens with a focus on integrated clinical interpretation. The question often is, with all the scores that are generated on the WRAML3, how does the clinician choose the "right" or "best" score(s)? This chapter attempts to tackle this important and complicated question.

LEVELS OF ANALYSIS

Vertical Interpretive Model

The WRAML3, like most tests of cognitive functioning, can be interpreted on several different levels. The familiar "top-down" or vertical analysis is often represented as a pyramid with the top representing the

---

Essentials of WRAML3 and EMS Assessment, First Edition.
Wayne V. Adams, David V. Sheslow, and Trevor A. Hall.
© 2024 John Wiley & Sons, Inc. Published 2024 by John Wiley & Sons, Inc.

test's global measure(s) and the base comprised of all the subtests contributing to the global measure(s). The middle of the pyramid often consists of the subgroupings of subtests forming conceptual indexes. So, for example, and as illustrated in Figure 5.1, most intelligence tests have one or two summary global scores, such as a Full Scale IQ for the WISC, then provide subordinate or contributing index scores such as Verbal Comprehension and Fluid Reasoning Indexes. Finally, at the base are the many subtests that similarly make up those sub- or contributing indexes.

The confirmatory factor analysis of the standardization data (found in Chapter 4 of the *Technical Manual*) supports this pyramidal interpretive model for use with the WRAML3. For its Standard Form, at the Immediate Memory pyramid apex is the General Immediate Memory Index (GIMI). The middle of the pyramid consists of the contributing Visual Immediate Memory Index (VisIMI), the Verbal Immediate Memory Index (VerIMI), and the Attention Concentration Index (ACI). The subtests comprising each of these Indexes form the base of the pyramid. Similar pyramids, albeit with fewer "bricks" at their base, can be fashioned for WRAML3's Delayed Memory, Recognition Memory, and Working Memory Indexes.

In a top-down analysis, the global measure is "king" because the greatest number of items (representing more sampling of memory

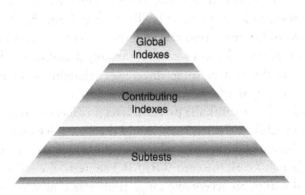

Figure 5.1 Illustration of a Top-down, or Pyramidal Approach to Interpretation.

functions) contributes to a global index, resulting in a test's aggregated measure having the greatest reliability (e.g., reliability for the WRAML3's General Immediate and General Delayed Memory Index is .93 and .91, respectively). That is, all test items from all related subtests are represented in a given general memory measure (i.e., General Immediate Memory, General Delayed Memory, and General Recognition Indexes). Another reason the royal global measure reigns is that it provides practical simplicity (think "Occam's Razor"). That is, it is easier to understand and work with a single estimate than multiple estimates (e.g., "His overall memory is at a level similar to others his age," vs. "His visual memory is at a level similar to others his age, his verbal memory is similar too, as is his average ability on rote memory tasks."). Despite these regal assets, a global Index is a summary statistic, and summaries can sometimes distort or omit meaning. Looking more deeply is sometimes necessary so that resultant interpretations do not suffer from overgeneralization, an inherent weakness of any global measure when there is excessive variability among its contributing indexes or subtests.

Accordingly, the top-down approach posits that should a global Index be "compromised" by excessive variability, the clinician should move down to the next level. Contributing indexes should then become the basis of interpretation since each has stronger reliability than its constituent subtests; WRAML3's contributing Immediate Indexes are the Visual Immediate, Verbal Immediate, and Attention/ Concentration Indexes whose reliabilities range from .81 to .93. This second level of interpretation can help the examiner uncover differential patterns of strength and weakness possibly disguised by the global index, but at the cost of somewhat lower reliability than using the global measure by itself.

Similarly, when the middle pyramid level is suspected to be compromised by variability, the clinician would then consider moving to the pyramid's base or subtest level, which, again, has a lower level of reliability (although for all the core WRAML3 subtests, the reliability level is still well within an acceptable range [immediate subtest reliabilities range from .71 to .92]).

At this point, it would be reasonable to ask what generally "compromises" an interpretive level to justify moving to a lower one. In this context, significant discrepancy between contributing scores would justify moving to a lower level of analysis. So, for example, if the scores found in Table 5.1 were obtained, the differences between Index scores may justify discounting or ignoring the GIMI, since the contributing VisIMI, VerIMI, and ACI scores are so discrepant, as determined by the calculated Index difference values found in Table A.18 of the *Administration* manual. Otherwise, one would interpret the GIMI as suggesting an overall average level of immediate recall. However, in our example, one of the contributing scores (VisIMI) shows well above-average recall, another shows low average recall (ACI), and the third index suggests an even lower score (VerIMI). The client nowhere showed *average recall* with the three constituent domains, yet the global immediate memory summary implies overall average recall ability. Using this GIMI to generate diagnostic opinions or remedial recommendations would likely lead to erroneous formulations.

In like manner, marked discrepancy between its two contributing subtests may again cause the clinician to disregard a mid-level Verbal Immediate Memory Index score, and look more closely at its subtest results for interpretation, despite yet another slight drop in reliability.

Table 5.1 Example of the Interpretive Impact of Index Discrepancies

Immediate Memory Index	Sum of Subtest Scaled Scores	Standard Score
GIMI	60	100
VisMI	31	132
VerMI	13	79
ACI	16	88

Note: GIMI = General Immediate Memory Index, VisIMI = Visual Immediate Memory Index, VerIMI = Verbal Immediate Memory Index, ACI = Attention Concentration Index.

You will notice that the WRAML3 employs dual criteria to verify apparent discrepancies and these have also been included in Table 5.2, namely levels of statistical significance and Base Rate. Hopefully, the discussion in Chapter 4 will allow those who previously were less familiar with these statistical concepts to see how they are used for discrepancy determination. Based on a hypothetical 10-year-old, Tables 5.2 and 5.3 expand Table 5.1, showing how the VerIMI is compromised because of a subtest score difference which is confirmed as being sufficiently discrepant to merit attention, justified by statistical significance and very low base rate. Those same criteria support the notion that the VisIMI and ACI would be retained for interpretative purposes because of the consistency found in their contributing subtests. A focus only on the GIMI or its contributing indexes alone would overlook any importance associated with the underlying VerIMI subtest discrepancy. Further, ignoring the index and subtest discrepancies sets the examiner up to ignore the important finding that the client generating these scores probably has a genuinely inconsistent set of memory abilities, and global generalizations about the examinee's expected memory performance would likely be misleading. Correspondingly, the need for rather tailored interventions is implied. Rapid Reference 5.1 provides a decision-tree summary of the Vertical Interpretive Model.

Parenthetically, as noted in a previous chapter, critical values and base rates for all possible discrepant comparisons are not provided in Tables A.18–A.23 of the WRAML3 Administration Manual because if all immediate, delayed, and recognition combinations of index and subtest comparisons were made available, it would exceed several hundred, a number making their clinical utility rather unwieldy. Instead, those comparisons typically of greatest interest are found in the cited tables. While less precise, when examiners are interested in a comparison that is not tabled, one can get a general sense of critical values and base rates noting those in the same "family" which should provide a general idea of the degree of discrepancy that your obtained score represents, and in many cases, may prove satisfactory for interpretive purposes. You will notice that there is, with a few exceptions, fairly similar critical values across index and subtest families of comparisons,

Rapid Reference 5.1

WRAML3 Interpretation: Vertical Level of Analysis Decision Tree

1. For any General Memory Index (Immediate, Delayed, or Recognition)
   - Subindex discrepancy?

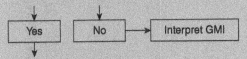

2. Go to subindexes (Visual or Verbal and Attention/Concentration for General Immediate Memory Index)
   - Subtest discrepancy for subindexes?

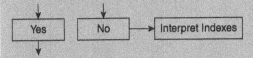

3. Go to individual subtests employing Process Scores as appropriate

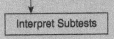

with those for the youngest and oldest cohorts being a bit smaller (i.e., fewer extreme scores) than those representing cohorts from 10 to 70 years of age. For example, statistically significant critical values across Immediate and Delayed Index comparisons are typically found with differences around 15 standard score points or more. Therefore, a nontabled standard score discrepancy of about 10 at the .10 level or 13 points at the .05 level could be considered statistically significant with reasonable confidence. For subtests, scaled score differences of about 3–4 points, by rule of thumb, could be reasonably estimated to

Table 5.2 Examples of Determining WRAML3 Subtest Discrepancies

Global Index and Contributing Indexes/Subtests	Standard Score					
GIMI	100					

	Index	Subtest	Qualitative Descriptor	Subtest Discrepancy (scaled score points)	Critical Value and *p*-value	Base Rate
VisIMI	132					
Picture Memory		16	Extremely High		3.63	
Design Learning		15	Very High	1 point	*p* > .10	> 25%
VerIMI	79					
Story Memory		4	Very Low		2.69	
Verbal Learning		9	Average	5 points	*p* < .05	< 5%
ACI	88					
Finger Window		8	Average		3.76	
Number/Letter		8	Average	0 points	*p* > .10	> 25%

Note: GIMI = General Immediate Memory Index, VisIMI = Visual Memory Index, VerIMI = Verbal Memory Index, ACI = Attention Concentration Index.

WRAML3 INTERPRETATION: LEVELS OF ANALYSIS 155

> ## ≡ Rapid Reference 5.2
>
> **Interpreting Obtained Differences**
>
> **Discrepancy Rules of Thumb:**
> - Suspect Index differences may be interpretable if > 10 standard score points
> - Suspect Subtest differences are interpretable if > 3 scaled score points
> - Confirm suspicions using tabled values for actual decision-making in clinical or research situations.

be different. A similar strategy can be employed with base rates consulting Table A.21 or A.23 in the *Administration* manual. Guidelines on how to calculate precise critical values and base rates for untabled discrepancies are found at the end of Chapter 2 of the *Technical* manual. The easiest method that also provides the greatest precision is to use the Q-Global scoring software!

Let us conclude this section with a few additional comments about discrepancies within the context of interpretation. First, all discrepancies are not alike. Some discrepancies are dramatic whereas others just "squeak by" the criteria the clinician has established. Obviously, the more extreme an obtained discrepancy, the more attention it merits as the clinician formulates interpretations and recommendations. This notion is illustrated in Table 5.1. The VisMI vs. VerMI discrepancy is screaming for attention. If the discrepancy were 30 points less, it would still be deemed psychometrically discrepant, but its functional impact for that examinee would be much moderated.

Second, a discrepancy within one level of the interpretive pyramid may compromise interpretation at that level as well as on the level(s) above it. So, for example, as we saw in Table 5.2, the discrepant VerIMI subtest results should temper interpretation of the VerIMI as well as of variables that use that index, in this case, the GIMI.

Table 5.3 Examples of determining WRAML3 Index Discrepancies

Index Comparisons	Standard Score 1	Standard Score 2	Difference	Critical .05 Value	Statistical Significance?	Base Rate
VisIMI *vs.* VerMI	132	79	53	13.47	Yes	< 2%
VisIMI vs. ACI	132	88	44	16.10	Yes	< 2%
VerIMI *vs.* ACI	88	79	9	14.69	No	> 25%

Note: GIMI = General Immediate Memory Index, VisIMI = Visual Immediate Memory Index, VerIMI = Verbal Immediate Memory Index, ACI = Attention Concentration Index.

Obviously, the more immediate indexes and/or subtests are affected by discrepancy, the more responsible use of the GIMI could be negatively impacted.

Third, a discrepancy can result from an idiosyncratic event such as a momentary distraction from a fire engine's passing, or a jump in anxiety because of sudden awareness about being late to a soccer game because testing is going longer than expected. Obviously, such chance instances can temporarily lower performance suggesting a "false positive" result within a subtest and possibly also impacting an index. At the risk of being redundant, always look at consistency of performance within and beyond a given test result before you put much credence in one or even two abnormal findings. For example, a low score on the immediate subtest but a higher score on the delayed subtest might question the relevance of the immediate subtest result. There is ample justification for being a skeptic when it comes to interpreting test results! The illogical "Consistency amongst Discrepancies" is what is sought!

Finally, just as discrepancies can be found at the index and subtest levels, there may also be unusual observations *within* a given subtest having clinical implications. That is, observed discrepancy in task approach may reflect emotional, behavioral, or neurological "variability." Remember from Chapter 4 that the WRAML3 has included many measures termed "Process" variables to aid the examiner in clarifying how the examinee arrived at a particular subtest score. When confronted with a discrepancy, or performance variability, it is important to discern an underlying process affecting the inconsistency that might lead to a more clear interpretation of the factors affecting the subtest or even index and, ultimately, a way to change the process. The Process Scores may help examiners provide a quantitative basis to test hypotheses around atypical intra-subtest performances.

Our top-down hierarchy of interpretation as well as discrepancy discussion thus far has focused on the immediate memory indexes and subtests. It bears repeating that the same interpretive points made can, and should be, extended to the Delayed Memory Index and its subtests as well as the Recognition Memory Index and its subtests.

Horizontal Interpretive Model

In addition to the top-down conceptual model for interpretation with the WRAML3, there is a second conceptual model to consider. As previously mentioned, there was a time in the not-too-distant clinical past when the assessment of immediate memory was thought to be a sufficient way of measuring memory. But, as we have observed, knowing that the level achieved for immediate recall may be quite different than recall demonstrated after 20 or 30 minutes. In fact, it has been argued that delayed recall may more accurately represent actual memory performance in everyday life. We also know that results from a delayed memory measure may sometimes not accurately reflect memory storage. Consequently, an alternative to the top-down analysis exists to help with such dilemmas, and might be called a "horizontal level of analysis." While not at odds with the top-down analysis, the "horizontal" perspective makes comparisons across immediate, delayed, and recognition performance indexes and subtests to also determine the presence of inconsistency (i.e., discrepancy) across findings. While it is expected that delayed recall will normally be somewhat weaker than immediate for both visual and verbal recall, when performance for Delayed Indexes and/or subtests is disproportionately weaker compared to immediate subtests, a top-down analysis alone will likely be inadequate for thorough diagnostic understanding.

A specific example illustrating the utility of the horizontal analysis is found in Tables 5.4 and 5.5. The first table provides the General Immediate, Delayed, and Recognition Index scores achieved by a hypothetical 19-year-old. Table 5.5 shows some of the possible discrepancies that could be evaluated. The results shown again question the clinical

Table 5.4 Illustration of Horizontal Analysis Data: Comparing Discrepancy Performance on General Immediate, Delayed, and Recognition Indexes

	General Immediate Verbal Index	Verbal Delayed Index	Verbal Recognition Index
Index Results	91	73	94

Table 5.5 Illustration of Evaluating Possible Discrepancies Found with Data of Table 5.4 using a Horizontal Analysis

Index and Subtest Comparisons	Standard Score 1	Standard Score 2	Difference	Critical Value .05	Statistical Significance?	Base Rate
GIMI vs. GDI	91	73	18	11.38	Yes	< 2%
GDI vs. GRI	73	94	21	11.80	Yes	< 2–5%
GIMI vs. GRI	91	94	3	14.10	No	> 25%

Note: GIMI = General Immediate Memory Index, GDI = General Delayed Index, GRI = General Recognition Index.

veracity of the GIMI as an estimate of overall memory since there appears to be considerable forgetting of the originally learned information 20–30 minutes later, specifically a decline of 18 standard score points; that difference meets statistical significance with a low base rate of occurrence sufficient to be considered a suspicious finding and worth paying attention to. However, Table 5.5 also provides evidence in the second and third rows that the Immediate memory information was not really forgotten since results of the Recognition Index suggest that much of that information had been stored. Since the Recognition score achieved differs little from GIMI performance, it is suggested that the information is stored, but cannot be reliably retrieved. It seems reasonable to hypothesize in this case that retrieval (vs. storage) of information is in some way impaired. This example shows how administering Delayed and Recognition measures yields more nuanced clinical formulations.

Empirically determining horizontal discrepancy is done in the same fashion described with vertical using Tables A.18 and A.19. Note that in the above example, the constituent subtests of each Index are assumed to not be discrepant with each; otherwise, the interpretation would be even more complicated. Other examples with greater complexity are provided in Chapter 7 as a discussion of both vertical and horizontal methods of interpretation are further considered.

Cautionary Words about Interpreting Discrepancy

The meaning and significance of differences between indexes deserve additional and cautionary comments. A 15-point Index difference seems substantial, although whether it will be noticeable clinically will likely depend on what is the overall level of the client's memory functioning. For example, a person who achieves a Verbal Delayed Memory Index of 140 with a Visual Delayed Memory Index of 125 demonstrates statistically different memory ability on the test, but that person (and observers) may go through life unaware of the relative weakness in Visual Memory because their "weakness" is still at a level far above the majority of age-mates. Plus, that client may well use compensatory memory abilities from the formidable verbal memory domain to assist when encountering especially challenging visual memory demands. Conversely, a person with Delayed Verbal and Visual Index scores of 70 and 55 may perceive a difference in remembering verbal versus visual information, but the disparity may not always be noticed by instructors or employers because of the marked degree of weakness that characterizes both domains. Plus, the area of relative strength may not be strong enough to noticeably compensate for an area of greater memory weakness. Generally, differences between index scores are increasingly noticeable and ecologically meaningful the greater the scores are found away from the extremes of the performance distribution. Therefore, finding a Visual Delayed Memory Index of 100 and a Verbal Delayed Memory Index of 80 may well be noticed by the examinee and by those living and/or working with them, in addition to the clinician who completed the evaluation. Accordingly, one "takeaway" message from this is that, depending on the reason for referral, clinicians should highlight the relevance of a detected difference, in part, based upon the perceived or actual importance of the difference for the various stakeholders. That is, sometimes a finding of statistical significance and low base rate can be overinterpreted. In such cases, clinicians may be excited about the discovery of a heretofore unknown weakness and use a significant portion of a report to discuss it, as well as generate recommendations related to its detection. However, the clinician should not be surprised and disheartened if the finding is apathetically received or its validity questioned by the examinee because the significant difference score is found in the extremes of the distribution and has little functional relevance, meaning, or credibility.

A second and perhaps more important cautionary comment relates to low-performance overinterpretation. We as clinicians sometimes forget that perfectly healthy (nonreferred) persons "fail" neuropsychological subtests. This has been demonstrated many times in a literature spanning more than 25 years (e.g., Heaton et al., 2004; Ingraham & Aiken, 1996; Schretlen et al. 2008). This research has consistently shown that when using standard test score cut-offs (e.g., 2 SDs below the mean) of commonly used measures (including memory measures), it should be expected that adults in nonclinical groups will typically exceed established cut-offs for 10–30% of the subtests administered. However, inadvertently, our training has wrongly taught us to expect "healthy" examinees (i.e., those included in standardization samples) not to score within impaired ranges. Therefore, the prudent clinician should be initially suspicious of any unusual finding (strength or weakness) and look for additional support to establish increased credibility for that aberrant score. Such support may come from consistency of results, such as, for example, with WRAML3, if visual memory weaknesses found with immediate recall are replicated with visual delayed recall, and from another test's results that also show (or have shown) visual processing weaknesses. In addition, client history should support the result as credible. So, with our visual memory weakness example, we would not expect to hear that the examinee "can drive to a new location once and thereafter she never gets lost getting there again." Nor would we expect bragging from the family about our examinee in times past, returning home to create wonderfully detailed sketches from memory of landscapes visited earlier in the day. So, to be good diagnostic detectives, we should not be overly swayed by evidence from one or two measures suggesting impairment unless that finding converges with other test results, history, and in-person observations. History generally trumps test results. Knowing how to weigh the importance of aberrant findings is a critical clinical skill. Be wary when encountering discrepant findings supporting discrepancies!

In summary, understanding the scores generated, as well as how to use those scores, and how to weigh the veracity of those scores are all skills needed to adequately appreciate the complexities of memory test interpretation for a given examinee. The WRAML3 attempts to offer the examiner a manageable sampling of memory data within the traditional evaluation context to allow them to feel confident in developing hypotheses and drawing conclusions about memory functioning. However, as illustrated in Chapter 7, integrating data from indexes, subtests, process variables, as well as other sources such as behavioral observations and history may significantly affect conclusions initially formed from a first glance at test results. In addition, consistency across these various data sources may, and likely should, affect the content and confidence the clinician has in any interpretive formulation. To come full circle, by administering the WRAML3 (and other cognitive measures), you as the clinician are tasked with obtaining, weighing, integrating, and then interpreting a body of information collected in the service of making accurate diagnoses and useful recommendations for those referred for memory assessment. As just mentioned, Chapter 7 will consider this challenge by presenting examples of this integrative approach being applied. But first, we will have a break in the discussion of interpretation in order to provide a chapter that briefly discusses the why, when, and how one might go about using abbreviated formats available for the WRAML3.

🐟 TEST YOURSELF 🐟

Interpretation: Levels of Analysis

1. **Whenever possible, global index scores should be used rather than subtest scores because**
   (a) Index scores have higher reliability
   (b) Subtest scores are smaller than Index scores
   (c) Factor analyses are done using Index scores
   (d) Index scores are easier to understand
   (e) There is less variability across Index scores
2. **Healthy young adults not belonging to a clinical group will not earn a memory Index score below:**
   (a) 105
   (b) 95
   (c) 85
   (d) 75
   (e) Any of these scores is possible

ESSENTIALS OF WRAML3 AND EMS ASSESSMENT

3. **Determining whether to use the General Immediate Memory Index rather than its Visual, Verbal, and/or Attention Concentration counterparts is an example of**
   (a) a horizontal analysis
   (b) a vertical analysis
   (c) an oblique analysis
   (d) a factor analysis
   (e) an effort analysis

4. **Deciding how best to interpret Immediate vs. Delayed vs. Recognition Indexes is an example of**
   (a) a horizontal analysis
   (b) a vertical analysis
   (c) an oblique analysis
   (d) a factor analysis
   (e) an effort analysis

Answers: 1a, 2e, 3b, 4a

Six

WRAML3 ABBREVIATED FORMATS

Mr. Jones was accidentally double-booked for re-evaluation for special education service reviews on Tuesday. Because both scheduled students were previously found functioning in the average range of intelligence, Mr. Jones decided to accommodate both by re-administering the most recent version of the Wide Range Achievement Test-5 along with the WRAML3 Brief version.

Mr. Smith was evaluated one month ago after falling off a ladder and sustaining a fractured femur and rib, as well as a concussion. At today's return visit, he was medically cleared to return to his management job, but his physician thought it prudent to also screen memory skills before discharge. Given the distance Mr. Smith needed to travel for his care, completion of such a screening during the current office visit was requested. Consequently,

---

Essentials of WRAML3 and EMS Assessment, First Edition.
Wayne V. Adams, David V. Sheslow, and Trevor A. Hall.
© 2024 John Wiley & Sons, Inc. Published 2024 by John Wiley & Sons, Inc.

166 ESSENTIALS OF WRAML3 AND EMS ASSESSMENT

the practice's psychologist was asked if it would be possible to "squeeze in" an evaluation that day. Because of the cancellation of another psychology appointment, a 60-minute slot could be made available, so the Screener version of the WRAML3 was scheduled.

Time was fleeting during Dr. Kay's school evaluation of James who was three years out from treatment for childhood leukemia. Dr. Kay administered the most recent versions of the Wechsler Intelligence Scale for Children and the Wechsler Individual Achievement Test, as well as a review of recently completed parent and teacher checklists. John's fourth-grade teacher questioned James' retention of reading material and class instruction. Because of time constraints to complete the evaluation and James' growing fatigue, Dr. Kay decided to use the WRAML3 Brief format to see if there was evidence for the teacher's concern.

Psychological assessments can vary from a multi-appointment, comprehensive neuropsychological evaluation for a new patient entering a rehab facility, to providing a brief re-evaluation to assure that there has been little change in status since a recent assessment. Given pressures for efficient and cost-effective client management without diminished outcomes, there is a growing trend toward shorter evaluation times which are achieved, in part, by using sound screening tools. Such is the trend with memory assessment as well. Examples of common situations leading to an abbreviated memory screening appear above. Those and other reality constraints such as demand for increased productivity, case complexity, limited evaluator time, possible forensic review, and reimbursement constraints may need to be considered when choosing which WRAML3 format is most appropriate for an evaluation referral. Stated differently, examiners are increasingly asking, "What should I administer that will adequately answer the referral question, satisfy the referral source, and do it in the least amount of time?"

However, within this current climate of streamlined evaluation, there arises a common dilemma. Namely, for efficiency, it is critical to determine, prior to evaluation, what information would be most pertinent. Yet the examinee's behavior and emerging test results during the testing session often generate additional questions that call for a change in the assessment plan. Fortunately, the WRAML3 was designed to have the flexibility to be used in both pre-planned comprehensive testing contexts, as well as those which unexpectedly arise as an evaluation evolves.

Accordingly, because of these contemporary challenges, this chapter focuses on when and how to best use the two abbreviated testing formats provided by WRAML3. As an alternative to the full multi-subtest Standard format, the battery also provides four- and two-subtest options. In this chapter, each abbreviated format will first be described detailing content, followed by general guidelines for use. And since all choices have costs, and usually "less is seldom more," the chapter concludes with a cautionary word as well as a case illustration of benefits and costs examiners should be aware of when considering using an abbreviated format.

SCREENER FORMAT

This four-subtest version is comprised of two Visual and two Verbal subtests, the same composition as the Screener from the WRAML2, and retaining the same name. Being comprised of the first four subtests of the WRAML3, it enjoys all the solid psychometric characteristics of those subtests, as well as yields the same Visual and Verbal Indexes as the Standard version. Akin to the General Immediate Memory Index associated with the Standard version, the Screener provides a Screener Memory Index yielded by combining the Visual and Verbal Index scaled scores using Table A.7 of the *Administration* manual. The same Record Form of the Standard administration format is used to record examinee responses. Figure 6.1 shows the Screener test structure graphically.

The Screener is designed so that examiners in the midst of the assessment can decide if a more comprehensive evaluation is warranted and, if so, administer the entire battery which can be done legitimately because the four Screener subtests and their order are the same as those

168 ESSENTIALS OF WRAML3 AND EMS ASSESSMENT

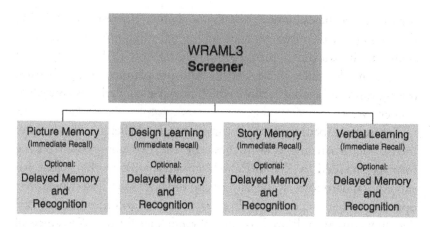

Figure 6.1 The Subtests that Comprise the Screener Format of the WRAML3.

used in the Standard version. Therefore, by adding the subsequent subtests of the Attention Concentration Index, the examiner would be able to administer the subtests in the order of standardization and obtain any or all of the various Indexes. That is, whether using just the Screener format or changing course and proceeding with the full Standard version, the examiner always has the option to administer the Delayed Recall and Recognition components of the battery assuming their associated mandated time intervals are observed. Therefore, the Screener format by itself shortens administration time but also provides the examiner with the alternative to complete more comprehensive testing should preliminary findings indicate that that is the preferred clinical course. This is an attractive option when the Screener version is being used for re-evaluation. That is, if the WRAML3 was administered a year or two earlier, using the Screener for re-evaluation makes sense unless the updated results start to show different levels of performance, at which point, the examiner might reasonably decide to re-do the entire battery.

The Screener Format may also be especially attractive option when credible information about attentional factors is already available from other sources. The reader will remember from our discussion in Chapter 4 that attention is an important initial ingredient in the memory/learning sequence and is therefore a WRAML3 focus using the two subtests comprising the Attention/Concentration Index. Accordingly, when attention/rote memory results are already available, the Screener format, comprised of the remaining WRAML3 immediate subtests may have appeal. However, the counterargument to be considered is that since examinees with attention difficulties often exhibit variability between testings, repeating attention measures that do not take a lot of time may provide a useful comparison with other attention results, indirectly examining attention variability.

> **DON'T FORGET**
>
> The first four immediate recall subtests of the Standard WRAML3 format comprise the Screener. It generally takes approximately 25 minutes to administer. Delayed Recall and Recognition options can also be exercised.

BRIEF FORMAT

When the goal of memory assessment is to gather a concise sample of memory functioning, or when examinee factors (e.g., fatigue) or extreme examiner time constraints apply, the examiner may wish to use the Brief format. Two subtests, one visual (Design Learning), and the other verbal (Story Memory), comprise this format (see Figure 6.2). These two subtests are the most reliable of the WRAML3, psychometrically supporting their use in a very abbreviated format. Administration time is approximately 10–15 minutes. Using the Brief format, the examiner will obtain estimates of both visual and verbal memory (and potentially, their Process scores), and by using Table A.15 of the *Administration* manual, obtain an overall estimate of global memory called the Brief Immediate Memory Index. While examinees may use the Standard format Record Form and Response Booklet for the Brief version's two subtests, to avoid waste, reduce costs, and add to examiner convenience, there are available a Brief Record Form and Brief Response Booklet that reproduce the relevant two-subtest portions (including optional subtests and Process components) from the corresponding parts of the Standard Record Form. That is, should the

170 ESSENTIALS OF WRAML3 AND EMS ASSESSMENT

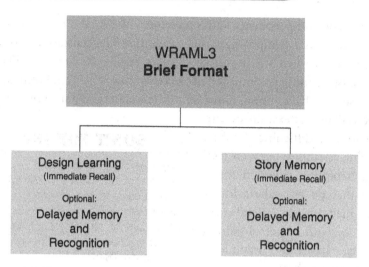

Figure 6.2 The Subtests that Comprise the Brief Format of the WRAML3.

examinee wish to use just a bit more time, Delayed Recall and Recognition counterparts of the Design Learning and Story Memory subtests can also be administered and scored using the Brief Record Form, assuming the mandated time intervals are observed. Consequently, Brief Immediate, Brief Delayed, and Brief Recognition Indexes can all be obtained using Tables A.16 and A.17 (*Administration* manual) using the Brief format's two subtests. Critical values and Base Rate comparisons between Immediate, Delayed, and Recognition components of the two subtests can be found in Tables A.29 and A.30, respectively. The capability to screen key memory functions in less than 15 minutes and then have the option to additionally focus on memory decay over time and recognition are major assets of the Brief format.

> **DON'T FORGET**
>
> Delayed Memory and Recognition components are optional parts of both abbreviated formats as well as the Standard format.

> **DON'T FORGET**
>
> The two subtests of the Brief are the most reliable of the WRAML3. Combined they take approximately 10–15 minutes to measure Immediate Visual and Verbal recall.

A WORD OF CAUTION

It is important to again underscore that while abbreviated assessments have a legitimate role in an evaluator's toolbox, even more caution is needed when using their results than when employing results obtained from an entire WRAML3 administration. As has been argued, testing provides an efficient and empirical basis for hypothesis building that can significantly assist diagnostic and remediation efforts. It follows then that fewer data points (less sampling and content breadth) reduce reliability and possibly validity; therefore, abbreviated measures can provide an incomplete and possibly distorted picture. For example, Working Memory is omitted from both abbreviated formats despite its known importance in academic endeavors. Also, a Performance Validity score cannot be computed using an abbreviated format.

Even though there are reasons to be cautious when using the abbreviated formats, it can be observed in Rapid Reference 6.1 that both the Screener and Brief formats yield scores that are less than one standard score point different from those generated using the full Standard administration format, and the respective scores are highly correlated. Therefore, in those instances where abbreviated versions are necessary, users can know that generally there is very good psychometric correspondence with the overall scores generated by the more comprehensive Standard format.

> **CAUTION**
>
> Time delays "built into" the Standard administration format still need to be observed when using Delayed and Recognition subtests as part of either abbreviated format.

ABBREVIATED FORMATS: CASE ILLUSTRATION

Earlier in the chapter, it was mentioned that "less is seldom more." Sometimes "less can be enough" but also "less can be misleading." Of the many tasks confronting an examiner, one of the most challenging is deciding, in session, when enough relevant information has been gathered to adequately answer the referral question. Below is a hypothetical amalgam of cases which shows results as if the same examinee took each of the three WRAML3 formats with no practice effects. The goal of presenting this case using this unusual approach is to illustrate the advantages and potential costs of using an abbreviated format.

ESSENTIALS OF WRAML3 AND EMS ASSESSMENT

> # ≡ Rapid Reference 6.1
>
> ### Comparison of Standard Score Differences and Correlations Between Standard Format Results and those Obtained by Brief and Screener Formats
>
> | | | | |
> |---|---|---|---|
> | Screener Index | 0.6 points $r = .92$ | | |
> | Brief Immediate Memory | 0.3 points $r = .84$ | | |
> | Brief Delayed | | 0.8 points $r = .90$ | |
> | Brief Recognition | | | 0.6 points $r = .90$ |

Reason for Referral

Jamal, a 10-year-old, presented for a brief evaluation of learning concerns, referred to by his fifth-grade teacher. Jamal's parents divorced several years ago, and he has had no recent contact with his mother. Jamal and his father moved to Delaware from rural North Carolina when the father was transferred to the state's Air Force base 6 months ago. Jamal's father reported that Jamal has had difficulties adjusting to his new school as he is finding fifth grade quite challenging.

History (Excerpted)

Important in Jamal's history, but not mentioned until the parent interview, was a car accident that occurred at the end of the summer prior to his start of fourth grade. Jamal was in a coma at the crash site and remained so for a day in the local hospital. Jamal was discharged after 4 days with his physicians being "impressed with his rate of recovery." Following his hospital stay, Jamal received homebound instruction for 2 weeks, after which he re-entered school. An academic evaluation was performed later that fall.

Prior to the accident, Jamal was reported to be a well-adjusted young man with better-than-average academic achievement. In fourth grade, post-injury, Jamal's progress faltered and by the end of the year, Jamal demonstrated some frustration across all academic areas. Jamal's teachers reported that he had difficulty organizing himself to complete assignments, study for exams, and handing in homework, all of which were uncharacteristic prior to the accident. No problems with attention or impulsivity were reported. Jamal also demonstrated limited carry-over from classroom lessons from week to week and required considerable review prior to a new lesson in a sequence. His teacher noted that sometimes Jamal would appear frustrated and would "just shut down."

An excerpt of Jamal's fifth-grade school evaluation is presented below but the focus of this case study is on the WRAML3 Abbreviated Formats. On the WISC-V, Indexes ranged from the very low to the average ranges.

WISC-V

Index	Standard Score
FSIQ	88
Verbal Comprehension	106
Visual Spatial	92
Fluid Reasoning	85
Working Memory	79
Processing Speed	75

174 ESSENTIALS OF WRAML3 AND EMS ASSESSMENT

WIAT-IV (*Initial and Re-evaluation Results*)

Subtest	Fall, Grade 4 Standard Score	Fall, Grade 5 Standard Score
Reading Comprehension	90	85
Word Reading	95	90
Numerical Operations	80	75
Math Fluency—Addition	89	84
Math Fluency—Subtraction	85	77
Math Fluency—Multiplication	79	69
Sentence Composition	88	87

Comparison of Jamal's Hypothetical Performance Using Each of the Three Available WRAML3 Formats

WRAML3 Subtest Options	Standard Format	Screener Format	Brief Format
Performance Validity Indicator	2 (Questionable)		
WRAML3 Global Indexes			
General Immediate Memory Index	72		
Screener Memory Index		81	
Brief Immediate Memory Index			88
Visual Immediate Memory Index	76	76	
Verbal Immediate Memory Index	91	91	
Attention/Concentration Index	66		
General Delayed Index	73	73	73
Visual Delayed Index	67	67	
Verbal Delayed Index	85	85	

WRAML3 Subtest Options	Standard Format	Screener Format	Brief Format
General Recognition Index	77	77	76
Visual Recognition Index	68	68	
Verbal Recognition Index	88	88	
Picture Memory			
Immediate	6	6	
Delayed	5	5	
Recognition	4	4	
Story Memory			
Immediate	9	9	9
Delayed	7	7	7
Recognition	7	7	7
Design Learning			
Immediate	6	6	6
Delayed	4	4	4
Recognition	5	5	5
Verbal Learning			
Immediate	8	8	
Delayed	8	8	
Recognition	9	9	
Finger Windows	5		
Number Letter	4		
Visual Working Memory	*Not administered*		
Verbal Working Memory	*Not administered*		
Sentence Memory	6		

Hypothetical Comparison of "Reasonable Inferences" Generated by Results from Standard, Screener, and Brief Formats by Jamal. (An "X" indicates the stated finding that would be available using the format associated with the column in which it is placed.)

Reasonable Inferences Derived from Test Results	Standard Format	Screener Format	Brief Format
Jamal exhibited a large difference between intelligence on the WISC-V (FSIQ = 88) and global memory on his General Immediate Memory Index (GIMI = 72). The GIMI includes visual, verbal, and attentional measures; the latter two areas appear to have a major negative impact on Jamal's learning.	X		
Note: Clinically, a memory measure is often a better predictor of future learning than an intelligence measure since the former examines *in situ* while much of an intelligence test measures what has already been learned. Therefore, in acute brain injuries, past performance may not be a good predictor of future performance. The WISC Processing Speed and Working Memory results do not reflect past learning, and so connote impaired processing not in agreement with the other IQ Index scores which are more associated with undisturbed past strengths.			
Found a significant difference between Immediate Verbal and Visual Memory in favor of the former. ($p < .05$).	X	X	

Reasonable Inferences Derived from Test Results	Standard Format	Screener Format	Brief Format
Found a significant difference between Immediate Verbal Memory and Attention Concentration Index ($p < .05$). In light of no concerns about attention, this may suggest weak sequencing skills as part of Jamal's overall academic weaknesses.	X		
A look at the Story Memory vs. Sentence Memory subtests may further support the "rote recall/sequencing weakness" hypothesis as "minor" errors in word order on Sentence Memory are penalized.	X		
Looking at WIAT-4 results suggests limited academic learning over the past year. Examining both subtests that required learning over trials, Jamal demonstrated a flat learning curve for Design Learning but a more typical learning curve for Verbal Learning suggesting weak nonverbal memory and organizational abilities even with repetition. This is consistent with his weaker math skills.	X	X	
An estimate of attention, or in this case, perhaps rote sequencing, was obtained using the same norms as those associated with verbal and visual memory so that direct comparisons can be made.	X		
Sufficient information was derived to suggest that Jamal will require considerable support for all academics given his poor memory skills.	X	X	X
Sufficient information was derived to suggest that Jamal will have memory issues affecting learning.	X	X	X

(*continued*)

ESSENTIALS OF WRAML3 AND EMS ASSESSMENT

Reasonable Inferences Derived from Test Results	Standard Format	Screener Format	Brief Format
Sufficient information was derived to suggest classroom Delayed Learning performance is more predictive than Immediate.	X	X	X
The complexity of Jamal's memory impairment is suggested by the findings.	X		
An estimate of effort is available using the Performance Validity Indicators. Jamal's PVI was "Questionable" because of his low ACI score and Visual Recognition Memory performance. But effort appeared good on the verbal tasks which reflected greater competency.	X		
All process scores are available to aid in examining the "how" an examinee approached a memory task to test some of the hypotheses put forward above.	X	X	

COMMENTARY

It is well known that a closed-head injury resulting from a car accident can result in very mild to very severe neuropsychological deficits. In Jamal's case, the pattern of test results suggests a rather complicated and intertwined pattern of neuropsychological strengths and weaknesses. While the WRAML3 Brief format suggested that Jamal exhibited significant deficits in memory to require classroom modification, the Screener format was more useful in beginning to identify some of the complexities. However, both abbreviated forms would likely have led to a recommendation for a more thorough examination of Jamal's learning and memory deficits. The Standard format findings better uncover the complexities apparent across immediate, delayed, and rote memory domains. Because of so much subtest discrepancy, global measures and isolated subtest results can be quite misleading. Immediate memory tasks showed verbal recall strengths (i.e., average performance) compared to visual.

That division of strengths remained delayed, albeit at lower levels for both sensory modalities. The recognition subtests indicated that the apparent weaknesses with delayed memory are not related to retrieval weaknesses. Attention/Concentration, Jamal's area of greatest consistent weakness no doubt plays a role in aspects of his inefficient learning processes, yet even that hypothesis is not consistently supported given his results with the Verbal Learning subtest which demands elements of rote learning and sustained attention. Clearly, this will be a challenging youngster to program for despite an encouraging Verbal Comprehension IQ score. Adding to the complexity, Jamal may make additional neurological progress related to his brain injury, and the results of this evaluation may change in a positive direction over the next 6–12 months. Interestingly, despite all of the scatter found on his memory profile, his GIMI of 72 (the third percentile) may be helpful in predicting a slow academic course as indicated by Jamal's very limited progress between fourth and fifth grades as suggested by the WIAT-IV findings.

TEST YOURSELF

Abbreviated Formats

1. **The Screener Format's typical administration time (without optional subtests) is about**
   (a) 5 minutes
   (b) 15 minutes
   (c) 25 minutes
   (d) 40 minutes
   (e) 55 minutes

2. **The Performance Validity Indicator is designed to be used with**
   (a) The Standard format
   (b) The Screener format
   (c) The Brief format
   (d) All of the above
   (e) Only the Standard and Screener formats

180 ESSENTIALS OF WRAML3 AND EMS ASSESSMENT

3. The Standard and Abbreviated formats have a correlation of what magnitude?

(a) Low

(b) Moderate

(c) High

(d) The magnitude of correlation depends on age and can be a, b, or c

(e) The correlation is unknown

4. The subtests with the highest reliabilities are

(a) Story Memory and Number Letter

(b) Picture Memory and Verbal Learning

(c) The two Working Memory subtests

(d) Story Memory and Design Learning

(e) Picture Memory and Story Memory

Answers: 1c, 2a, 3c, 4d

Seven

INTEGRATED INTERPRETATION OF THE WRAML3

et us start this chapter by briefly summarizing the essence of interpretation presented in Chapters 4 and 5 since that will be foundational for much of this chapter's content. You will remember that to organize test findings, it is likely worthwhile to conduct a vertical interpretation within each General Memory Index using the criteria of statistical significance and reasonable base rate in order to determine which level of interpretation to employ. Whenever possible, the choice should be to use the most global index, and this is true for the General Immediate, Delayed, and Recognition Indexes. But when discrepancies between indexes or subtests are identified using the above criteria, then lower levels of analysis may be indicated. A similar strategy should also be employed when using the recommended horizontal analysis in order to carefully examine different components of an examinee's memory processing.

Essentials of WRAML3 and EMS Assessment, First Edition.
Wayne V. Adams, David V. Sheslow, and Trevor A. Hall.
© 2024 John Wiley & Sons, Inc. Published 2024 by John Wiley & Sons, Inc.

It was also said that to formulate credible hypotheses that will lead to sound diagnostic and remediation formulations, WRAML3 test results should be integrated with other findings derived from examinee history, prior test results, current input from significant parties such as teachers, parents, spouses, and work colleagues, and the examiner's own clinical observation.

INTERPRETATION USING CASES AND COMMENTARY

With these interpretive notions in mind, let us move on to examining various WRAML3 results and how they might prove to be clinically useful. What follows are several cases, each illustrating possible ways WRAML3 scores and auxiliary input can be integrated so as to best contribute to a diagnostic formulation. Efforts have been expended to make each of the illustrations briefer than typical case studies which tend to be fairly lengthy in order to be comprehensive; in so doing, such cases can be rather difficult to wade through. Instead, we are presenting shortened versions of various cases chosen to highlight specific interpretive ideas related to the WRAML3. And since test data often can be interpreted in a variety of ways, a commentary section follows each case examining the basis for a diagnostic statement or presenting potential shortcomings or an alternate perspective to the interpretation provided, or generating additional recommendations that the test's findings might justify. As a reminder, for those also wanting the more traditional case study format for review, almost 30 pages describing 5 cases are provided at the end of the *Technical Manual*. In the current chapter, the authors have tried to offer additional information beyond what is found in those longer case studies so that by using both, a more thorough clinical understanding of how to use the WRAML3 effectively will result. The reader will notice that other than the WRAML3 results, complete test data sets of other measures typically included in an evaluation are sometimes truncated or absent; the cases that follow have been intentionally abbreviated to improve the heuristic value of a specific set of WRAML3 results while not generating a case that is unnecessarily lengthy.

CASE A: ADHD?

This case is presented since it involves one of the most common referral concerns for children, ADHD. It illustrates how, when "crunched for time," a clinician can use the Brief Format of the WRAML3 to add useful information to test results already gathered in order to achieve a more nuanced diagnostic formulation. The case illustrates one condition that can mimic attention difficulties but has a different basis. It also shows progressive hypothesis testing as results suggest diagnostic "clues" that deserve follow-up testing.

Reason for Referral

Sam, aged 11 years, 2 months, was referred to by his sixth-grade teacher and parents for an opinion on whether he may have an attention disorder. Depending on results, recommendations for classroom management strategies were requested. Because there was a counseling appointment slot available due to cancellation, it was agreed that the relatively short interval available would be used to start exploring possible explanations for the referral concern.

Relevant Background

Sam's perinatal, birth, and early developmental histories were all benign. He entered kindergarten at age 5 and no academic or behavioral concerns were noted then or in first through third grades. However, in fourth grade, some concern was registered about Sam's finishing classroom work and homework, especially longer, multi-stepped assignments. These concerns persisted into fifth grade along with some others related to Sam's reading comprehension and ability to complete math assignments (especially word problems). Last summer, IQ and academic testing were completed by a private practitioner. She found overall intellectual ability to be within the average range (Full Scale = 108), but somewhat lower achievement in reading comprehension than that score would predict (standard score = 95). Math achievement was variable; the mechanics were on grade level, but word problems and lack of

184 ESSENTIALS OF WRAML3 AND EMS ASSESSMENT

mastery of pre-algebra content brought down the overall score. The psychologist completing the evaluation felt that if Sam had ADHD, it was not at problematic levels given her observations of his work style and demeanor during the evaluation. Since continuing academic struggles were noted early in sixth grade, a referral was made for evaluation. Sam's mother reports his need for greater assistance with and monitoring of homework than she remembers providing Sam in the lower grades. Particularly challenging are extended assignments requiring planning, such as group projects and book reports. Recently, Sam seemed to struggle at first to independently complete a new chore (washing his own clothes) that he agreed to do in exchange for increased allowance, but after some parental "coaching" for a few weeks, Sam is now independently completing the task successfully. Leisure time enjoyment includes model building of old ships, as well as playing sports with friends in the neighborhood.

Test Administered and Results

Table 7.1 Sam's Results from the Brief Version of the Wide Range Assessment of Memory and Learning, Third Edition

Subtest	Immediate Scaled Score	Delayed Scaled Score
Design Learning	8	8

Design Learning Process Scores:
   Trials (age cohort scores in brackets)
     Raw Scores: T1 = 23[21], T2 = 35[36],
       T3 = 39[49], T4 = 44[59]; Delay = 42[36]
Learning Slope (20) = base rate of ≤15th percentile
Quadrant Analysis: not significant		

Story Memory	9	7

Story Memory Process Scores:
   Verbatim scaled score = 11
   Gist scaled score = 09
   Story C scaled score = 10; Story D = 8		

INTEGRATED INTERPRETATION OF THE WRAML3 | 185

Table 7.1 (continued)

Subtest	Immediate Scaled Score	Delayed Scaled Score
Additional Subtests included:		
Finger Windows	10	
Number Letter	11	
Visual Working Memory	6	
Verbal Working Memory	7	
Global Scores		
	Brief Immediate Memory Index	91 (27th percentile)
	Brief Delayed Memory Index	85 (16th percentile)
	Attention/ Concentration Index	103 (58th percentile)
	Working Memory Index	80 (9th percentile)

Informal Writing Task

Sam's attempt to write a story ("Write me a story about this picture and be sure it has a beginning, middle, and end.") produced five simple sentences in 5 minutes despite what appeared as interest. Sam appeared to have some difficulty self-organizing and seemed to benefit from gentle examiner prompts. Handwriting was legible and overall appearance was neat; adequate spacing between words and correct spelling was observed. The story was rather concrete describing the picture with a simple partially evolving plot. Subjective overall impression of the product was adequate mechanics but lacking in content development and imagination.

Clinical Impressions and Recommendations

WRAML3 results, found in Table 7.1, and the writing sample, history, and observations all support the contention that Sam is not demonstrating

186 ESSENTIALS OF WRAML3 AND EMS ASSESSMENT

an attention disorder. Part of the evidence lay in lack of academic concerns until fourth grade, good handwriting, enjoyment of tasks that require sustained attention (ship-building, math computation, competing chores independently), and strength in short-term memory tasks highly demanding of sustained attention. The pattern of performance on Design Learning was of interest since Sam started at an age-appropriate level on Trial 1, but thereafter showed less recall on each successive trial compared to age-mates. His learning slope score confirmed that while starting well, his last learning trial was significantly below expectations. This pattern is not the usual one found in youth with ADHD, who tend to struggle with large amounts of stimuli presented all at once on Trial 1, especially when a perceptual-motor response is the output mode. One explanation of the obtained pattern of today's and prior test results may relate to insufficient involvement of executive functioning since improving performance over trials on Design Learning demands both memory ability as well as skills to develop an effective strategy that will increase recall with a novel task. Both Trial 1 and the Delayed Memory score would suggest that visual memory, per se, is not a weakness. However, to improve performance over trials, both problem-solving strategies as well as rote memory rehearsal are needed. To test the "frontal lobe" hypothesis, the Attention/Concentration and Working Memory subtests were administered. Unlike what is observed with many students with ADHD, Sam's performance on short-term rote memory tasks (Finger Windows and Number Letter) was well within normal limits. (Such performance would also suggest good effort being extended during testing.) However, both Working Memory subtests were poorly performed. These tasks require good short-term memory skills complemented by good executive skills. It appears that the latter weakness may impact achievement. This conjecture is further supported by Sam's completion of the Story Memory subtest, which showed an overall average score but noticeably better Verbatim scores than Gist, not a typical pattern for those with ADHD. In terms of longer-term memory, it seems that Sam adequately retains visual and verbal information that is initially encoded.

Given the results, it is recommended that additional evaluation of executive skills be completed soon. If those results show levels of weakness as today's findings would predict, then there would be a more empirical basis to conclude that Sam's academic struggles are at least in part due to executive functioning delays or inefficiencies. Such weaknesses would explain increasing academic difficulty over the last few years as demands progressively increase for independent problem-solving, time management, and development of strategies that were successful in dealing with areas of struggle especially when not provided by parents or teachers. Reading comprehension may also be affected as "reading between the lines" inference and greater semantic subtlety increasingly characterize the content of assigned reading. Similar challenges would be experienced with novel word problems in contrast to learning math operations that for the most part remain constant once learned.

Assuming the results support the executive functioning hypothesis, there are a number of remediation plans that should prove helpful for Sam. In addition to providing strategies to solve immediate classroom challenges, helping Sam learn how to independently generate and employ effective problem-solving skills should help him use his intellectual and memory abilities more productively. Focus on teaching metamemory skills might help Sam prepare for a learning task. At home, since there is good involvement in completing assignments, working of organizational strategies like PQRS; preview, question, review, and summarize might help. Some brief counseling might also be useful in helping Sam and his parents develop a plan that will prevent Sam from growing dependent on parental strategizing for him so much and instead will equip the parents with ways to help Sam develop those strategies himself, but with opportunities for parental suggestions when needed. Growth in this area will be important before he begins junior high school. Working short-term with a tutor on how to be a less passive reader, but to develop skills to read for comprehension might be a good use of time over the summer (i.e., "coaching" to implement the PQRS suggestion mentioned above).

Commentary

A number of interesting hypotheses with supportive reasoning suggest that ADHD may not be the best way to characterize Sam's ongoing struggles. Thinking about executive functioning as a source of Sam's issues also might have merit as a strategy for planning helpful interventions undertaken by teachers and parents.

The evaluation described above represented a good use of limited examiner time, generating potentially useful conclusions by integrating prior test results, history, and new memory data, especially those most related to attention demands. Interpreting the test data fast enough to then add the Attention Concentration as well as Working Memory subtests to evaluate the emerging hypothesis related to executive functioning is a good example of following the clues. Unlike that observed with many students with ADHD, Sam performed well on the short-term rote memory tasks (Finger Windows and Number Letter) but poorly when executive demands were added with the Working Memory subtests.

Yet, there may be support for an alternative diagnostic view. Sam may not be particularly inattentive when presented with a short stimulus array, or be impulsive or distracted by extraneous stimuli for brief periods, but he does share some of the DSM-5's ADHD symptom list such as having difficulty following through on instructions or finishing tasks once begun, and difficulty organizing tasks and activities. Executive dysfunction and ADHD, when conceptualized, are often found in the same sentence. It may well be that ADHD, like many diagnoses, will eventually be seen as falling on a spectrum with impulsivity, distractibility, and executive dysfunction. Minimally, Sam's presentation could be seen as consistent with the neurological (i.e., frontal lobe) differences theorized in those diagnosed with ADHD.

Nonetheless, from a descriptive and treatment perspective, seeing Sam's weakness as "executive dysfunction" has promise. Working on strategy development and organizational approaches as noted above is a sensible plan. But practically, many school ADHD protocols and "help books" for parents will also have useful suggestions for this young man even though the diagnostic name may not exactly fit. For example, school interventions are commonly available for his symptoms like "not following through on instructions, failing to finish schoolwork, and reluctance to do tasks that require mental effort over a long period of time." As more seasoned clinicians know, a simple diagnosis of ADHD is not so simple!

CASE B: LEARNING DISABILITY?

This case involves a school re-evaluation of a 10-year-old child named Clare who has had a history of academic struggle since first grade. The purpose of this case is to illustrate (1) an appropriate use of an abbreviated form of the WRAML3, (2) an occasion of a non-correspondence between intellectual and memory performance, and (3) parental, and to some degree, teacher unawareness of the impact of intellectual disability.

History/Current Status

An initial testing during early second grade resulted in a WISC-V Full Scale IQ of 65 with little variability across the contributing indexes, other than a relative strength on the Digit Span subtest. A measure of Adaptive Functioning yielded a standard score of 70. Special educational services were judged appropriate approximately a month following that evaluation and shortly thereafter those were extended and have been maintained since. A routine 3-year re-evaluation was recently scheduled to assess Clare's progress which her teacher remarks "has been disappointing." Clare's parents expressed hope that these new and the prior test findings could explain why she was still not at grade level given the considerable remedial efforts teachers, parents, and Clare seem to have expended over the years.

Medically, Clare was born prematurely, and was in a neonatal intensive care unit for about a week before going home. Motor and language milestones are remembered by the parents as being somewhat delayed compared to an older sibling's development. Overall, Clare has been a healthy youngster with relatively few days missed from school because of illness. Her favorite leisure-time activities are doll play, TV watching, and going to a playground near home. While friendly and outgoing, she gravitates toward playing with younger children when at the park and is frustrated when age mates leave her to play by themselves. She recently has been working on setting the table at home for supper times earning an allowance, and has gradually improved with daily coaching, mastering all parts of that chore in about 2 weeks.

190 ESSENTIALS OF WRAML3 AND EMS ASSESSMENT

The school psychologist planned an evaluation session that included the re-administration of the prior intelligence and adaptive functioning measures, along with academic testing. A learning/memory screening was also included in an effort to more thoroughly address the parents' concern about Clare's lack of academic progress.

Results

Results of the re-administered WISC-V and prior measure of Adaptive Functioning yielded results commensurate with expectations based on the initial tests' results; that is, all index standard scores continued to be found in the 60–70 standard score range and no outlying subtest scores from this range were noted. Therefore, the developmental course suggested by the earlier results seems to be the resultant trajectory. Updated results of the academic measures demonstrated reading, math, and spelling scores at the mid-third-grade level, corresponding to the standard scores generated by the WISC results. Table 7.2 displays the results of the computer printout associated with the Brief format of the WRAML3.

Summary, Clinical Formulation, and Conclusions

WRAML3 results show a somewhat mixed picture of memory competencies, most of which suggest significant weaknesses. The major exception was performance on the immediate component of the Design Learning subtest. It was hypothesized that immediate visual memory skills especially for rote recall are a relative strength, at times allowing Clare to give an impression she is understanding content. However, both reasoning and delayed recall ability are significant weaknesses that negatively impact new learning.

To evaluate that hypothesis, the Verbal Learning, Finger Windows, and Number Letter subtests were administered two days after the testing reported above, with the results noted in Table 7.3. The results support the notion that Clare's rote memory skills are noticeably better than her IQ would predict. That is, the three rote subtests found in Table 7.3 are within or close to the average range of immediate memory

Table 7.2 WRAML3 Brief Format Printout from its Scoring Software for Clare's Performance (Used by Permission. Copyright © 2021 NCS Pearson, Inc. All rights reserved.)

Subtest Score Summary

		Scaled Score		
Subtest	Raw Score	Brief Immediate Memory	Brief Delayed Memory	Brief Recognition Memory
Design Learning	125	8		
Story Memory	15	4		
Design Learning Delayed	26		5	
Story Memory Delayed	8		3	
Design Learning Recognition	17			4
Story Memory Recognition	26			4

Index Score Summary

Index	Sum of Scaled Scores	Index Score	Confidence Interval (95%)	Percentile Rank
Brief Immediate Memory	12	76	70–85	5
Brief Delayed Memory	8	64	59–76	0.8
Brief Recognition Memory	8	63	59–80	0.7

(*continued*)

Table 7.2 (continued)

Visual and Verbal Subtest Comparisons

Subtest Comparisons	Scaled Score 1	Scaled Score 2	Difference	Critical Value (.05)	Significant	Base Rate
Design Learning vs. Story Memory	8	4	4	2.62	Y	≤10%
Design Learning Delayed vs. Story Memory Delayed	5	3	2	3.22	N	–
Design Learning Recognition vs. Story Memory Recognition	4	4		4.48	N	–

Immediate/Delayed Recall Comparisons

Subtest Comparisons	Scaled Score 1	Scaled Score 2	Difference	Critical Value (.05)	Significant	Base Rate
Design Learning vs. Design Learning Delayed	8	5	3	3.12	N	–
Story Memory vs. Story Memory Delayed	4	3	1	2.74	N	–

Delayed Recall/Recognition Comparisons

Subtest Comparisons	Scaled Score 1	Scaled Score 2	Difference	Critical Value (.05)	Significant	Base Rate
Design Learning Delayed vs Design Learning Recognition	5	4	1	4.04	N	–

Story Memory Delayed vs. Story Memory Recognition	3	4	–1	3.75	N	–

Retention Score

Trial Comparisons	Raw Score 1	Raw Score 2	Difference	Mean (*SD*)	Base Rate
Design Learning Delayed Total—Design Learning Trial 4	26	42	–16	–2.4 (5.4)	≤5%

Process Scores—Design Learning

	Raw Score	Mean (*SD*)	Base Rate
Trial 1	16	21.5 (9.8)	–
Trial 2	27	36.7 (12.8)	–
Trial 3	40	49.2 (13.8)	–
Trial 4	42	56.4 (12.5)	≤15%
Delayed	26	54.0 (13.1)	≤5%
Learning Slope (Trial 4–Trial 1)	26	34.9 (10.8)	–
Upper Left Quadrant	32	35.3 (16.3)	–
Upper Right Quadrant	24	33.1 (14.0)	–
Lower Left Quadrant	34	39.6 (14.3)	–
Lower Right Quadrant	25	34.9 (12.3)	–

Table 7.3 Clare's Performance on Additional WRAML3 Subtests that Focus on Immediate Rote Memory

Subtest	Scaled Score
Verbal Learning Trials: 5[5], 7[8], 8[10], 8[11]; 5[9] *(Age cohort medians in brackets)*	8
Finger Windows	7
Number Letter	9

ability, as was reflected in the WISC-V Digit Span Forwards performance, as well as the Immediate Design Learning task. Likewise, Story Memory Verbatim content was remembered noticeably better than Gist. All these findings would suggest that Clare is able to perform near the low end of the average range when rote recall is the output demand, but when meaningful content or generating a strategy to enhance learning apart from rote recall, this young lady shows marked deficits. This, then, affects delayed recall which is found within the range that Clare's IQ score would predict. Therefore, Clare often initially gives the impression of recalling much to which she is exposed, but after a short interval, the recall of that information is much reduced compared to same-age peers (as can be seen in Figure 7.1). The memory and IQ components together better explain why Clare seems to initially "master" a lesson being worked on one-on-one, but the next day the amount retained is much less than expected. While this may be a frustrating result for Clare and to those working with her, it may also provide a hint as to ideas for hobbies or even future work that accentuate immediate responsiveness and minimize delayed and contextual requirements, especially in visual memory tasks.

Beyond communicating these results to Clare's teachers, it seems that a conference with the parents is indicated with the objective of sensitively reviewing the results briefly, and spending more time on the meaning and ramifications of what seems to be a confirmed diagnosis of Intellectual Disability. It appears that the parents are not sure why, with so much hard work on everyone's part (including theirs and

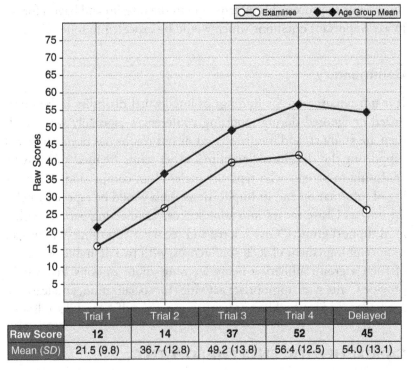

Figure 7.1 Clare's Design Learning subtest results across five recall trials.
(Used by Permission. Copyright © 2021 NCS Pearson, Inc. All rights reserved.)

Clare's), she has made a disappointing amount of progress. A discussion about diagnosis may have occurred three years ago following that evaluation, but, if so, it seems important aspects of the intellectual disability were not well understood. Emphases should include Clare's interpersonal strengths, as well as a time of how best to utilize available resources to optimally support Clare as well as her parents. Emphasis during the parent conference should include academic concerns, but as importantly, paths to learning and fulfillment in non-academic areas as well, both in school and outside. A few well-chosen written materials about Intellectual Disability should be given to the parents at the end of the conference. A follow-up conference may also be indicated given the potential emotional impact of these results. The follow-up would allow the parents to process this information in the interim and have a forum to ask important questions which would be expected to follow.

Commentary

It is not uncommon for findings of intellectual disability to be minimized or ignored during reporting conferences especially when children are younger, and if only one set of test results has been generated supporting this diagnosis. Sometimes other terms are used and may be confusing to parents who typically prefer clear, compassionate reporting of information and its implications. This would be especially helpful now as Claire moves into adolescence. Connecting parents with a local support group ("Give it a try and see what you think.") is also an important ingredient of such conferences, with two desirable outcomes of such a group affiliation being learning about options that would provide Claire with appropriate activities for socialization, and learning methods to aid her building independence with self-help skills at home.

CASE C: HEPATIC ENCEPHALOPATHY

This case is included to demonstrate the use of memory testing to judge the potential value of debriefing sessions as well as psychotherapy sessions with certain clients. It also highlights the importance of memory results for treatment planning. The case and subsequent commentary illustrate how one set of results can be interpreted differently, leading to a discussion of what may be intra-psychic processes at play within clinicians influencing their interpretation of test results. Rather than a traditional set of tabled results in a formal report, the data in this case are relayed in a format more suited for a referral from a physician.

Mr. R
Age: 59
Education Level: 12 and some college
Ethnicity: White-Hispanic

Reason for Referral

Mr. R was referred by his psychotherapist and family physician for a neuropsychological evaluation in order to gain clarity about his cognitive status. This information is needed for recommendations related to presenting medical advice, conducting vocational planning, and recommending couple therapy.

Current Status

About 6 months ago, Mr. R experienced motor and cognitive decline, presumably related to hepatic encephalopathy. While there has been medical improvement since then, Mr. R still presents with complaints of gross- and fine-motor deficits, balance problems, difficulty with concentration, fatigue, word finding, and memory deficits. Both physical and cognitive symptoms have delayed his returning to his job as a pipefitter and union supervisor. Mr. R requested an opinion of his competency for returning to work.

Summary of Relevant Background

Mr. R has a medical history that includes borderline diabetes, hypertension, heart disease, obesity, cirrhosis, chronic pain, hearing problems, and allergies. He experienced a problem with alcohol abuse for many years but reports quitting drinking 3 years ago. Other drugs were denied, other than nicotine (cigarettes). Mr. R graduated high school but reports not liking school starting in seventh grade. He reports disliking English classes but liking shop and math. No special education services were reported being requested or extended. Mr. R reports being in a satisfying relationship with his wife who has not been employed outside the home. His past hobbies included fishing, camping, and shooting. He has volunteered with Wounded Warriors and the Boy Scouts. Mr. R indicated that those who know him well would use the following words to describe areas of strength: fairness, reliability, and self-sufficiency. He presents as an amiable and friendly participant willing to attempt all tasks. Among a listing of 20 potential adult life stressors, Mr. R endorsed two: addiction and job instability. No prior psychological testing is reported.

Selected Test Results

Mr. R's results from his Neuropsychological Assessment

Wechsler Adult Intelligence Scale – Fourth Edition (WAIS-IV)

Composite Index	Standard Score
Verbal Comprehension	100
Perceptual Reasoning	69
Working Memory	77
Processing Speed	65
Full Scale	75

Delis-Kaplan Executive Functioning System Trail-Making Test

	Seconds	Scaled Score	Errors
Visual Scanning	44	4	0
Number Sequencing	142	1	0
Letter Sequencing	59	9	0
Number-Letter Switching	240 (*terminated*)	1	3
Motor Speed	61	7	0

Wisconsin Card Sorting Test: 0 Categories, 39 correct, all trials administered

Test of Memory and Malingering: Trials 1 and 2: borderline acceptable (some apparent confusion with the task)

MMPI-2 RF: Uninterpretable. Difficulty maintaining sustained attention and perseverative responding evident. Some confusion with the task noted.

INTEGRATED INTERPRETATION OF THE WRAML3 | 199

Everyday Memory Survey (EMS)

(Validity acceptable for both versions)

	T Score	Percentile
Self-Report	48	42nd
Observer-Report (wife)	28	<1st

WRAML3 Key Diagnostic Findings (as found in Table 7.4):

- Performance Validity adequate to interpret results
- Differences found between Visual and Verbal Immediate memory, with the latter within normal limits but marked weakness with the former
- Both poor visual and verbal Delayed Recall and poor Recognition performance compared to peers (Extremely Low to the low end of the Low Average ranges)
- Relative strength in Immediate rote and meaningful verbal recall (Story Memory, Sentence Memory) but it significantly erodes over time; impressions based on immediate memory will therefore overestimate actual verbal recall
- Extent of test results deficits may be slightly exaggerated because of overall slow processing speed; significant slowing in most tasks likely to have functional consequences
- Executive functioning shows striking weakness and likely affects ability to form organizational strategies that would assist recall
- No evidence of storage vs. retrieval discrepancy contributing to poor performance
- Lack of client awareness of everyday functional recall struggles

WRAML3 Interpretation (excerpted from a letter sent to the two referral sources mentioned above):

Dear Drs. X and Y:

Thank you for your referral of Mr. R for neuropsychological evaluation in order to obtain findings that would assist in this patient's

Table 7.4 Wide Range Assessment of Memory and Learning, Third Edition (WRAML3)

Performance Validity = 1, Indeterminate (Indicators: ACI = 0, Recognition of 16 = 1)			

General Indexes:	Immediate	Delayed	Recognition
	76	61	67

Subtests	Scaled Score	Subtests	Scaled Score
Visual Immediate Memory	65	Verbal Immediate Memory	97
Picture Memory	5	Story Memory	10
Design Learning	3	Verbal Learning	9
Visual Delayed Recall	56	Verbal Delayed Recall	76
Picture Memory	4	Story Memory	7
Design Learning	1	Verbal Learning	5
Attention/ Concentration	81		
Finger Windows	5		
Number Letter	9		
Visual Recognition	70	Verbal Recognition	72
Picture Memory Recognition	6	Story Memory Recognition	7
Design Learning Recognition	4	Verbal Learning Recognition	4
		Working Memory	75
		Visual Working Memory	5
		Verbal Working Memory	6
		Additional Optional Subtest	
		Sentence Memory	11

ongoing treatment under your care. The following is a summary of that evaluation, and Mr. R has given written permission to share these comments with you; a debriefing session with Mr. R occurred yesterday and a brief summary was provided to him to take with him following that meeting. Specific test results are available to you should you wish to review those. If you have additional questions, please do not hesitate to call.

The Performance Validity Indicator derived from the WRAML3 suggested that Mr. R gave credible effort suggesting test scores are usable for interpretive purposes.

Testing results imply that Mr. R is demonstrating significant impairment in both short- and longer-term memory tasks, compared to age-mates, and there is a greater-than-expected memory decay over time in both Visual and Verbal memory domains. There is evidence suggesting that immediate recall of verbal narratives such as that found in conversation and reading comprehension is a relative strength (near the 35th percentile), but unfortunately, his recall does not maintain with the passage of time, falling to the 5th percentile after a half hour. The immediate verbal recall findings suggest that initial impressions during talk therapy or a medical consultation may overestimate what Mr. R may retain after such sessions. Providing an oral outline prior to discussions and both an oral and written concluding summary highlighting important points that can be subsequently reviewed should prove very useful for Mr. R to meaningfully participate in his treatment. However, weak executive skills along with poor recall will limit his amount of effective problem-solving and concept generalization toward treatment goals. Attention/concentration will challenge memory encoding over time, and so shorter but more frequent therapy sessions will likely prove more helpful than using the typical one-hour format. However, slower overall processing speed will provide an additional challenge with briefer sessions because of Mr. R.'s slow pacing.

With respect to retirement, I endorse the decision Mr. R recently made that it would be best to retire rather than return to his prior job that has numerous memory demands and decisions that need to be made at a fast pace in an environment with numerous distractions. Instead, I wonder if there might be a role for him as a volunteer in a supportive environment that can capitalize on his rich skill set. Mr. R has reasonably good social skills and desires to interact but may misinterpret and forget aspects of social interactions. Consequently, the volunteering experience could serve as a valuable therapeutic and diagnostic focus for future therapy sessions if reliable communication between the volunteer site and the therapist could be established. Since recall and problem-solving are areas of relative weakness, Mr. R will likely need some help in planning and implementing what may possibly be new experiences in volunteerism and other novel pursuits. Habitat for Humanity or a local sheltered workshop may be a promising option for sharing his past construction experience with compassionate and monitoring support available.

Driving is a very important activity for Mr. R's sense of independence. Therefore, an evaluation is recommended with a driving instructor in order to determine Mr. R's current capacity given detected spatial, processing speed, and memory weaknesses. Part of that evaluation would be assessing competence in driving locally as well as outside his immediate community using a GPS, given his relative verbal strengths and visual/spatial and problem-solving weaknesses.

The Everyday Memory Survey (EMS), a rating measure of competency with everyday tasks making memory demands (e.g., recalling ingredients of a familiar recipe or the channel for a favorite TV show) was administered. Mr. R's perception of his memory impairment is quite different from his wife's. This is one area of conflict that became a focus of therapy. Hopefully, the results (and above suggestions) from this evaluation will provide a basis for developing action plans on how best to proceed. Helping Mr. R's wife better understand the challenges memory, pacing, and problem-solving present in everyday life would likely de-escalate conflict now being experienced by the couple. Also, including Mrs. R as part of "the team" when developing home-based strategies might decrease frustration and potential conflict. The action plan developed should be written out so Mr. R can review it at home when needed.

Commentary

This psychologist presented an abridged version of a patient evaluation with hepatic encephalopathy. Since this condition can be episodic, and result in some degree of recovery, my comments are solely based on this client's current status as reported above.

While the Verbal Immediate Memory Index showed some sparing, the Delayed and Recognition memory scores are each suggestive of impairment. It may appear that Mr. R can respond appropriately in conversation, but "where it counts" (after a brief interval) verbal recall is deficient. Similarly, while his IQ measure might suggest an "island" of strength in verbal intelligence, much of the score is based upon prior learning. Today's verbal recall results may be a better gauge of Mr. R's need for support in new verbal learning situations.

Taken together, findings from his most recent test data and the memory weaknesses reported on Mrs. R's EMS, it appears that significant accommodations will be needed for Mr. R to adapt to the world around him. Not only were pervasive memory weaknesses found, but Mr. R's EMS results suggest limited insight into these deficits. Recommendations around driving and volunteering were mentioned, and I applaud a driving evaluation recommendation. However, driving is predominantly visual and spatial sets of tasks. While learning the use of a GPS would help with finding his way to and from desired destinations, learning and remembering how to use a GPS and developing other problem-solving skills often needed to travel raises safety concerns for me.

The other recommendation about volunteering is also a concern, but less so. It may be that older, more rehearsed memories may still be present and would allow skill mentoring in a shop class. Mr. R himself would need to be carefully monitored at the outset to be sure he demonstrates caution and competency with the shop equipment and when interacting with students. Possibly giving a "demonstration" of what he feels competent teaching (without students) would be a place to start. If it could be made to work, it would be a valuable experience for both Mr. R and the recipients of his years of experience.

Continuing psychological support has value, especially with the aids mentioned to enhance the experience. Including his spouse in a debriefing session and later in counseling sessions should help her better understand the nature of what is interpreted as her husband's peculiar and "stubborn" ways. Mrs. R may well find herself in a caretaker role and that will require some adjustment. A dementia support group with other spouses may be helpful even though that diagnosis is technically incorrect.

To examine possible "remission" of symptoms, a re-evaluation in a year is suggested.

CASE D: DEMENTIA LIKELY?

This case is included for a variety of reasons. First, it is not an uncommon referral to those working with a geriatric population. Second, it provides an example of re-evaluation to determine if decline has occurred faster than an age-appropriate rate. Third, it demonstrates when the Performance Validity Indicator (PVI) should be ignored, and the results believed despite the "Questionable" rating its indicators mandate. The case also demonstrates the natural collaboration between a psychologist and physician in order to achieve greater diagnostic clarity.

Current History and Reason for Referral

Pat, an 82-year-old male, was referred to for a follow-up neuropsychological evaluation. Two years ago, his neurologist made a tentative diagnosis of early signs of Parkinson's disease and/or Lewy Body Dementia (LBD). At that time, Pat was showing some mild coordination difficulty, some difficulty walking as well as intermittent struggles with planning and organizing tasks that were previously mastered, like using a cell phone or using tools for a simple repair task. There were times when he was quite clear but then would become confused. For example, Pat has recently been asking about his parents who were long ago deceased or asking if they are coming to take him to his childhood home. When told about their death, he becomes upset. Pat also recently reported communicating with his parents or "characters" from his Philadelphia childhood. At this time, when possible, family avoids directly answering his questions about them as he can become somewhat belligerent.

Previously, Pat was able to sustain attention for long periods and had a love of reading the classics. In the months before the tentative diagnoses, attention would vary somewhat but more recently, Pat has been unable to consistently follow a 10-minute radio show and has considerable difficulty learning new spatial tasks. For example, when he visited his son, he could not remember how to get to his bedroom from the kitchen even after several "practice trials."

Prior to his diagnosis, Pat was a high school teacher and had been living alone. Pat has five children who live near him and are active in caring for him. While he is independent for many of his daily activities, more recently, a family member has been "living" with Pat in his home on a rotating basis because of perceived decline in cognitive functioning, most noticeable over the last year. Family is often uncertain about Pat's status as "one day he is doing great and on another, he seems lost." Pat has also demonstrated a marked increase in anxiety that can accelerate into agitation. This, in part, may be exacerbated by insomnia that has become more common. His family is considering placement in an assisted living residence in the community to meet Pat's current and future needs. Pat began taking Zoloft to help with the anxiety and Xanax (as needed) when markedly upset. The family is careful with Xanax as Pat has recently demonstrated some difficulties with balance and ambulation.

Brief History

On his previous neuropsychological evaluation 18 months ago, there was evidence of mild cognitive impairment relative to premorbid functioning. On the Wechsler Adult Intelligence Scale-IV, Pat earned a Verbal Comprehension Index at the 53rd percentile (VCI 101) and a Perceptual Reasoning Index at the 7th percentile (PRI 78). As expected, he performed poorly on tests traditionally thought to be sensitive to visual perceptual/spatial tasks and tasks involving executive functioning

206 ESSENTIALS OF WRAML3 AND EMS ASSESSMENT

(e.g., Stroop Test, Trails Test). Pat earned a master's degree, was a high school history teacher and had a love of books, suggesting that the average VCI might represent some loss of functioning. Nonverbal reasoning was impaired and found within the Borderline range consistent with his suspected diagnosis of LBD. Pat's family requested re-evaluation in order to update information to aid with a "conversation" around planning for Pat. Results related to Pat's memory performance are presented in Table 7.5 which shows data from the current as well as the initial WRAML3 evaluation 18 months prior.

[Note: Several other tests were included in this brief evaluation (e.g., Delis-Kaplan Executive Functioning System, Wisconsin Card Sorting Test), and were consistent with negative changes in executive functioning. For comparison purposes, data from the two administrations of the WRAML3, separated by 18 months, are presented in the table below. While attempted, the Working Memory subtests were discontinued on both occasions as it appeared that Pat was frustrated by the difficulty of the tasks.]

Summary and Clinical Formulation

The Performance Validity Indicator (PVI), an estimate of effort, was found to be "Questionable." In Pat's case, the PVI is attributable to his poor ACI performance and confusion when completing the Recognition subtests of the WRAML3 (particularly the Design Learning subtest). That is, his degree of impairment affected the utility of the score.

- Pat's General Memory Indexes (Immediate, Delayed, and Recognition) showed a 12- to 18-point decline in standard scores over 18 months. Each is suggesting that memory ability now is near the 1st percentile. Further, for this age cohort, norms have a somewhat inadequate floor for low performers; that psychometric quirk then somewhat underestimates to degree of impairment. Pat's lowest scaled scores are thus affected.
- Interestingly, along with a 10-point decrease in Pat's Verbal Immediate Memory Index score between evaluations, a look at the subtest data shows increased disorganization in recalling the stories as well as recalling the word list from Verbal Learning.

Table 7.5 Pat's performance on the *Wide Range Assessment of Memory and Learning, Third Edition*

Performance Validity Indicator = 2 = questionable *(see text)*…

	Current	Prior	Current	Prior	Current	Prior
	Immediate		Delayed		Recognition	
General Indexes	66	81	64	76	62	80

Subtests	Scaled Score	Scaled Score	Subtests		Scaled Score	Scaled Score
Visual Immediate Memory			**Verbal Immediate Memory**			
Picture Memory	4	7	Story Memory		8	9
Design Learning	4	6	Verbal Learning		7	9
Visual Delayed Recall			**Verbal Delayed Recall**			
Picture Memory	5	7	Story Memory		7	8
Design Learning	3	5	Verbal Learning		4	6
Attention/Concentration						
Finger Windows	6	6				
Number Letter	7	8				
Visual Recognition			**Verbal Recognition**			
Picture Memory Recognition	4	8	Story Memory Recognition		7	8
Design Learning Recognition	3	6	Verbal Learning Recognition		4	7
			Working Memory		Attempted	Attempted
			Additional Optional Subtest			
			Sentence Memory		7	5

Compared to his prior evaluation when visual memory was found more negatively affected than verbal, that trend continues, but shows similar decline in both.
- Figure 7.2 illustrates Pat's decrease in his learning ability. Both the Design Learning and Verbal Learning subtests examine performance across four trials of the same stimuli (and the delay trial). Pat's weak performances on these learning subtests appear to be indicative of poor recall and possibly inefficient executive functioning, both consistent with neurological degradation. Previously on the Design Learning subtest, Pat demonstrated an approximation of a learning curve across trials. On the current Design Learning subtest, Pat demonstrated a relatively flat learning curve across all four trials and no savings on the Delay Trial. On the Immediate Verbal Learning subtest, Pat performed better but still failed to recall any words on the Delay trial. Thus, after a 20- to 30-minute delay, there was little evidence of recall. Unfortunately, these findings would predict that Pat will have

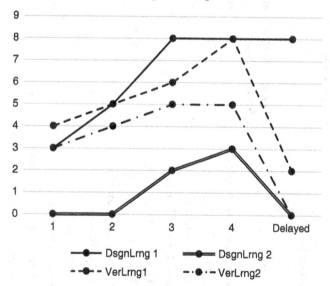

Figure 7.2 Design and Verbal Learning Subtest Performance over Trials for Pat.
Note: DsgnLrng1 = testing from 18 months ago and DsgnLrng2 = current; same for VerLrng 1 and 2.

significant difficulty learning and retaining the new information he encounters in the days ahead.

- A measure of everyday memory (The Everyday Memory Survey) was also administered to Pat and a trusted family member prior to each evaluation. While Pat subjectively endorses some level of decline in completing numerous common tasks independently, there is a more severe rating from a knowledgeable observer of Pat's ability to cope with the everyday tasks he confronts. Safety concerns were flagged in the completion of this measure. Other family members concurred with the survey's findings.

Conclusion

The data from the WRAML3 and the EMS document that both cognitive and functional/behavioral abilities have, consistent with family suspicion, manifested a marked decline evidenced in the two evaluations. The evidence now points more to LBD or a combination of it and Alzheimer's disease rather than Alzheimer's alone. Pat's gross-motor deterioration is also concerning and while not part of today's evaluation, the clear association between Parkinsonism and LBD will obviously likely be addressed by his neurologist.

At this point, Pat is reported to exhibit significant levels of anxiety that are helped with medication. Additional behavioral symptoms also concern the family. Given the decline in cognitive function and the likely trajectory of behavioral and emotional issues with LBD, planning now for additional support in the future will be important since Pat is likely to require increasing assistance for tasks of daily living. Safety is now of increased concern as memory and other cognitive functions have undergone considerable decline.

CASE E: ACADEMIC STRUGGLE AND AN IEP

Most school psychologists are familiar with the process of developing an Individual Educational Plan (IEP). The authors wanted to include this case (1) for those unfamiliar with IEPs, to provide a sampling of

210   ESSENTIALS OF WRAML3 AND EMS ASSESSMENT

the typical IEP document (with an extended WRAML3 analysis), and (2) for those involved in this process, it might provide some insights as to how the WRAML3 might aid in developing useful recommendations.

The following data were excerpted from an actual IEP. The original is quite lengthy (14 pages), written in "legalize" and contains a large amount of narrative. For this reason, only parts of the IEP are presented below. The Annual Measured Academic/Functional Goals (which were impressive) was omitted. The WRAML3 is presented in detail with "bulleted" important findings. A conclusion by the authors is provided, though it was not included in the original document.

Student: D	**Gender:** M	**DOB** 05/20/2016		**Age** 7–0
Native Language: English		**School:** Bronx Elementary	**Grade** 2	

Reason/Agreement for Meeting

Reason: Eligibility Determination with IEP
Determination: Eligible for Special Education and Related Services
Meeting Date: 05/23/2023
Annual Review Date: 5/22/24
Re-evaluation Date: 5/22/26
School Year: 2022–2023; 2023–2024
Classification: Specific Learning Disability
Placement Category: General Education Setting
Start Date: 06/02/2023–05/22/2024

Previous Evaluation Results

Speech/Language Evaluation (Excerpted)
Results of evaluation indicated strength in single-word vocabulary. Picture cues assisted with word finding. Weaknesses include understanding sentences and lengthy utterances, organizing utterances for expression to generate original sentences. Difficulty following

INTEGRATED INTERPRETATION OF THE WRAML3   211

directions, understanding linguistic concepts, and understanding various sentences. Low to moderate deficits in Receptive Language and Language Structure Indexes. D performed at the low to moderate range Expressive Language Index and Language Structure Index. Questions about auditory memory were raised during today's evaluation from both observation and test data.

Psychological Evaluation (Excerpted)

WISC-V	Score	Percentile
Full Scale I. Q.	92	30
Fluid Reasoning	108	66
Verbal Comprehension	88	21
Processing Speed	94	34
Visual Spatial	105	63

Educational Evaluation

Woodcock-Johnson-IV Test of Achievement (Excerpted)

	Score	Percentile
Broad Reading	78	7th
Reading Comprehension	72	3rd
Reading Fluency	75	5th
Broad Math	85	16th
Math Calculation	92	29th
Math Problem Solving	78	7th

Present Level of Academic Achievement

Reading:

D receives 1 : 1 assistance during reading activities. He is able to read on his own with assistance to decode words. He needs assistance staying focused and keeping his place when reading. D struggles with comprehending what he has read and answering comprehension questions. D struggles to answer WH questions, and his answers are frequently off-topic.

Writing:

During writing, D has shown improvement and is able to write five sentences with prompting and assistance. We have been using a graphic organizer to organize his thoughts and include a topic sentence, three details, and a closing, but he sometimes needs support maintaining a singular focus and varying sentence beginnings. When working independently, graphic organizers are helpful when writing to a specific writing genre (narrative, opinion, and explanatory); however, he requires support from a teacher to organize his thoughts and prompt him through the writing process.

Math:

During math, D benefits the most from one-on-one instruction, free from distraction, practicing repetition and review of the concept. When a new concept is introduced, D needs step-by-step instruction with visuals and modeling. After guided practice, he can typically complete problems independently with only verbal prompting such as "what do you do next?" With word problems, we are working on breaking them down into small parts and circling important information and keywords to decide which operation we must use to solve the word problem.

How does the student's disability affect involvement and progress in the general educational curriculum?

D demonstrates weaknesses in reading and reading comprehension, as well as in receptive and expressive language skills.

Parent Concerns

Parents are concerned about D's ability to communicate clearly, as well as his reading skills. They also reported that he can be very shy and they are concerned about his ability to socialize with his peers.

INTEGRATED INTERPRETATION OF THE WRAML3 213

Special Education Programs	Location	Subject	Frequency/Period	Duration	Dates
Pull-out of Classroom	Resource Room	Language Arts	5 times weekly	80 minutes	06/02/2023–05/22/2024
(replacement In-class Resource)	General Education Classroom	Math	5 times weekly	60 minutes	06/02/203–05/22/2024
Related Services					
Speech/ Language Therapy	Pull-out of Classroom	Sp. Therapy	2 times weekly	30 minutes	06/02/2023–5/22/2024
		Group (not to exceed 5)	1 time weekly	30 minutes	

Wide-Range Assessment of Memory and Learning, 3rd Edition

Performance Validity Indicator = 1, Indeterminate (Indicators: ACI = 0, Recognition of 16 = 1)

General Indexes (not reported; see text)	Immediate	Delayed	Recognition
	–		–

Indexes and Subtests	Standard Score	Indexes and Subtests	Standard Score
Visual Immediate Memory	**100**	**Verbal Immediate Memory**	**77**
Picture Memory	11	Story Memory	5
Design Learning	9	Verbal Learning	8

(continued)

214 ESSENTIALS OF WRAML3 AND EMS ASSESSMENT

Visual Delayed Recall	100	**Verbal Delayed Recall**	74
Picture Memory	10	Story Memory	4
Design Learning	10	Verbal Learning	8
Visual Recognition	100		
Picture Memory Recognition	11		
Design Learning Recognition	9		
Attention/Concentration	80	**Verbal Recognition**	72
Finger Windows	6	Story Memory Recognition	5
Number Letter	4	Verbal Learning Recognition	9
		Working Memory	75
		Visual Working Memory	8
		Verbal Working Memory	4

Process Subtests
Story Memory
Scaled Scores: Gist = 3 Verbatim = 7

Additional Optional Subtest
Sentence Memory   7

Trials (D and [age cohort])

Subtest	1	2	3	4	Delayed
Design Learning	24 [21]	36 [36]	44 [49]	50 [56]	45 [54]
Verbal Learning	6[5]	6 [8]	7 [10]	7 [11]	4[9]

WRAML3 Key Diagnostic Findings and Analysis:

Unlike most subtests that evaluate what the examinee has previously learned, the WRAML3 actually allows the psychologist to watch the examinee learn and remember *in situ*. Watching D perform the Story Memory subtest and contrast that performance with the Picture Memory subtests provided a window into both his language issues and nonverbal strengths. Further, note that D's poor NL and FW performances, in the face of good attention abilities, allow the examiner to hypothesize difficulty with sequencing less meaningful data, consistent with his academic learning disability.

- General Indexes were not reported as there were significant differences between all Verbal and Visual Indexes. It should be noted that all Visual Indexes were found within the Average range.
- Visual and Verbal Immediate memory were found to be significantly different from each other ($p < .05$) with a base rate of occurrence of less than 10%.
- Both poor Verbal Delayed Recall and Verbal Recognition performance were found particularly weak compared to peers. Importantly, there was a nonsignificant difference between the Immediate and Recognition Indexes suggesting cueing may have limited benefit on D's verbal processing issues.
- Relative weakness was also found on the ACI Index. D was observed to maintain good focus, particularly on visual subtests (consistent with the absence of teacher concern in this area). It appeared that the source of the poor NL and FW performances was difficulty with sequencing less meaningful data. This is consistent with the reading and spelling deficits demonstrated on academic testing on Woodcock-Johnson. It may be that the sequencing difficulties will have a greater impact on D's math achievement as he progresses through the grades. Initial math facts for addition and subtraction are not as dependent on sequencing operations as are multiplication and division. This is

suggested by D's weaker Math Problem Solving than Math Calculation achievement on the WJ-IV.

- Difficulty with sequencing meaningful or semantic verbal information was also observed on the Story Memory. D had difficulty organizing the details of the story coherently. In fact, regarding the process variable, Gist and Verbatim on the Story Memory subtest, most of the credit earned was from remembering details (Verbatim scaled score 7) rather than the storyline (Gist, scaled score 3).
- There was some improvement when the amount of verbal information to be recalled was reduced. On Sentence Memory subtest, D earned a scale score of 7 compared to a Story Memory scale score of 5. Of course, both of these scores represent concerns around a language processing disorder. From an "auditory memory" perspective, functionally, D's ability to understand and process contextual verbal information will exert a marked effect on his ability to recall language-based content. Verbal memory deficits will also affect recall from longer reading selections. Keeping messages brief, supported nonverbally, and practiced would be helpful.
- Nonverbal subtest performance was consistently found within the average range and suggested that visual cuing, picture support, and creative support nonverbal would be a useful mode of assistance.

Summary and Recommendations

Using the WRAML3 data, the psychologist was able to support D's diagnosis of a language-based learning disability. The clear discrepancy between verbal and nonverbal performance allowed the psychologist on the team to advocate for an increase in services for D. This included both individual and group language therapy as well as both pull-out and in-class resource support for Reading/Language Arts areas.

While no significant concerns were raised at the IEP conference, his teacher noted that D demonstrated increasing reserved participation with peers in the classroom. During the IEP, there was a discussion that centered around a possible relationship between the increasing language demands of second grade and D's difficulty expressing himself in social situations. It was agreed that emotional functioning should be monitored.

D's parents are very involved and registered concern about his language as well. D's parents noted that many of the men on dad's side of the family were "generally quiet" and tended to work in craft fields where language demands are minimized. Further, during the conference, parents reported learning disabilities in the family history. Parents were shown graphs of the Design Learning and Verbal Learning subtests to illustrate their son's marked strengths and weaknesses. They were also shown the Story Memory Record Form from where the psychologists numbered the details reported as D retold the story. The disorganization and dearth of details recalled were illustrative. They agreed to supplement his school services with private speech and language therapy so that they can learn how to best help.

Additional accommodations recommended at the IEP meeting are included as below:

Additional Recommended Accommodations

- Allow for repetition and/or clarification of directions, as needed
- Reinforce verbal directions with visual cues
- Provide multi-sensory instruction
- Additional time to complete classroom tests/quizzes
- Small group administration of classroom tests/quizzes
- Read test aloud (items and directions). Allow for oral responses when appropriate
- Provide books on CD or read-aloud computer software
- Break down tasks into manageable units
- Provide study guides
- Frequently check for understanding
- Modified tests/quizzes (word bank, fill in the blank, etc.)
- Use graphic organizers

Commentary

The case study nicely illustrates the utility of the WRAML3 in detecting language-based learning difficulties. I would stress the implications of the weakness uncovered since by third grade, they will noticeably affect D's reading and listening skills as more content-oriented subjects like history and science become part of the curriculum. Looking at the Verbal Learning Trial scores is rather sobering for both immediate as well as delayed recall. The Sentence Memory subtest shows that accurate recall of sentences with easy vocabulary starts to deteriorate once sentence length exceeds seven words (with clear implications for instruction). These findings (and D's demonstrated areas of strengths) need to be communicated in a meaningful fashion to his teacher(s) as they prepare lesson plans. Accordingly, the LD specialist, speech and language pathologist, and classroom teacher should be given time to actively brainstorm possible interventions that could be implemented in the classroom. In a sense, they might think of D as a 7-year-old from a foreign country arriving in the United States with the rudiments of English but not yet having proficiency with the language; with that perspective, how might they approach teaching this child? (Note the daunting language demands embedded within several of the "Accommodations Recommended" listed above, possibly suggesting current misunderstanding of D's verbal memory and language impairments.)

Consistent with the idea of utilizing "visual assists" that appeared in the IEP narrative, teachers should be generating concrete possibilities that could be incorporated when teaching reading and math basics, but even more so to be used in content-laden instruction. D risks being left behind in content areas because of slow-developing reading, math, and listening fundamentals. Using a video presentation of a historical event or streaming a science discovery that provides visual assistance along with verbal narrative may be methods worthy of being tried and evaluated. Exploring computer software options (especially in math) would be another example of more visually oriented approaches to instruction. Obviously, all such interventions should not be tried at once; prioritizing a list of reasonable possibilities, and then experimenting with those that seem most promising should be a fruitful approach. Given D's visual reasoning and visual memory scores, it would seem likely that any instruction that can receive auxiliary visual supplement would be much better recalled and comprehended. Perhaps as an aid to help D's parents understand his verbal memory/processing skills, the Table of Age Equivalents in WRAML3's *Administration Manual* may be helpful in communicating that D performed like most pre-kindergarteners.

I would modify the recommendation for monitoring emotional status to actually making referral to a mental health specialist with a goal of building a plan that would prevent an already shy child from becoming even more withdrawn and discouraged. The approach would have to be different from that of many school counselors since "talk therapy" would not be this child's strong suit. Hands-on activity that would allow brief, simple verbal exchanges should work better, such as "For next week, I want you to take three pictures of things that make you happy and three that make you sad." There is not much documentation of what this child does well, and that would be an important avenue to explore. If he does well in art, certain sports, games, or other leisure-time activities, those may become the best sources for tailoring emotional support and a language therapy curriculum. The parents may welcome the counselor's insights about how home interactions and attempts to be "helpful" could be modified to have a more positive emotional and academic impact.

Successes and failures of various "interventions" tried in and out of school this year should be recorded and passed on to next year's educational team since these language-based weaknesses will likely persist in the coming years.

Eight

EVERYDAY MEMORY SURVEY: OVERVIEW, ADMINISTRATION, AND SCORING

This chapter starts the second section of this book. While the *Everyday Memory Survey* (EMS) has been mentioned at various points in the preceding chapters, little has been said of its format, content, or use. This and the next chapter will examine the EMS more closely, and describe why it should and how it can be used with more traditional memory tests such as the WRAML3.

EVERYDAY MEMORY

Everyday memory is the naturalistic expression of memory operations utilized in daily life. In other words, everyday memory can be described as functional behavioral expressions of organic memory substrates. Examples of everyday memory include the ability to remember such life events as appointments, familiar routines, where items were placed, financial due dates, and other common recall demands. In a sense,

---

Essentials of WRAML3 and EMS Assessment, First Edition.
Wayne V. Adams, David V. Sheslow, and Trevor A. Hall.
© 2024 John Wiley & Sons, Inc. Published 2024 by John Wiley & Sons, Inc.

much of what is on one's "to-do" list is comprised of everyday memory demands. The term "ecological validity" has been used to describe the EMS's content because it reflects common memory tasks of everyday

> **DON'T FORGET**
>
> The EMS measures everyday memory, which is the application of memory skills to meet the challenges of daily life.

life. The EMS was intentionally designed to be user-friendly by incorporating brevity, readability, ease of administration and scoring, and clinical applicability while maintaining psychometric integrity.

EMS OVERVIEW

The EMS is a psychometrically sound, self-report questionnaire designed to assess subjective judgments of everyday memory performance in order to evaluate, monitor, manage, and ultimately treat adults with known or potential memory impairment. At present, the EMS is only available for an adult population. For persons under the age of 18 years, the memory demands of everyday life change throughout childhood and adolescence, and thus would rightly require multiple forms to capture the evolution of everyday demands throughout development. Plus, many of the everyday memory demands for 5- to 18-year-olds are anchored in school-related interactions, and thereby become confusingly entwined with intelligence, learning anomalies, curriculum structure, parenting practices, and other substantial confounds.

Conceptual support for the need to assess everyday memory can be traced to the International Conference of Practical Aspects of Memory in 1978 (Gruneberg, Morris, & Sykes, 1978; Neisser, 1982). At those meetings, Neisser (1978) shared his belief that research on memory lacked the needed focus on how memory is actually used in daily life. Since then, there has been considerable interest and perhaps even controversy in research related to functional memory loss and preservation following neurological illness or insult. In essence, the controversy centered around the lack of correspondence between formal/traditional memory measures and memory questionnaires targeting real-life performance. Intuitively, it seemed that the formal and functional measures of memory should be highly related. Yet, research (Hertzog & Hultsch, 2000) suggested that the range of memory deficits caused by stroke, car accident, or dementia and the varied neuropsychological measure of memory only result in slight, positive associations. The clinical needs for patient care, therefore, resulted in the conclusion that to be most complete and most helpful, the psychological assessment of "memory" *should* include both standardized testing and a measure of "real life memory." This conclusion led to interest in co-developing the EMS with the revision of the WRAML3.

A wide array of practical applications exists for the EMS that complements traditional memory test measures, such as the WRAML3. These include, but are not limited to: (1) screening for memory challenges in settings such as primary care clinics, specialty medical clinics, memory centers, retirement communities, rehabilitation facilities and clinics, and community centers; (2) identifying specific tasks of memory struggle for a given examinee, thereby inviting meaningful tailored recommendations using rigorous test findings that often are underutilized; (3) monitoring everyday memory gains and/or declines post-treatment for a neurologic illness or injury; and (4) generating ecologically meaningful serial/longitudinal research data related to neurological or pharmacological outcomes.

Because those with memory loss may not be able to consistently rate functional memory skills accurately, the EMS has two formats which can be used independently, but are intended to be used in tandem. The *Self-report* and *Observer* formats elicit two different and important subjective perspectives providing a broader understanding of perceived memory competency germane to the demands of everyday life. The *Observer* form should be completed by someone well-acquainted with the person whose everyday memory is being evaluated. More information on how to select appropriate observer raters is presented later in this chapter. Both the *Self-report* and *Observer* forms consist of 25 content-parallel items that are written at the 5th-grade reading level, and each takes about 10 minutes to complete. Examples of questions found on the two EMS forms are provided in Rapid Reference 8.1 (these items are illustrative examples only and not items actually on the scale). Rapid Reference 8.2 summarizes important EMS components being discussed in this chapter.

Embedded Performance Validity Indicator

As noted in Chapter 3, demonstrated veracity of responses is essential for all test measures. This is particularly important for self-report and other third-party measures like the EMS. Relying on subjective ratings

---

≡ Rapid Reference 8.1

Example of the EMS for Self-Report and Observer Formats

(using sample items not included on the EMS)

	Never	Rarely	Some times	Often	Almost Always
Self-Report Format					
I forget where I park my car.	[0]	[1]	[2]	[3]	[4]
I lose important things like keys, wallet, or purse.	[0]	[1]	[2]	[3]	[4]
Observer Format					
This person forgets where the car is parked.	[0]	[1]	[2]	[3]	[4]
This person loses important things like their phone, wallet, or purse.	[0]	[1]	[2]	[3]	[4]

≡ *Rapid Reference 8.2*

EMS General Description and Overview

Focus	Designed to measure subjective impressions of everyday memory performance
Formats and Content	Two forms: *Self-Report* and *Observer*, each has 25 parallel items each consisting of a single sentence.
Ages	Designed to measure everyday memory in persons aged 18- to 90-years of age
Norms	The EMS normative sample is representative of the US English-speaking population of individuals aged 18–90 years. An analysis of data gathered by the US Census Bureau American Community Survey (US Census Bureau, 2017) provided the basis for stratification along the following variables within each age group: gender, race/ethnicity, socioeconomic status (as indicated by parent education level for ages 18–24 years or personal education level for ages 25 and older), and geographic region. The EMS was developed and normed along with the WRAML3, sharing 39% of cases on the *Self-Report* form and 42% of cases on the *Observer* form between the two instruments. By sharing standardization samples in this way, the authors hoped to psychometrically align traditional, formal testing results (i.e., the *WRAML3*) with subjective everyday memory performance (i.e., the *EMS*).
Uses	Intended for both clinical applications in identifying, monitoring, and remediating memory impairment, as well as for research purposes.
Administration	Approximately 10 minutes for respondents to complete.
User Qualifications	Designed for use by clinical psychologists, psychiatrists, physicians, physician assistants, nurse practitioners, school psychologists, and other educational, medical, or mental health professionals. Also, in many cases, clinical social workers, speech/language therapists, licensed professional counselors, school counselors, and similarly trained individuals have the background and experience needed to use the EMS.

targeting everyday memory increases the likelihood of response distortion due to idiosyncratic influences such as rater demographic background, cultural norms, possible secondary gain, inattentiveness/ random responding, influential events occurring prior to testing, or a lack of task understanding. To address this issue, the EMS includes a pair of extreme but plausible items that can help detect compromised validity of the obtained responses, or alert clinicians to a serious symptom that occurs in only a small percentage of the nonclinical population. Of note, the two items do not contribute to the EMS Score for both the *Self-Report* and *Observer* forms. More will be said of this safeguard in the next chapter that focuses on uses and interpretation of the EMS.

Psychometrics

Extensive information related to development, standardization, reliability, and validity of the EMS is found in Chapters 4 and 5 of its *Manual*. Nonetheless, several especially relevant psychometric characteristics will be highlighted here so that users can see at a glance that the EMS meets the high standards professionals have rightly come to expect for nationally standardized instruments.

Standardization. Well before standardization, the three-year research program leading to the publication of the EMS was an iterative process, with three phases of development leading to further refinements of the instrument. The first phase of development involved a comprehensive review of the research literature on memory, with a specific emphasis on everyday memory. As a result of the review, a pilot version of the EMS was developed, critiqued, and further refined, and preliminary data was gathered using targeted populations. With further refinements, the resultant items were administered with the WRAML3 pilot administration (as discussed in Chapter 3) with the goal of generating a final version to be used for standardization. A total of 113 *Self-Report* forms were collected. Also, a pilot study included a small clinical sample of individuals diagnosed with Alzheimer's disease. The resulting data were then examined for potential bias with respect to sex and

226 ESSENTIALS OF WRAML3 AND EMS ASSESSMENT

ethnicity, and psychometric qualities. After several additional analyses and reviews designed to ensure good construct coverage, a final set of 46 parallel items for the EMS *Self-Report* and *Observer* forms were chosen for standardization.

The normative sample consisted of 920 *Self-Report* and *Observer* forms divided into 6 age groups representative of the US 2017 Census data with respect to age, gender, race/ethnicity, education level, and geographic location. The selection of the final 25 items was based on the analysis of data collected during standardization using classic test theory models in that items with problematic frequency distributions, low point-biserial values (i.e., < .1), high standard errors of measurement (i.e., >.4), or poor clinical sensitivity were eliminated. The EMS authors' clinical judgment was also used to ensure construct coverage and clinical utility.

Reliability. Data from the EMS standardization sample (see Table 5.4 in the EMS *Manual*) show strong internal consistency across all age groups for both the *Self-Report* ($r = .92$) and *Observer* ($r = .94$) forms. This is true for both nonclinical participants in the standardization sample as well as those with a reported clinical classification of Mild Cognitive Impairment/Early-Stage Alzheimer's Disease or Major Depressive Disorder in two special study group samples. In addition, test–retest correlations for the *Self-Report* ($r = .81$) and *Observer* ($r = .82$) forms indicate the EMS provides stable results over time.

Validity. Information included in Chapter 5 of the EMS *Manual* details demonstrated validity for the EMS in the areas of content, internal structure across forms, and for its sensitivity to detect differences between matched controls and those in clinical groups known to have memory impairments. As expected, individuals with Mild Cognitive Impairment/Early-Stage Alzheimer's Disease showed significantly more difficulties with everyday memory tasks on both the *Self-Report* and

> **DON'T FORGET**
>
> The EMS is a psychometrically sound tool that can be utilized for multiple applications by any professional with formal training and experience with memory disorders, their assessment, and treatment.

Observer forms. Similarly, individuals with Major Depressive Disorder also showed significantly more difficulties with everyday memory tasks compared to those in their matched control group on both the *Self-Report* and *Observer* forms. The EMS *Manual* also presents

> ## DON'T FORGET
>
> The *Observer* and *Self-report* formats of the EMS yield different subjective perspectives germane to memory performance in everyday life, and can be used in assessment, monitoring, and remediation efforts.

information on its interrelationships with WRAML3 performance; this will be detailed in the next chapter.

User Qualifications, Responsibilities, and Cautions

As indicated in its *Manual*, the EMS should only be used by trained clinicians and/or researchers who, at a minimum, have had formal coursework in psychological testing and measurement and understand the basic psychometrics that underlie test use, development, and interpretation. Users should also have familiarity with the assessment of memory-related impairments as well as a background in adult development and age-related cognitive changes. Although the EMS is designed for use by clinical psychologists, neuropsychologists, psychiatrists, physicians, physician assistants, nurse practitioners, school psychologists, and other educational, medical, or mental health professionals, use is not restricted to these professions. In many cases, clinical social workers, speech/language pathologists, licensed professional counselors, and similarly trained individuals have the background and experience needed to interpret results of the EMS. Importantly, users of the EMS should be familiar with the principles presented in the *Standards for Educational and Psychological Testing* (American Educational Research Association [AERA], American Psychological Association [APA], & National Council on Measurement in Education [NCME], 2014), as well as with the more recent updates, and should endorse standards for the ethical use of educational and psychological tests. All users should review the EMS *Manual* carefully, including the specific issues related to administration, interpretation, psychometric integrity, and test security.

> ## CAUTION
>
> This and the following chapter should not be used as a substitute for the information found in the *Everyday Memory Survey Manual*, which must be utilized in order to more thoroughly understand its psychometric basis, guidelines for administration, and interpretation.

Although the EMS can be administered and scored easily by a range of personnel, responsibility for interpretation must be assumed by a professional who realizes the limitations of screening and diagnostic procedures that are based on self and other third-party rating scales.

ADMINISTRATION AND SCORING

A solid understanding of how to administer, score, and interpret the EMS is essential if its users want to make the most of the information it can provide. Chapter 9 of this book provides a comprehensive commentary related to interpretive strategies and the wide-ranging uses the EMS affords, in both the clinical and research arenas. However, this section provides information related to administration and scoring. Proper administration and careful scoring are obviously needed in order to obtain trustworthy survey results.

> ## DON'T FORGET
>
> Proper administration to English-speaking adults who can read at least at the 5th-grade level, and careful scoring are both needed in order to obtain trustworthy results.

Examinees and Observers

The EMS is intended for US English-speaking adults aged 18–90 years, with at least a 5th-grade reading level. To state the obvious, the EMS *Self-Report* form should be completed by the person whose everyday memory is being evaluated. The EMS *Observer* form should be completed by someone who has knowledge about the daily behaviors of the person whose everyday memory is being evaluated. More specifically, the person completing the EMS *Observer* form is expected to have a high degree of familiarity with the examinee, having had ample opportunity to have

EVERYDAY MEMORY SURVEY 229

≡ Rapid Reference 8.3

Guidelines for Those Qualified to Serve as an EMS Observer

Those qualified to complete an EMS Observer Form should have:

- **frequent and recent contact** (usually at least weekly) with the person whose everyday memory is being evaluated.
- interacted for a relatively **long duration** (at least several months) with the person whose everyday memory is being evaluated.
- opportunities to observe the person being evaluated in a **variety of settings** assessed by the EMS.

---

recently observed their behavior in typical life situations. Ideally, the respondent completing the *Observer* form will be a spouse, significant other, sibling, close friend, adult child living nearby, or a familiar care provider. Rapid Reference 8.3 summarizes guidelines from the EMS *Manual* on how to appropriately identify acceptable observer raters.

In addition, it is perfectly acceptable, and sometimes preferable, to have EMS ratings obtained from multiple qualified observers across multiple times. Using multiple sources of information about the person whose everyday memory is being evaluated has the potential to enhance the EMS input by generating data from multiple settings and perspectives.

Administration

As is true with any psychological assessment, establishing good rapport between the examiner and the examinee is a vital first step. Effectively establishing rapport with a wide adult age range should be in the clinical repertoire of the person administering both survey forms. One important caution to proffer here is, given the implications of perceived or real declines in memory performance, some examinees may be worried or uncomfortable about being evaluated, even by a friend or loved one. A suggested set of introductory directions for the examinee and observer are provided in Chapter 1 of the EMS *Manual*, but those can be somewhat tailored to be more reassuring, or to offer calming support in areas about which the examinee may be unduly concerned. Sometimes including a brief explanation of how the results will be used can increase willingness. When hesitancy is encountered, simply add something like "Some folks may be concerned about filling out forms like this, but your thoughts and opinions are very important in helping us understand how things are going for you."

Further, when administering both the *Self-Report* and the *Observer* forms, the examiner should utilize the introduction scripts referred to above, emphasizing the importance of completing all the items. Both forms also provide brief instructions at the top of the front page just below the area where demographic information is recorded. It is acceptable to respond to any examinee questions raised by the scripts as well as provide reassurance when encountering signs of unease. Once started, most examinees take only around 10 minutes to complete the survey.

Although it is always preferable for the EMS to be completed one-on-one in a controlled setting, some circumstances may require a respondent to complete the EMS remotely. This can be accomplished in one of two ways: (1) by utilizing a formal parcel service, or (2) by utilizing the EMS publisher's online administration and scoring system, Q-global. Helpful guidelines for some of the unique challenges that may arise with remote administration are presented in Chapter 1 of the *Manual*. Additionally, the items may be read aloud if needed, with the examiner recording the response on paper or directly using Q-global. Reading may be done orally by the examiner or by using the audio provided via the online administration option. Of note, to assist those taking the EMS via oral administration, Appendix D in the EMS *Manual* provides a visual depiction of the item response options. The EMS publisher allows examiners to reproduce that page as needed in order to provide the respondent with a physical reminder of the response options available while they listen to the items.

Scoring

With only 23 true items on the EMS, all, or nearly all, are needed to be completed in order to optimize the validity of the EMS Score. The standardization of the EMS allows for up to three missing items before the form is considered to be invalid, although the examiner is encouraged to work with respondents to ensure all items are completed whenever it is possible. If missing items do exist, then an adjustment to the EMS total raw score is made by adding a raw score of 1 point to the raw score subtotal for each missing item. Conveniently, the digital administration option eliminates the possibility of missing data by requiring respondents to complete all test items before submitting a completed form.

The paper-based *Self-Report* and *Observer* forms require the EMS to be scored by hand. The EMS is scored in the same way regardless of whether the examiner is scoring the *Self-Report* or the *Observer* form. The front of the form captures rater responses and the back provides tools to aid in the summarization of the results. A scoring summary table (Figure 2.1 in the EMS *Manual*) and Score Profile grid (Figure 2.4 in the EMS *Manual*) are provided directly on the EMS forms to help calculate the raw score as well as space to record the corresponding T score and percentile rank. Extra grid space is provided to record results from multiple administrations and/or multiple raters.

Responses to all the items on the EMS (excluding the two embedded performance validity items) are used on the back of the form by totaling the number of each response option endorsed, the options being: *Never, Rarely, Sometimes, Often,* and *Almost Always.* The raw score totals are then weighted: multiplied by 0 for *Never,* multiplied by 1 for *Rarely,* multiplied by 2 for *Sometimes,* multiplied by 3 for *Often,* and multiplied by 4 for *Almost Always.* All weighted raw scores are then summed. That total is then converted into the EMS Score, which is an age-referenced T score ($M = 50$, $SD = 10$) obtained by utilizing the normative tables in Appendix A of the EMS *Manual.* Percentile ranks are also provided. As most readers will likely know, percentile ranks are used to determine how frequently a particular T score may be found in a nonclinical population and what percentage of nonclinical individuals are likely to express more impairment on the construct of interest.

For the EMS, low T scores are associated with more difficulties with everyday memory tasks, while high scores are associated with fewer difficulties. More detailed, step-by-step scoring instructions are provided along with examples in Chapter 2 of the *Manual*. More nuanced interpretative details related to the EMS Score, raw scores, and individual items are discussed in the next chapter.

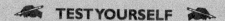

TEST YOURSELF

Everyday Memory Survey: Overview

1. **The correlation between traditional test results and those from functional measures of memory like the EMS has generally been shown to be:**
   (a) highly positive (+.75 and higher)
   (b) moderately positive (+.50 to +.70)
   (c) modest (+.20 to +.30)
   (d) moderately negative (-.50 to -.70)
   (e) highly negative (-.75 and lower)

2. **The EMS can be used for all the following except:**
   (a) Screener for memory challenges in settings such as primary care clinics
   (b) Tailoring practical recommendations for examinees
   (c) Diagnosing dementia in older adults
   (d) Monitoring everyday memory gains and/or declines post-treatment
   (e) Longitudinal research

3. **All of the following are true except:**
   (a) Examinees often "fake bad" on the *Self-Report* form.
   (b) The *Observer* form should be completed by someone well-acquainted with the person being evaluated.
   (c) Multiple raters for the *Observer* form are encouraged.
   (d) *Self-Report* and *Observer* formats are intended to be used together but could be used independently.
   (e) The EMS is normed for adults aged 18–90 years of age.

Answers: 1c, 2c, 3e

Nine

USES AND INTERPRETIVE CONSIDERATIONS FOR THE EVERYDAY MEMORY SURVEY

Building on the information in Chapter 8, this chapter focuses on principles, guidelines, and strategies for interpreting the *Everyday Memory Survey* (EMS). The chapter concludes with a clinical case illustrating the use and application of the EMS.

USES

As highlighted in the preceding chapter, the EMS is designed to be used in the assessment, monitoring, management, and treatment of adults with known or potential memory impairment. As such, the EMS may be regularly used to screen for memory challenges in a wide variety of settings. The EMS may also be readministered to monitor progress in clinical as well as research settings. One of the most promising uses for the EMS is how it can be utilized to document real-world manifestations

---

Essentials of WRAML3 and EMS Assessment, First Edition.
Wayne V. Adams, David V. Sheslow, and Trevor A. Hall.
© 2024 John Wiley & Sons, Inc. Published 2024 by John Wiley & Sons, Inc.

DON'T FORGET

The EMS provides the opportunity to identify and more deeply explore examples of perceived, concrete everyday memory challenges, often in tandem with findings derived from traditional performance-based memory measures!

of memory impairment often left unexplored in traditional performance-based memory assessment. That is, the EMS can serve as a bridge between formal test data and concrete interventions using input from both the examinee as well as a familiar third party.

INTERPRETATION OF THE EMS

Critical Items

The first thing an examiner needs to do once the EMS is completed is take note of the four "Critical Items." These items are nested within the 25 items comprising the EMS. As mentioned in Chapter 8, two critical items relate to the believability of the responses provided in the survey. If either of these items is endorsed at any level beyond "Never," the examiner has reason to question whether the examinee (and/or the observer) is inattentive, has a negative response set, lacks understanding, internalizes excessive worry, is expending inadequate effort, is not reading items or is not doing so carefully, or is exaggerating their memory deficit. Regardless, in such cases, the examiner must utilize clinical judgment to determine whether proceeding with scoring and interpretation of the survey is justified given the endorsement of a very low probability event. Critical Item endorsement should trigger examiner caution in interpreting the survey's results.

If the examiner makes the determination that proceeding with scoring and interpretation of the survey is unwarranted, then consideration of how to proceed should occur. Sometimes, like in a research context, a conversation with the examinee or observer may not be necessary; nonetheless, the survey data should be excluded from the research dataset. In clinical situations, a conversation about the examiner's concerns regarding accurate item endorsement is warranted. For example, the examiner might say something like the following: "I noticed some of your responses on the survey to be somewhat unusual. Would it be alright for us to talk through some of them?" From there, asking the examinee or observer to share the rationale for their response might then lead to a conversation about attention, motivation, and other potential confounds. There is no perfect way to approach such a sensitive situation, and as such, the examiner must be clinically prepared to work through what comes from the conversation. What is uncovered in that process may be more important in understanding and helping the examinee or observer than an EMS's valid score!

While examiners are encouraged to interpret results from the EMS cautiously if there is any reason to question the respondent's response accuracy, it is also important to note that a wide variety of factors can influence ratings on the *Self-Report* form—even something, for example, as simple as an examiner forgetting their reading glasses.

The other two Critical Items are intended to flag concerns about examinee safety. Again, if endorsed at frequencies greater than "Never," again more information is needed from the examinee or the observer to make a clinical determination of how to proceed. As with the two validity items, if ratings on either of the safety items elicit examiner concern, there is a need to make a determination about the examinee's safety. If clinically indicated, a supportive care plan would then be implemented. This is usually done collaboratively with observer, examinee, and other involved persons contributing.

It should be noted that oral administration of the EMS is an option, and enables the examiner to monitor the examinee's (or observer's) understanding of the items. This format may then become the basis for a portion of the typical clinical interview (see Chapter 2 in the EMS *Manual* for more details about this approach). When administering the EMS verbally, it is important to read the items as they appear on the forms using a neutral tone. As noted above, discrepancies between raters generally the *Observer* form more faithfully reflects everyday behavior, but, even then, the *Self-Report* form can provide important information as to the examinee's perception of current functioning. Further, because consistent results between raters allow for greater confidence in the

PUTTING IT INTO PRACTICE

The EMS may be particularly useful when monitoring fluid conditions such as recovery from brain injury or decline in dementia.

findings when *Observer* and *Self-Report* discrepancies occur, it is always preferable to utilize multiple EMS *Observer* raters when possible (more about this approach is discussed later in this chapter).

Examining Results

As is the case with all psychometric instruments, information gleaned from the EMS is best understood within the context of other relevant information. As mentioned in an earlier WRAML3 discussion, information useful to interpreting EMS findings includes but is not limited to psychosocial, medical, and educational histories, as well as an understanding of any cultural issues that may affect the presenting problem. It is also important to remember that the EMS is not, by itself, a diagnostic tool and thus should be used in isolation to diagnose specific memory-related neurological conditions. Nonetheless, in order to maximize the EMS's potential and to effectively interpret the information it provides, users are encouraged to have a robust familiarity with memory research, especially the relationship between everyday memory and formal memory test results; more discussion about that relationship as well as context is also presented later in this chapter. Lastly, remember that the EMS is a subjective rating scale designed to measure observable memory deficits. As such, examiners should have a working understanding of how to use and interpret rating scales. Remember, ratings, especially ratings evaluating a sensitive area such as memory, are influenced by personal expectations and perceptions, emotional factors, as well as the multiple cognitive subsystems needed to satisfactorily complete the tasks nested within given EMS items.

DON'T FORGET

Interpretation of the EMS is best done only by well-trained clinicians within the context of other auxiliary information.

USES AND INTERPRETIVE CONSIDERATIONS 237

After the EMS is scored and no endorsements of *Critical Items* are noted, the process of interpretation can begin using the overall T score (also referred to in the EMS *Manual* as the EMS Score). As shown in Rapid Reference 9.1, there are four descriptive classifications based on the Total EMS score.

The first step is to determine whether the examinee's EMS Score warrants further interpretive analysis. Because the EMS is a "deficit-based" instrument, little concern is generated with average or above ratings other than noting "within normal limits"; higher EMS Scores do not necessarily suggest strength in everyday memory functioning. Therefore, if the EMS Score is >45, and is judged to be valid as described above, then no further interpretive consideration is indicated. However, an EMS Score of 45 or greater should be deemed within normal limits only if that result is true for both the *Self-Report* and *Observer* forms. If one or the other EMS Score is ≤44, then the examiner should proceed with deeper levels of analysis and interpretation. In fact, there are data showing that significant discrepancies between observers and examinees often suggest greater likelihood that the examinee has significant memory impairment (Edelman, Fulton, & Kuhn, 2004).

≡ *Rapid Reference 9.1*

T-score Ranges and Corresponding Classifications of Functioning

T scores	Percentile Ranges	Descriptive Classification
≥45	≥28th	Age-Appropriate Everyday Memory
40–44	15th–27th	Mild Difficulties with Everyday Memory
29–39	2nd–14th	Moderate Difficulties with Everyday Memory
≤28	<2nd	Significant Difficulties with Everyday Memory

Low Scores

The primary focus of interpretation will be for EMS Scores below 45. As examiners assume, the likelihood of a serious memory deficit increases as the EMS Score decreases. Although the EMS is not a comprehensive diagnostic tool, it is often used as a screener to identify examinees who may be experiencing memory-related problems. As such, an EMS Score of ≤44 should prompt consideration for a more comprehensive neuropsychological and perhaps even a neurological evaluation. This is particularly germane given the natural history of such memory disorders as Alzheimer's Disorder that manifest memory weaknesses long before a formal diagnosis is made. Obviously, if the EMS is the initial screener, a decision about the need for a comprehensive work-up increases in importance the lower the EMS Score. Making judgments related to EMS scores falling in the mild to moderate range may be a bit more challenging. To aid in the decision-making, examiners will benefit from (1) comparing EMS Scores across multiple points in time, such as every 3, 6 or 12 months; (2) discussing what was behind more severe ratings to individual items from the examinee and/or observer; and (3) contrasting the findings with other test results, clinical observations, and history.

Multiple Responders and EMS Re-Administration

Examiners should always compare the EMS Score on the *Self-Report* form with the EMS Score on the *Observer* form. To support this practice, each paper form of the EMS includes a visual display called the Scoring Profile. This allows the examiner to plot ratings from the *Self-Report* and *Observer* EMS Scores side-by-side and over time when there are re-evaluation results. As well there is space for comparison ratings over time for re-evaluation results. Up to three subsequent administrations can be entered. In some cases, information gathered from multiple observers can indicate the consistency of an examinee's everyday memory challenges across different environments, which should lead to the development of context-specific intervention recommendations. The Scoring Profile grid appears in Figure 2.4 in the EMS *Manual* and a sample appears here in Figure 9.1.

USES AND INTERPRETIVE CONSIDERATIONS 239

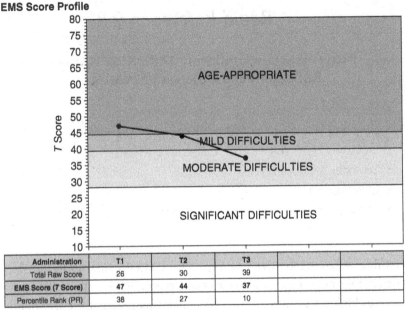

EMS Score Descriptive Classifications
Suggested ranges of interpretation for the EMS are as follows:

T Scores	Percentile Ranks	Descriptive Classification
45 and above	28 and above	Age-Appropriate Everyday Memory
40–44	15–27	Mild Difficulties With Everyday Memory Tasks
29–39	2–14	Moderate Difficulties With Everyday Memory Tasks
Below 29	Below 2	Significant Difficulties With Everyday Memory Tasks

Score Comparisons Over Time

Comparison	1st Score	2nd Score	Difference*	Significant (.05)
Earliest-to-Most Recent Reports Selected (T1-to-T3)	T1 = 47 (on 08/05/2021)	T3 = 37 (on 08/05/2021)	–10	Yes
Two Most Recent Reports Selected (T2-to-T3)	T2 = 44 (on 08/05/2021)	T3 = 37 (on 08/05/2021)	–7	No

*A positive difference indicates a decrease in symptoms and/or symptom frequency over time; a negative difference indicates an increase in symptoms and/or symptom frequency over time.

Figure 9.1 Q-global EMS Output Related to Observed Decline over Three Administrations.

In addition, the digital (i.e., Q-global) version of the EMS compares the difference between EMS Scores between the *Self-Report* and *Observer* forms with statistical values derived from the inter-form analyses to determine if obtained differences are "real" or possibly due to random effects or measurement error. A significant result suggests a

240 ESSENTIALS OF WRAML3 AND EMS ASSESSMENT

≡ Rapid Reference 9.2

Factors that Often Influence Differences Between Self-Report and Observer EMS Scores

- Length of time observer has known the examinee
- Length of time observer has recently spent with the examinee
- Demands of the setting when observer is present
- Self-rater memory deficits
- Observer bias
- The evaluation context (e.g., medical, legal, etc.)

credible difference between ratings. The EMS Manual indicates that correlations between examinees and observers are generally in the moderate to high ranges ($r = .40$ to $.73$), suggesting reasonable correspondence between the two forms should be expected. Rapid Reference 9.2 presents a listing of factors that most often influence differences uncovered between the *Self-Report* and *Observer* forms.

Individual Items

While individual items are narrow samples of behavior that typically lack generalizability, if done with caution and careful thought, an analysis of specific items can aid EMS interpretation. Subjective analysis of items that converge may help with planning targeted interventions and recommendations. Any EMS item endorsed as *Often* or *Almost Always* provides the examiner with specific examples of everyday memory challenges that warrant further inquiry via interview and/or further assessments. For example, the examiner may be able to determine a pattern of behavior related to a given environmental context that may negatively influence the examinee's ability to recall, such as a change in residence or medication. That kind of knowledge has immense value when interpreting results as well as personalizing an intervention strategy. Moreover, because the *Self-Report* and *Observer* rating forms are parallel in content, it is easy to compare the same items across raters.

When the examiner detects variability across raters, typically the examinee is underestimating the degree of memory dysfunction. Yet, as noted above, there are times when observer bias, observer impairment, or observer "agenda" results in disagreements with the examinee who made provide a more accurate picture of true memory decline. Second and third sources are always in fashion.

As another interpretative tool, the Q-global version of the EMS has the capacity to determine if the difference between EMS Scores from a single rater (examinee or observer) from one administration (Time 1) to another administration (Time 2) is statistically significant. This level of analysis helps examiners determine if obtained changes in ratings are due to random effects or measurement error (see Figure 9.1 for an example). When EMS Scores differ significantly over time, this suggests a decline or improvement in perceived memory difficulties. Tracking this change longitudinally helps examiners provide evidence-based data upon which to base extended discussions with the examinee and their family for possible alterations in plans for care.

Contextual Factors and Histories

As with any assessment tool, the EMS requires an analysis of the multiple contextual and interpersonal factors that have the potential to influence examinee and observer recall. For example, it is well known that memory is a vulnerable cognitive system for those who have experienced a critical neurologic illness or injury, especially during the early stages of recovery. Therefore, the EMS Scores for persons acutely recovering from such an illness or injury may be temporary, not accurately reflecting the examinee's ultimate level of recovery and should, accordingly, be interpreted with caution and not used for prognostic purposes. Nonetheless, the results can be very useful indicating the current domains which need therapeutic focus. Such information would be most welcome by an occupational therapist, home health professional visiting the examinee's residence, and, of course, family members.

Additional contextual factors that are important to consider while interpreting EMS results include sociological determinates of health such as economic stability, access to and quality of education, access to and quality of healthcare, access to healthy and affordable food, the safety of the neighborhoods where people live, and availability of family and friends, and supportive community resources.

Integrating Objective and Subjective Findings

The comprehensive assessment of memory functioning often includes neuropsychological measures that directly evaluate memory as well as questionnaires that assess subjective perceptions of memory functioning in daily life, like the EMS. When interpreting the data, examiners using the EMS in concert with traditional tests of memory should be aware of their complementary roles. As previously mentioned, a substantial body of literature reports modest to moderate correlations between subjectively reported and performance-based cognitive ability measures (Freund & Kasten, 2012; Herreen & Zajac, 2017; Uttl & Kibreab, 2011; Toplak, West, & Stanovich, 2013). This likely occurs for a variety of reasons. First, items on most surveys encapsulate multidimensional cognitive measures, whereas memory tests focus on a narrower band of performance. For example, forgetting where one parks one's car is in part a complex memory task incorporating multiple other processes such as spatial skills, attention, level of anxiety, and executive function, not to mention sociological influences such as availability of safe parking spaces. Few, if any, test results contain all these overlapping inputs and therefore that difference limits substantial correlation between them. Second, subjectively reported scores tend to be negatively skewed in nonclinical samples (i.e., everyone perceiving they are above average!); this is not typically true for performance-based cognitive ability measures. When correlations involve skewed distributions they are typically low. While small to large positive correlations were observed between WRAML3 Index Scores and *Self-Report/Observer* EMS Scores, this was mostly true within the older age groups. This may result from less skewed distributions often found within an older population because of normal memory loss. Consequently, it should be understood that both objective and subjective evaluative findings do not provide redundant information. Therefore, if the goal of clinical evaluation is to gain a full picture of the examinee's memory functioning, a combination of objective and subjective measurement is appropriate in order to better understand that person's memory strengths and weaknesses, and provide tailored recommendations that are useful and will be received as meaningful by the examinee.

This chapter will conclude with an illustration of how the brief time investment required by the EMS can yield additional useful information not readily available from results provided by traditional memory test batteries.

CASE EXAMPLE: TRAUMATIC BRAIN INJURY

Brief History

Luke is a 19-year-old white male who is being medically followed through a multidisciplinary clinical care program due to a traumatic brain injury he sustained when he was 14 years old. Briefly, Luke was admitted to the trauma intensive care unit following a motor vehicle collision in which he was a restrained passenger in a vehicle that was struck on the driver's side by a large truck. Imaging initially revealed significant injury including diffuse axonal injury; intraparenchymal hemorrhage of the right basal ganglia, right temporal lobe, frontal lobes (right greater than left), and right sylvian fissure; likely additional hemorrhagic contusion at the inferior right temporal gyrus; contusion at the right orbital roof; possible ischemia of the right caudate/putamen; and bilateral parietal-occipital hematomas.

As part of his ongoing care, Luke had previously participated in three neuropsychological evaluations over the course of four years. At his most recent follow-up assessment, both Luke, at age 19 years, and his mother (who attended the appointment with him) expressed ongoing concerns about learning and memory, especially related to keeping up with college coursework.

WRAML3 Screener Results

Interpretation and Commentary

Given the variability found across Luke's WRAML3 subtest performance, the examiner chose to focus on the subtest scores instead of overall Index scores. Aside from ongoing struggles with noncontextual visual memory (i.e., Design Memory results), Luke's WRAML3 scores showed him to have again uniformly improved immediate, delayed, and cued recall memory abilities despite the lengthy passage of time since his severe brain injury. Compared to his previous assessment, Luke demonstrated some increase in his ability to encode, store, and recall visual and verbal information. Significantly, though, Luke's current performance comparing immediate and recognition trials suggests that he does not consistently have access to verbal content but when cued, his performance markedly improves. Important as well, Luke's performance across immediate and recognition trials suggests stronger encoding and consolidation abilities related to contextual verbal memory than previously seen.

Similarly, Luke also demonstrated significant improvement across visual memory measures using meaningful stimuli. In comparison to his previous evaluation, Luke's performance across visual immediate recall and recognition trials represents an area of substantial improvement (e.g., previous performance fell within the very low score range). While Luke continues to struggle freely recalling complex but meaningful visual information after a delay period, his performance on the Recognition trial suggests he is able to better encode and consolidate visual information. With regard to recall of much less meaningful visual material, Luke continued to demonstrate significant difficulty across immediate, delayed, and recognition trials with his performance generally falling in the low average to very low ranges. Given the severity of injury to the right parietal lobe, this will likely be an area of persistent difficulty for Luke. Nevertheless, he and his mother reported developing remedial strategies to partially compensate for this area of weakness, including reviewing verbal discussions of the visual materials

USES AND INTERPRETIVE CONSIDERATIONS 245

(e.g., diagrams and illustrations) found in class lectures using the instructor's PowerPoint presentations.

While one can certainly generate some meaningful memory remediation strategies based on Luke's history and WRAML3 results, in this case, the EMS as an additional measure was especially helpful. Specifically, even though both Luke and his mother verbally reported ongoing memory concerns, there were notable differences between their EMS Scores. This is clinically meaningful given the strong correlation commonly observed between the EMS *Self-Report* and *Observer* Scores for Luke's age cohort. As noted in Table 9.1, there is more than a full standard deviation difference between the two EMS Scores.

Table 9.1 Luke's WRAML3 Test Results Excerpted from a Larger Neuropsychological Assessment Battery

WRAML3 (Screener Format)				
Subtest		Scale Score	**EMS**	*T* Score
Picture Memory	Immediate	(6)[a] 9	*Observer Report* (Parent)	24 (<1st percentile)
	Delayed	(5) 6		
	Recognition	(5) 8	*Self-Report*	42 (21st percentile)
Design Memory	Immediate	(3) 4		
	Delayed	(4) 5		
	Recognition	(5) 4		
Story Memory	Immediate	(4) 9		
	Delayed	(4) 5		
	Recognition	(3) 9		
Verbal Learning	Immediate	(10) 13		
	Delayed	(6) 7		
	Recognition	(5) 7		

[a] Scores in parentheses were obtained 15 months earlier.

246 ESSENTIALS OF WRAML3 AND EMS ASSESSMENT

Additional discussions during a follow-up interview led the examiner to conclude that Luke's mother had more awareness and insight about Luke's daily memory challenges than did Luke, which is not surprising given the nature of Luke's brain injury. This suggests that guidance may be needed in assisting Luke in employing strategies to adjust to his memory deficits, some of which he may be unaware. An additional inference from the EMS was that Luke is hesitant to disclose aspects his ongoing struggles.

At the EMS item-level, his mother's responses suggested that Luke was experiencing ongoing challenges with general forgetfulness, such as getting lost on his way to familiar places, remembering what he had read, misplacing things, and remembering new concepts. Luke also endorsed relative difficulties in forgetfulness and needing to write things down to reduce the likelihood of forgetting; however, Luke did not endorse struggles related to getting lost, remembering new concepts, or repeating himself. When Luke's WRAML3 results were viewed through the EMS Score "filter," his pattern of performance made more sense and thus led to subsequent therapeutic conversations with both Luke and his mother about other real-world examples of memory challenges he is experiencing in his college curriculum.

Learning from the EMS that Luke was hesitant to discuss some of his cognitive challenges, we gently moved into this issue resulting in a meaningful conversation between the examiner, Luke, and his mother. Additional concerns emerged such as (1) maintaining focus during times when concentration is needed; (2) remembering where on campus all of his classes are, (3) studying for tests and "knowing the content," then "forgetting" what he has studied for short-essay questions (extra time allotted to him for test taking did not help with this challenge); (4) remembering when he had started tasks, like laundry; and (5) feeling confused about what he was supposed to be doing at different times during the day.

Notably, the aforementioned challenges were not reported during the initial clinical interview or available from formal testing results. It was only after the EMS items were being discussed that these additional

USES AND INTERPRETIVE CONSIDERATIONS   247

(and important/relevant) daily life examples were mentioned. When asked about that, Luke commented, "I was a little worried about what you might think if I talked about those things." Rapport between the examiner and Luke was strong given that they have known each other for five years; nonetheless, it took going through items on the EMS to create the opportunity for Luke to feel confident enough to talk about his ongoing memory problems. Thereafter, several practical strategies were collaboratively generated so that Luke could share them with the professionals supporting his progress through the campus learning center. With little prompting Luke was able to conclude that using his phone alarm would help in remembering when to start tasks like laundry; similarly using his phone calendar at the end of class to record relevant upcoming events should prove especially helpful. Further, given the benefit of cuing, a recommendation for multiple-choice testing was made whenever feasible. In addition, Luke and his mother agreed to some short-term therapy sessions that would focus on more therapeutic ways to remind, encourage, and express feelings, as well as jointly problem-solve in a more constructive manner. Luke also thought once those sessions were finished, it would be useful to recommence individual therapy given the social and academic challenges and frustrations being experienced at school.

🪐 TEST YOURSELF 🪐

EMS Interpretation

I. **The *Critical Items* on the EMS are there to alert the examiner to:**
   (a) the most important everyday memory problems.
   (b) a possibility that the EMS score might not be valid.
   (c) personality traits of the examinee.
   (d) potential safety issues that need attention.
   (e) both b and d

248 ESSENTIALS OF WRAML3 AND EMS ASSESSMENT

2. Which EMS score warrants careful interpretive analysis?
(a) T score of 75
(b) T score of 60
(c) T score of 40
(d) T score of 50
(e) T score of 97

3. Which of the following is true of the EMS?
(a) Scores on the Self-Report and the Observer forms are seldom similar.
(b) A notable difference between scores on the Self-Report and the Observer forms should be investigated.
(c) The Self-Report score is typically lower than the corresponding score on the Observer form.
(d) The Observer score is typically lower than the corresponding score on the Self-Report form.
(e) An examiner should normally avoid using more than one "observer" rating an examinee

4. EMS outcomes are meant to:
(a) supply a fuller understanding of a person's memory when used with a traditional memory test.
(b) replace optional scores on the WRAML3 when necessary.
(c) only be used to inform treatment plans until a more traditional test of memory can verify results.
(d) monitor memory change (both positive and negative) over time.
(e) Both a and d

Answers: 1e, 2c, 3b, 4e

Ten

Q&A WITH THE AUTHORS

The authors thought it would be an interesting and helpful way to end this volume by offering a Q&A chapter mostly consisting of questions often asked by former trainees (residents and post-docs), colleagues, and those who attended our presentations or workshops. Some questions are technical, others clinical, and a few are semi-personal. Hopefully, the content will help review and tie together some of the themes of this work, as well as provide a useful and enjoyable conclusion to this work. It is hoped that the content below will add to what you have learned throughout this book and enable you to better serve those who come to you with the hope that testing will provide the information needed for them to find a path to wiser problem-solving, greater self-understanding, increased wholeness, and more joyful accomplishment in the living of life.

Essentials of WRAML3 and EMS Assessment, First Edition.
Wayne V. Adams, David V. Sheslow, and Trevor A. Hall.
© 2024 John Wiley & Sons, Inc. Published 2024 by John Wiley & Sons, Inc.

249

THE WRAML3 IS A BIG TEST! WHAT'S THE EASIEST WAY TO LEARN IT?

Agreed, the WRAML3 is a big test; we demur to say that there is not an easy way to learn it. The training rubrics provided for each of the subtests (found in Chapter 4) contain 161 items. That is, there are at least that many decision points to get right in a proper administration of the WRAML3, and that does not include the many additional details included in the test guidelines, or the use of the Process scores. Add to that the important clinical skills such as establishing rapport, maintaining motivation, and making useful observations, and then one can soon understand why learning a test like WRAML3 can be a daunting challenge. However, it is doable, and here are a few suggestions that should help: (1) Be serious about wanting to administer it competently, which means actually scheduling a realistic amount of time to achieve that goal; remember that distributed practice leads to better learning than massed practice! (2) Break the learning task into manageable parts (sound familiar?!); (3) Read the Administration *Manual carefully; (4) Select a subtest (usually the first), digest the administration guidelines and read the directions out loud as if a client were sitting across from you; repeat until it is done smoothly and feels comfortable; (5) Find a volunteer, maybe a trainee or fellow colleague wanting to learn the test too; alternatively, find one within the age range of those you commonly test; (6) Using the informed and consenting volunteer, administer one or more subtests you believe you administer competently; digitally record your performance and soon after the testing, use the subtest rubric(s) to assess competency; (7) When competency is achieved, move along in like fashion with the remaining subtests; (8) start adding one or two WRAML3 subtests to your actual testing of clients so you start getting a feel of how the subtest compares to other assessment tools with which you have clinical expertise; determine what the WRAML3 provides that is redundant and what are contributions beyond what you already obtain from the familiar tests you already use and value; (9) As you near completion of rotating all the WRAML3 subtests into your testing batteries, look for someone to teach parts of the WRAML3 to, such as externs, interns, or post-docs, because teachers usually learn more from teaching than students; alternatively, give a presentation on the test to a small group of fellow professionals; (10) start using the WRAML3! (11) Find or create a professional group that discusses testing cases, and share WRAML3 cases that puzzle you or have interesting findings, (12) start to supervise WRAML3 testing while maintaining humility!*

THE WRAML WAS THE FIRST STANDARDIZED AND NATIONALLY NORMED TEST OF MEMORY FOR CHILDREN AND ADOLESCENTS. WHAT ORIGINALLY LED YOU TO EMBARK ON THE DEVELOPMENT AND STANDARDIZATION EFFORT?

Wayne and David were pediatric psychologists working at a children's hospital in the 1980s. Part of each week we were both involved with an evaluation service that included consultation to a Rehabilitation unit. For many of the head injured clients we saw, there was no standardized test to evaluate children's memory, an area very important as children are discharged and returned to school. We adapted parts of various existing measures that had a memory component but found what we gathered was a less than satisfactory solution. One day, over lunch, we were again complaining about how frustrating it was to assess memory in this manner since most all the rehab youngsters we saw clearly had memory deficits. An older and very wise social worker sitting with us at lunch put down her coffee cup, looked us in the eyes and said, "Will you guys stop whining and do something about it!" That terse but sound advice was taken, and the original WRAML was released in 1990!

HOW DID THE WRAML GET ITS NAME?

Wide Range *was a product line that was developed and sold by a local test publisher (e.g., the WRAT (Wide Range Achievement Test) is a product of that company). Dr. Gary Wilkerson, the incoming president of the company played racquetball with Wayne, who jokingly claims he "threw a few games" to get a test proposal meeting! Wide Range was willing to take a chance on two testing newbies, provided excellent support, and in return the original test title, "Test of Learning and Memory," became the* Wide Range Assessment of Memory and Learning.

HOW LONG DID THE ORIGINAL WRAML TAKE TO DEVELOP COMPARED TO THE WRAML3?

There were about five of us working on the original version including a statistical consultant. David even sketched the pictures for Picture Memory before handing them to a real artist for the final renderings! We started out with a possible 21 different subtests, and gradually whittled them down to 9. The process took almost four years from inception to publication. The WRAML3 (with Pearson) had a group of 25 involved with 3 core staff plus the authors, and from initial draft to publication took almost 5 years. Across the three WRAML editions we learned an amazing amount about item sampling, pilot testing, standardization, statistical analyses, and a hundred other things that go on behind the scenes to create psychometrically sound measures that we test users too often take for granted. In the process, we also met numerous amazingly talented people, many of whom remain good friends.

YOU HAVE SAID THAT THE WRAML IS ONE OF THE BEST DIAGNOSTIC INSTRUMENTS TO ASSESS ADHD. WHY?

Several times in the text we have mentioned that most cognitive tests assess past learning (e.g., vocabulary). With the WRAML, the examiner gets to observe new learning with an examinee over a chunk of time to observe variations in the ability to sustain focus, remain free from external distraction and sustain effort when "confronted" by challenging tasks both immediate and delayed. This period of observation may be analogous to teacher observations which make teachers such valuable resources for reporting.

While there are group data confirming that ACI performance is lower for those with ADHD, it is the observable behavior in the testing session that we find particularly valuable for parent conferences and report writing. For example, we have seen the youngster with ADHD who gets most of the first half of a story but misses the whole second half, or the teen who gets two different scaled scores for the two stories presented, or the adult with ADHD who becomes overly focused on parts of a feature and fails to regard the whole scene. It is these kinds of observations that can be quantified with Process Scores, providing both quantitative and qualitative impressions. To be clear, the WRAML3 or its ACI component should not be considered procedures that, by themselves, diagnose ADHD. But throughout the battery there are ample opportunities to formulate as well as confirm those suspicions. By the way, some of us believe that ADHD is not a deficit (connoting "chronic deficient") but rather a dysregulation where variability is the rule. If that is true, being able to observe possible individual variability across a variety of attentionally demanding tasks should have important clinical utility.

HOW DO YOU FEEL ABOUT STUDENTS USING THE WRAML3 INTERPRETIVE REPORT SOFTWARE?

The intention of the Interpretive Report (IR) is to give users, especially new clinicians, hypotheses to mull over. Being new to the instrument, unfamiliar examiners may not initially be able to juggle the various conceptual combinations across all 17 WRAML3 subtests plus Process Scores. Consequently, the IR should assist all users by generating possibilities that seem to match a particular pattern of scores. Some of those score patterns might have been unrecognized by examiners, or for more experienced users, may have been overlooked, given the pace most clinicians keep. Therefore, the IR is a tool that is part idea generator and part reminder. But it is a starting place. Until artificial intelligence becomes much more sophisticated, computer software is unable to match the product created by human integrative thinkers who can take WRAML3 findings and join them with other test findings (at times, including personality results), observations, and history, integrating the best from both the clinical and empirical worlds. What is not intended is the IR being used as "an authority" in interpretation, but instead a catalyst. For the authors, finding whole sections cut from an IR report and unquestioningly pasted into an official report is always a disheartening discovery, especially when contradictory data are ignored.

HOW SOON CAN I RE-ADMINISTER THE WRAML3?

The answer to the question is related to the topic of reliability; that is, when can I re-administer the test again and expect, all things being equal, that I will get the same result. A partial answer is found in Rapid Reference 3.5,

254 ESSENTIALS OF WRAML3 AND EMS ASSESSMENT

which shows a representative sampling of WRAML3 Indexes and subtests with their respective coefficient alpha values (a complete listing is found in Table 3.2 of the Technical manual). Those correlations indicate high reliability, and suggest that examiners should expect to obtain reasonable agreement in test-retest scores, all things being equal. However, all things are not typically equal and a substantial contributor to differences in a non-clinical sample is practice effect. The extent of that impact can be seen in a sampling of subtest scores presented in Rapid Reference 10.1. Those difference scores range from almost 0 to 2.6 scaled score points. Those scores were obtained from the test-retest study completed during standardization (Table 3.6 in the **Technical** manual). Therefore, we know the memory "savings" for re-testing occurring an average of 30 days later, the interval used in that study. However, most clinicians would not repeat testing 30 days after the original administration. Instead, most clinicians might be interested in a re-evaluation in 6- to 12-months or longer following the initial testing. Unfortunately, we do not have data to know how much practice effect there still might be for that longer interval, but undoubtedly performance would reflect less recall than what is found for a 30-day delay. That prediction is supported by test-retest data from WRAML2 which had a 49-day separation between testing days and yielded subtest differences that are generally about half of those obtained with the 30-day test-retest

---

⇐ Rapid Reference 10.1

Test-Retest Scaled Score Differences for Several WRAML3 Subtests

PicMem	DsgnLrng	StMem	VL	FW	NL	VisWM	VerWM
1.9	2.6	2.0	2.2	0.7	0.5	0.1	0.4

Note: PicMem = Picture Memory, DsgnLrng = Design Learning, StMem = Story Memory, VL = Verbal Learning, FW = Finger Windows, NL = Number Letter, VisWM = Visual Working Memory, and VerWM = Verbal Working Memory.

interval. As would be expected, rote memory tasks of WRAML3 (i.e., FW, NL, VisWM and VerWM) showed very little practice effect, whereas the most meaningful material (i.e., StMem) had a difference of 2.6 scaled score points. Clinically, in our experience, when using a 6-months interval, most examinees will express some recognition of the task but not much recollection of the specific content. Just to be conservative, we tend to favor a one-year "rule-of-thumb" as a reasonable interval for routine re-evaluations, but less than that for evaluations assessing memory recovery, such as those re-administered following a brain injury. There is a unique twist with memory test re-administration and is related to the question that was asked. It was briefly touched on in Chapter 3. Since typically, re-evaluations are completed with examinees who have some suspected or known memory loss, re-administering the test and getting a somewhat inflated result from practice effects actually makes the concern about re-testing quandary moot. That is, if the examinee can remember the testing content from some months ago and thereby earn a higher score, that "inflated" score is, in fact, a useful measure providing evidence that the examinee can retain novel information over a significant span of time. And, if that is true, while the score might be a bit higher than if there was no initial testing, that score nonetheless allows the clinician to know that there has been reasonable memory recovery.

THE WRAML3 PERFORMANCE VALIDITY INDICATOR (PVI) IS BASED UPON PERFORMANCE ON THE FOUR RECOGNITION SUBTESTS AS WELL AS THE TWO ACI SUBTESTS. HOW CAN I KNOW IF AN EXAMINEE IS FAKING BAD OR SIMPLY NOT MOTIVATED TO PERFORM IF I DON'T ADMINISTER ALL OF THOSE SUBTESTS?

The PVI is not available unless all Recognition and ACI subtests are administered. However, because of circumstances such as time pressures, client fatigue, as well as adequate performance on Delayed subtests, the examiner may choose not to administer the Recognition subtests. When that happens, there is the ACI indicator that might, by itself, serve as a reasonable PVI estimate. That is, standard scores of 70 and lower on the ACI suggest that the examiner should consider questionable effort unless the examinee

256 ESSENTIALS OF WRAML3 AND EMS ASSESSMENT

might otherwise be expected to score this low, such as with those with marked Intellectual Disability or those who have recently sustained a significant brain insult. So, unless history and clinical observation would create a justification for a client's ACI score to be 70 or below, that low score by itself might justify considering non-optimal effort. The rationale for that contention is found in Table 4.23 in the Technical Manual which shows that the ACI by itself has sensitivity of .67 (67% of people who actually are showing poor effort will produce an ACI score of 70 or below) and specificity of .98 (98% of those who earn a score above 70 will be showing reasonable effort). And those levels of sensitivity and specificity will yield a 96% correct diagnostic classification of a large group half of whom are not giving forth good effort and half who are. However, without both PV indicators being employed, caution is warranted. Caution is also advised if there is marked variability between the two ACI subtests. For example, working with a person with severe hearing impairment could produce a Number/Letter subtest score so low that the ACI would be found below 70 despite an adequate Finger Windows score. In this extreme example, a solid familiarity with the client's history would prevent misinterpretation of minimal effort being expended (and, in this instance, prevent inferring poor verbal memory ability based on the likely results from the Verbal Index subtests).

I "GOOGLED" EVERYDAY MEMORY SURVEY AND FOUND A 2004 PUBLICATION AUTHORED BY DR. HALL. IS THAT POSSIBLE?

Yes, that is true! This is Trevor Hall responding and thanks for asking. I'm happy for this opportunity to highlight the importance of meaningful mentorship! Truth be told, the 22-year-old, wannabe-professional-snowboarder version of me had no business applying to graduate school in Clinical Psychology during the fall of 1999. Even so, that version of me did... thankfully. Dr. Wayne Adams took a chance (I still have no idea as to why...!) and allowed me to join his lab as a graduate student. Under Wayne's mentorship, I easily "caught the psychometric bug" which was a far (and dare I say, very nerdy) cry from high alpine backcountry! Jokes aside, words cannot express how grateful I am for that to have happened! The original version of the EMS was the result of my dissertation research, which started around the time the WRAML2 was released. Wayne was always interested in what WRAML results might "look like" in the everyday world; hence, the concept for the EMS was born! Had I known then about the amount of work that goes into developing a psychometrically sound measure like the EMS, I might not have chosen such an enormous task for my dissertation, but that "psychometric bug" has super powers! I learned so much during that time about instrumentation, statistics, evaluation, standardization, validation, and more. The research passion forged during the late Friday afternoon meetings with Wayne (fondly dubbed WTWW – Wasting Time with Wayne because of their wide ranging discussions) has continued being an influential part of my professional life ever since. Naturally, when the question was asked about my willingness to resurrect and revise the original EMS as the WRAML3 was being developed, I could not resist! The rest, as they say, is history.

WHY IS THERE NO LONG-TERM MEMORY SUBTEST?

The question begs the related question of, how long ago should the content of a long-term memory subtest have occurred to qualify as a test of long-term memory? There is no general agreement on an answer to that query. Clearly, long-term memory has to be longer than immediate recall. But is 20-minutes, 20-days or 20-years adequate? Also embedded in selecting a proper time span is a heavy cultural component since the content of a test should be available to all in the standardization sample, and that becomes very difficult in a fast-paced, diverse, mobile society of varying ethnic and socio-economic experiences. How can the examiner be sure certain content was learned at a given level of exposure by an examinee months or years ago? While we could teach unique content like found in Story Memory to an examine in response to that concern, and then test recall one or more years later, are clients, examiners, or researchers willing to wait that long to obtain an answer? Plus, will the examinee remember or be willing to show up for an appointment scheduled that far out? Plus, there is no guarantee that the once unique content will not be contaminated by exposure to a popular TV series or breaking news story that coincidentally

258 ESSENTIALS OF WRAML3 AND EMS ASSESSMENT

shares some of the same content. So, for a variety of logical, psychometric, and practical challenges, long-term memory tests have not been developed.

The question could be approached in different way: how well do the WRAML3 subtests predict longer-term memory functioning? We know from WRAML2 and WRAML3 results that immediate and 20- to 30-minute delayed recall scores are highly correlated in non-clinical samples (generally with the range of .85–.90). Ebbinghaus's pioneering research would also suggest that the 30-minute delay is pretty highly correlated with recall 24 hours later. One of our students showed in his dissertation that contextual WRAML3 subtests (Story Memory and Picture Memory) have reasonably credible recall and recognition even a week later. The few very long-term longitudinal studies do report cognitive testing results, and most show that IQ and other cognitive measures (including some memory tasks) have relative continuity, that is, the top achievers remain top achievers, and those in the middle or lower end of the distribution tend to retain their relative positions. So, while long-term memory tests do not exist, it is reasonable to believe that for persons from non-clinical groups, the results of a Delayed Recall Index provides a reasonable estimate of much longer-term memory performance.

WHY WAS NO AUTISM SPECTRUM DISORDER GROUP INCLUDED AMONG THE VARIOUS CLINICAL SAMPLES THAT WERE OBTAINED AND WHOSE DATA ARE INCLUDED IN THE VALIDITY CHAPTER OF THE WRAML3 TECHNICAL *MANUAL*?

We would like to provide an impressive justification for this absence like, Autism Spectrum Disorder (ASD), being a wide spectrum, has too much developmental and clinical variability to constitute an identifiable, homogeneous group for inclusion that psychometrically would allow adequate generalization. And while there is some truth to that, the real answer is simpler. While trying to limit the problem of clinical variability in our ASD sampling effort, the COVID pandemic arrived and forced an end to data collection. Fortunately, a large enough sample for the WRAML3 standardization was already obtained before Pearson halted data collection; the same was true for the other clinical groups scheduled for data collection. However, that was not the case for the ASD sample. Given the publication deadline, we went with the clinical groups for which the test data were already collected, which unfortunately did not include an adequate sample for the ASD group.

Having said that, though, based on previous WRAML editions and clinical experience, we would predict better visual than verbal memory scores, better rote than meaningful learning, better Verbatim than Gist memory, somewhat better Recognition than Delayed Recall and, yes, lots of variability across test scores. A recent study with high IQ children with ASD reported results supporting this conjecture (Santini et al., 2022). Is there someone out there interested in a research topic combining ASD and memory, and has access to a well-defined ASD sample of reasonable size?!

HOW SHOULD I USE THE QUALITATIVE DESCRIPTORS (SUCH AS "AVERAGE" OR" EXTREMELY LOW" SCORE) FOUND IN ONE OF THE WRAML3 MANUALS?

Terms like Extremely High or Very Low are provided as WRAML3 "qualitative descriptors" and are suggested to be used when wanting to communicate a level of functioning to others who are not familiar with statistical terms like standard score or percentile. Consequently, the qualitative descriptors found in the Administration manual (Table 4.1) are arbitrary terms intended to convey approximate meaning to the lay public. As such, the descriptors are not evidence-based and alternative terms found with other tests may be equally appropriate. The divisions found between WRAML3 descriptors are roughly based upon standard deviation units and are intended to convey a general level of performance with words that are respectful, descriptive, and understandable to laypersons reading reports or participating in debriefing conferences, such as parents or clients. Correspondingly, we intentionally avoided using labels associated with several IQ instruments given the potential confusion that might create.

HOW SHOULD I USE THE AGE EQUIVALENTS FOUND NEAR THE END OF THE ADMINISTRATION MANUAL?

In a word, carefully! Like with the Qualitative Descriptors discussed above, Age Equivalents (found in Table A.28 of the Administration *manual) are designed to help convey a general understanding of performance to a lay audience. The scores are generated by using mean raw scores for a given subtest, and then "smoothing" the distribution statistically to fill in as many holes as possible in all those distributions. So, it is reasonable to say, using the table, that a person earning 12 raw score points on the Finger Windows subtest performed as well as a majority of seven-year-olds, meaning that the majority of seven-year-olds earn around 12 points on that subtest. A 10-year-old who also scores 12 on that subtest would also earn an age equivalent of a 7-year-old, but that does not mean that the 10-year-old remembers like a 7-year-old. The processing of the two children is probably rather different despite achieving identical scores. While, in our example, the age equivalent would communicate the concept of relative delay, such communication may or may not be accurate since some impairments are due to delay but others attributable to disorder or both delay and disorder. (Disorder implies that the impairment results in processing that is different from that of the younger child, not just immature.) Further, several subtests have gaps despite the statistical smoothing making exact score assignments for the age equivalents difficult or impossible. So, for example, with Finger Windows a raw score of 14 spans the range from an early 9-year-level to almost to a mid-10-year level. Therefore a 9-year-old earning that score could be described as Average, High Average, or Very High given that range. Consequently, the Age Equivalents are approximations intended to communicate general estimates. When used for something beyond that, the user is likely going beyond what a reasonable empirical basis allows. Further, since there are more gaps between age divisions the older one goes in the table, one has to be increasingly cautious the older the examinee; that is one reason the chart ends at age 22-years. Finally, as the Table A.28 states, the items, and thus the memory demands made by the subtests for 5- to 9-year-olds sometimes contain somewhat different items than found in subtests for those 10-years and older; this is true for 11 of the 17 subtests. So, there is no credible evidence provided in the WRAML3 manuals that justifies one saying with any certainty that an examinee of age 10 is or is not performing like a 7-year-old. The bottom line is that Table A.28 is provided because it has some overall utility communicating an estimate of performance, but it is not based upon the same precision found with standard scores, nor should one extrapolate additional meaning beyond using an Age Equivalent to convey a gross age estimate of typical subtest score achievement for a given age.*

IF I DON'T HAVE TIME TO DO AN ENTIRE WRAML3 ADMINISTRATION, IS IT OKAY TO GIVE JUST A FEW SUBTESTS?

As noted in several chapters of this book, departing from the Standard, Screener, or Brief Formats is sometimes necessary, but the more one departs from the standardized method of administration, the more one has to be cautious about interpreting the results obtained. Clinically, the authors do not find that giving a subset of subtests seems to make too much difference other than occasionally the level of fatigue expressed by examinees. (This assumes that if delayed or recognition subtests are part of that subset, that the 20- to 30-minute delays have been observed.) Nevertheless, recognize that there is no empirical basis upon which to argue that the results yielded when giving a few subtests are the same as the results obtained using the standardized procedure associated with one of the three WRAML3 formats provided.

WHAT DOES THE WRAML3 SAY ABOUT THE DEVELOPMENTAL TRAJECTORY OF MEMORY? WE KNOW THAT IN OLD AGE, MEMORY DECLINES. DOES THAT DECLINE START THEN OR EARLIER, AND IS THE DECLINE THE SAME FOR VISUAL AND VERBAL MEMORY?

The question is a good one, and probably requires at least a small treatise to adequately discuss! However, Figure 10.1 will provide a reasonable response given space limitations and attention capacity at the end of this book!

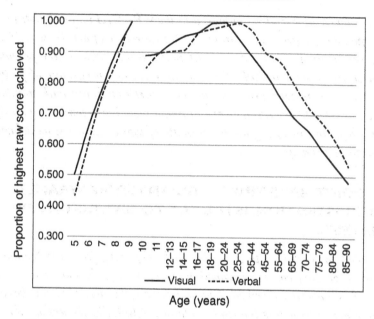

Figure 10.1 Age trajectories for performance on WRAML3 Visual and Verbal Delayed Indexes.

Figure 10.1 shows Results for the Delayed Memory subtests. These are featured because your question is generally asked within the context of longer-term memory. However, the findings with Immediate Memory and Attention/Concentration are fairly similar to those being described here with Delayed Memory.

In order to make sense of the trajectory of memory, some kind of statistical variable(s) need(s) to be generated. In our case, the curves are generated by plotting the percentage of the maximum raw score earned per Index by the highest performing age-cohort of the standardization sample. The percentages are found on the vertical axis in decimal form, so 1.00 represents 100%, .900 represents 90%, etc. Age is found on the horizontal axis, ranging from five-years to an 85- to 90-years age band. The solid line represents composite results from the Visual Delayed Index (comprised of Picture Memory and Design Learning) and the dotted line represents the Verbal Delayed Index (comprised of Story Memory and Verbal Learning).

The first thing to notice is the very steep increase in both visual and verbal memory from ages 5- to 9-years. Visual and verbal recall both exhibit a similar impressive spike. This reflects the enormous increase in recall capacity across these ages, an especially encouraging finding for teachers and parents, and corresponds to what most of us know about how fast and easily children acquire and retain new information. The increasing efficiency may be due to improvement in memory processing itself, but also probably captures growth in executive functioning that corresponds to the maturing of many pre-frontal cortex connections during this age range. With better problem-solving skills, children will start gradually developing strategies that will aid in increasing recall beyond the limits imposed by rote learning capacity (7 ± 2 bits of new information).

At age 10, remember that a portion of the test content shifts to a different set of items and is indicated by a break in the lines. The steep increase for the younger group is based on the metric of percentage of maximum total earned, so not surprisingly, the 9-year-old group achieved the highest performance, and so earned 100%. As would be expected memory continues to increase past age nine, although the trajectory is more gradual than previously, achieving asymptote around 18–24 years of age for visual memory, and starts a slow and steady decline thereafter. Of interest, there is not an accelerating pace of decay once the "senior years" are reached. A similar pattern is seen for verbal memory, although the scores maximize about 5 years later than visual, and then start a decline that parallels visual memory.

Figure 10.2 is similar showing the developmental trajectories of the two immediate, rote recall subtests of the Attention/Concentration Index, Finger Windows and Number Letter. Since the subtests' administration is the same across the age span, the curves are uninterrupted in contrast to the Indexes appearing in Figure 10.1. The trajectories' similarity in the two Figures is striking in that again the visual subtest, Finger Windows, achieves maximization earlier than the verbal subtest (Number Letter), and starts to decline in parallel fashion at the expected point of decline, namely about 5 years after the visual. Very similar patterns are also seen with the Visual and Verbal Working Memory subtests, as well as the Immediate Visual and Verbal Indexes. It may be a point of interest that the

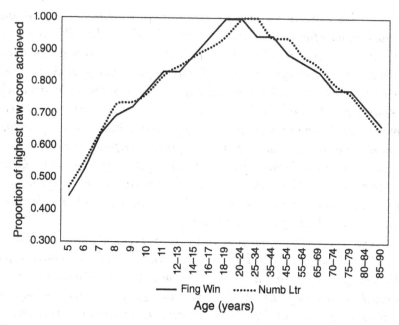

Figure 10.2 Developmental trajectory (across age cohorts) of Finger Windows and Number Letter subtest performance of the WRAML3.

Design Learning subtest starts its downward trajectory as expected (starting at the 25–30 year age band), but the downward pace for this subtest is more precipitous than any of the other subtests.

Looking at Figure 10.2, it appears that by 85-years of age, rote memory scores are at a comparable level as those achieved by eight- to nine-year-olds. While not displayed, it is of interest to note that among the content-laden subtests, and as might be expected, the more meaningful tasks (Picture Memory and Story Memory) have a slower rate of decay compared to less meaningful (Design and Verbal Learning).

It is often surprising to readers that memory decline starts to be documented earlier than expected, including age ranges often thought to be "years of our prime." Similar studies using IQ subtest performance also show declines in visual reasoning and spatial skills (i.e., Fluid Intelligence) beginning well before various components of verbal reasoning (i.e., crystalized Intelligence), although the spatial reasoning does not start its declining trajectory until at least 10 years after the start of visual memory decline, and verbal intelligence seems to be the most insulated from decay, often found lower but close to younger ages well into people's 60s (Salthouse, 2012), which allows them to write books about testing even at more advanced age!

ARE THERE ADDITIONAL FACTORS RELATED TO INTERPRETATION THAT USERS OF THE WRAML3 AND/OR THE EMS SHOULD CONSIDER?

Yes, additional contextual factors that are important to consider while interpreting results include sociological influences (e.g., economic stability, access to and quality of education, access to and quality of healthcare, access to healthy and affordable food, the safety of the neighborhoods where people live, and availability of family as well as supportive community resources) because such things affect a wide range of health, daily functioning, and quality of life outcomes and risks. Further, the field of psychology has recognized that the use of broad categories, such as race, educational level, and sex/gender, is inadequate, and can obscure reliable assessment of many of the underlying social determinants that can result in unintended consequences for the people we as clinicians are seeking to help. More research is needed to establish appropriate characterization of social determinants and the use of this information in normative data for common psychological, educational, and neuropsychological tests. As such, the authors strongly encourage users of the WRAML3 and/or the EMS to stay current on advances made in this very important area.

REFERENCES

Adams, W., & Sheslow, D. (2021). *Wide range assessment of memory and learning* (3rd ed.). San Antonio, TX: NCS Pearson.

AERA, APA, & NCME (2014). Standards for Educational and Psychological Testing: National Council on Measurement in Education. Washington DC: American Educational Research Association.

American Educational Research Association (AERA), American Psychological Association (APA), & National Council on Measurement in Education (NCME). (1999). *Standards for educational and psychological testing*. Washington, DC: American Psychological Association.

American Educational Research Association, American Psychological Association, & National Council on Measurement in Education. (2014). *Standards for educational and psychological testing*. Washington, DC: American Educational Research Association.

Angelopoulou, E., & Drigas, A. (2021). Working memory, attention, and their relationship: A theoretical overview. *Research, Society and Development, 10*(5), e46410515288–e46410515288

Atkinson, R.C., & Shiffrin, R.M. (1968). Human memory: A proposed system and its control processes. In *Psychology of learning and motivation* (Vol. 2, pp. 89–195). New York: Academic Press.

Essentials of WRAML3 and EMS Assessment, First Edition.
Wayne V. Adams, David V. Sheslow, and Trevor A. Hall.
© 2024 John Wiley & Sons, Inc. Published 2024 by John Wiley & Sons, Inc.

Babikian, T., Merkley, T., Savage, R. C., Giza, C. C., & Levin, H. (2015). Chronic aspects of pediatric traumatic brain injury: Review of the literature. *Journal of Neurotrauma, 32*(23), 1849–1860.

Bäckman, L., Jones, S., Berger, A. K., Laukka, E. J., & Small, B. J. (2005). Cognitive impairment in preclinical Alzheimer's disease: A meta-analysis. *Neuropsychology, 19*(4), 520–531.

Baddeley, A. (1992). Working memory. *Science, 255,* 556–559.

Baron, I., Fennell, E., & Voeller, K. (1995). *Pediatric neuropsychology in the medical setting.* London: University Press.

Bender, L. (1938). A visual motor gestalt test and its clinical use. *American Orthopsychiatric Association Research Monograph* (Vol. 3). New York: American Orthopsychiatric Association.

Benton, A. L. (1946). *Benton visual retention test.* New York: Psychological Corp.

Benton, A. L. (1974). *The revised visual retention test* (4th ed.). New York: Psychological Corp.

Blumenfeld, H. (2021). *Neuroanatomy through clinical cases.* Sunderland, MA: Sinauer Associates.

Burkhart, S., & Adams, W.V. (2011, November 16–19). *Using short-term memory measures to assess long-term memory in early Alzheimer's disease.* National Academy of Neuropsychology Annual Convention, Marco Island, FL, United States.

Buschke, H., & Fuld, P. A. (1974). Evaluating storage, retention, and retrieval in disordered memory and learning. *Neurology, 11,* 1019–1025.

Churchill, J. D., Stanis, J. J., Press, C., Kushelev, M., & Greenough, W. T. (2003). Is procedural memory relatively spared from age effects? *Neurobiology of Aging, 24*(6), 883–892.

Corkin, S. (2002). What's new with the amnestic patient, HM? *Nature Reviews, Neuroscience, 3,* 153–160.

Cullum, M., Kuck, J., & Ruff, R. (1990). Neuropsychological assessment of traumatic brain injury in adults. In E. D. Bigler (Ed.), *Traumatic brain injury* (pp. 129–163). Austin, TX: Pro-Ed.

Cytowic, R. (1996). *The neurological side of neuropsychology.* London: MIT Press.

Dehn, M. J. (2015). *Working memory assessment and intervention.* Hoboken, NJ: John Wiley & Sons.

Ebbinghaus, H. (1885). *Uber das Gedachtnis.* Leipzig: Duncker.

Edelman, P., Fulton, B. R., & Kuhn, D. (2004). Comparison of dementia-specific quality of life measures in adult day centers. *Home Health Care Services Quarterly, 23*(1), 25–42.

Ek, U., Fernell, E., Westerlund, J., Holmberg, K., Olsson, P. O., & Gillberg, C. (2007). Cognitive strengths and deficits in schoolchildren with ADHD. *Acta Paediatrica, 96*(5), 756–761

Farias, S. T., Harrell, E., Neumann, C., & Houtz, A. (2003). The relationship between neuropsychological performance and daily functioning in individuals with Alzheimer's disease: Ecological validity of neuropsychological tests. *Archives of Clinical Neuropsychology, 18*(6), 655–672.

FERPA. (1974). *Family educational rights and privacy act.* Washington, DC: U.S. Department of Education. https://ww2.ed.gov/policy/gen/guid/fpco/ferpa/index.html.

Fox, R. S., Zhang, M., Amagai, S., Bassard, A., Dworak, E. M., Han, J., Kassanits, Y. C., & Miller, C. H. (2022). Uses of the NIH Toolbox® in clinical samples: A scoping review. Neurology: Clinical Practice. 12(4), 307–319.

Freund, P.A., & Kasten, N. (2012). How smart do you think you are? A meta-analysis on the validity of self-estimates of cognitive ability. *Psychological Bulletin, 138*(2), 296–321.

Frise, N. R., & Adams, W.V. (2010, August 12–15). *Validating a new procedure for measuring long-term memory.* American Psychological Association Annual Convention, San Diego, CA, United States.

Fuster, J. M. (1995). *Memory in the cerebral cortex: An empirical approach to neural networks in the human and nonhuman primates.* Cambridge, MA: MIT Press.

Ghabanchi, Z., & Rastegar, R. E. (2014). The correlation of IQ and emotional intelligence with reading comprehension. *Reading, 14*(2), 135–144.

Gillberg, C. (1995). *Clinical child neuropsychology.* Cambridge: Cambridge University Press.

REFERENCES 269

Gruneberg, M. M., Morris, P. E., & Sykes, R. N. (1978). *Practical aspects of memory*. London: Academic Press.

Green, P., & Flaro, L. (2003). Word Memory Test performance in children. Child Neuropsychology, 9(3), 189-207. Obviously, a change in text citation will be needed as well.

Hall, T. A., Adams, W., & Sheslow, D. (2021). *Everyday memory survey*. San Antonio, TX: NCS Pearson, Inc.

Hall, T., Greene. R., Lee, J., Leonard, S., Bradbury, K., Drury, K., Recht, G., Randall, J., Norr, M., & Williams, C. (2022). Post-intensive care syndrome in a cohort of school-aged and adolescent ICU survivors: The importance of multidisciplinary follow-up in the acute recovery phase. *The Journal of Pediatric Intensive Care. J Pediatr Intensive Care DOI: 10.1055/s-0042-1747935*.

Haberlandt, K. (1997). *Cognitive psychology* (2nd ed.). Boston: Allyn & Bacon.

Heaton, R. K., Miller, S. W., Taylor, M. J., & Grant, I. (2004). *Revised comprehensive norms for an expanded Halstead-Reitan Battery: Demographically adjusted neuropsychological norms for African American and Caucasian Adults*. Lutz, FL: Psychological Assessment Resources, Inc.

Herreen, D., & Zajac, I. T. (2017) The reliability and validity of a self-report measure of cognitive abilities in older adults: More personality than cognitive function. *Journal of Intelligence*, 6(1), 1.

HIPPA. (1996). *Health insurance portability and accountability act of 1996. HIPPA for professionals*. Washington, DC: U.S. Department of Health and Human Services. https://www.hhs.gov/hipaa/for-professionals/index.html.

Hertzog, C., & Hultsch, D. F. (2000). Metacogniton in adulthood and old age. In F. Craik & T. Salthouse (Eds.), *The handbook of aging and cognition* (pp. 417–466). Mahwah, NJ: Lawrence Erlbaum Associates.

Ingraham, L. J. & Aiken, C. B. (1996). An empirical approach to determining criteria for abnormality in test batteries with multiple measures. *Neuropsychology, 10*, 120–124.

Institute on Aging. (2023, August 30). Understanding different types of dementia. https://www.nia.nih.gov/health/infographics/understanding-different-types-dementia.

Jefferson, A. L., Paul, R. H., Ozonoff, A., & Cohen, R. A. (2006). Evaluating elements of executive functioning as predictors of instrumental activities of daily living (IADLs). *Archives of Clinical Neuropsychology: The Official Journal of the National Academy of Neuropsychology, 21*(4), 311–320.

Kirkwood, M. W. (2015). A rationale for performance validity testing in child and adolescent assessment. In M. W. Kirkwood (Ed.). *Validity testing in child and adolescent assessment: Evaluating exaggeration, feigning, and noncredible effort* (pp. 3–21), New York: Guilford Press.

Kleeren, L., Hallemans, A., Hoskens, J., Klingels, K., Smits-Engelsman, B., & Verbecque, E. (2023). A critical view on motor-based interventions to improve motor skill performance in children with ADHD: A systematic review and meta-analysis. *Journal of Attention Disorders, 27*(4), 354–367. https://doi.org/10.1177/10870547221146244.

Knight, R. (1992). *The neuropsychology of degenerative brain diseases.* Mahwah, NJ: Lawrence Erlbaum.

Koeppen, J. A. (2018). *The role of astrocyte specific regulation of Ephrin-B1 in refining hippocampal circuits during memory formation.* Riverside: University of California.

Kolb, B., & Whishaw, I. Q. (2021). *Fundamentals of human neuropsychology* (8th ed.). New York: Worth Publishing.

Larrabee, G. J. (2012). Performance validity and symptom validity in neuropsychological assessment. *Journal of the International Neuropsychological Society, 18*(4), 625–630.

Lashley, K. D. (1950). In search of the engram. *Symposium of the Society for Experimental Biology, 4*, 454–482.

Leonard, S., Hall, T., Bradbury, K., Holding, E., Wagner, A., & Williams, C. (2022). Preliminary evidence of memory dysfunction in youth with moderate-severe versus mild complicated traumatic brain injury and matched controls using the Wide Range Assessment of Memory and Learning, 3rd Edition (WRAML3). *The Journal of Pediatric Neuropsychology, 8*, 178–190.

Lezak, M., Howieson, D., Bigler, E., & Tranel, D. (2019). *Neuropsychological assessment*. New York: Oxford University Press.

Li, C. M. F., Robinson, L. R., & Tam, A. K. H. (2019). Addressing post-traumatic amnesia – Recommendations for improving patient lives after brain injury. *The Journal of Trauma and Acute Care Surgery*, *86*(6), 1033–1038.

Lippa, S. A. (2018). Performance validity testing in neuropsychology: A clinical guide, critical review, and update on a rapidly evolving literature. *Clinical Neuropsychologist*, *32*(3), 391–421.

Luria, A. R. (1966). *Higher cortical functions in man* (B. Haigh, Trans.). New York: Basic Books.

Luria, A. R. (2006). *The mind of a mnemonist*. Cambridge, MA: Harvard University Press.

Maass, W., & Markram, H. (2002). Synapses as dynamic memory buffers. *Neural Networks*, *15*(2), 155–161.

Mapou, R. L., & Spector, J. (Eds.). (1995). *Clinical neuropsychological assessment: A cognitive approach*. New York: Plenum Press.

McCarthy, D. (1972). *McCarthy scales of children's abilities*. New York: Psychological Corp.

Miller, G. A. (1956). The magical number seven, plus or minus two: Some limits on our capacity for processing information. *Psychological Review*, *63*, 81–97.

Miller, M., Bigler, E., & Adams, W. (2003). Comprehensive assessment of child and adolescent memory: The Wide Range Assessment of Memory and Learning, the Test of Memory and Learning, and the California Verbal Learning Test-Children's Version. In C. R. Reynolds & R. W. Kamphaus (Eds.), *The handbook of psychological and educational assessment of children, Vol. I, intelligence, aptitude, and achievement—second edition* (pp. 275–304). New York, NY: Guilford Press.

Mitchell, A. J. (2008). The clinical significance of subjective memory complaints in the diagnosis of mild cognitive impairment and dementia: A meta-analysis. *International Journal of Geriatric Psychiatry*, *23*(11), 1191–1202.

Mlinac, M. E., & Feng, M. C. (2016). Assessment of activities of daily living, self-care, and independence. *Archives of Clinical Neuropsychology*, *31*(6), 506–516.

Mochizuki-Kawai H. (2008). Neural basis of procedural memory. *Brain and Nerve*, *60*(7), 825–832.

National Institute on Aging. (2022, December). *What is dementia? Symptoms, types, and diagnosis*. www.nia.nih.gov/health/what-is-dementia.

Nayar, K., Ventura, L. M., DeDios-Stern, S., Oh, A., & Soble, J. R. (2022). The impact of learning and memory on performance validity tests in a mixed clinical pediatric population. *Archives of Clinical Neuropsychology: The Official Journal of the National Academy of Neuropsychology*, *37*(1), 50–62.

Neisser, U. (1982). Memory: What are the important questions. In Neisser, U., Memory observed: Remembering in natural contexts, New York: W.H. Freeman, 3–19.

Newsome, M. R., Durgerian, S., Mourany, L., Scheibel, R. S., Lowe, M. J., Beall, E. B., Koenig, K. A., Parsons, M., Troyanskaya, M., Reece, C., Wilde, E., Fischer, B. L., Jones, S. E., Agarwal, R., Levin, H. S., & Rao, S. M. (2015). Disruption of caudate working memory activation in chronic blast-related traumatic brain injury. *NeuroImage. Clinical*, *8*, 543–553.

Papagno, C., & Trojano, L. (2018). Cognitive and behavioral disorders in Parkinson's disease: An update. I: Cognitive impairments. *Neurological Sciences*, *39*(2), 215–223.

Pitcher T. M., Piek, J. P., & Hay, D. A. (2003). Fine and gross motor ability in males with ADHD. *Developmental Medicine and Child Neurology*, *45*(8), 525–535.

Prigatano, G. P. (1978). Wechsler Memory Scale: A selective review of the literature. *Journal of Clinical Psychology*, *34*, 816–832.

Reeves, D., & Wedding, D. (1994). *The clinical assessment of memory*. Berlin: Springer-Verlag

Reitan, R. M., & Wolfson, D. (1985). *The Halstead-Reitan neuropsychological test battery: Theory and clinical interpretation*. Tucson, AZ: Neuropsychology Press.

Rey, A. (1941). L'examen psychologique dans les cas d'encephalopathie traumatique. *Archives de Psychologie*, *28*, 286–340.

Rey, A. (1958). *L'Examen clinique en psychologie.* Paris: Presses Universitaires de France.

Reynolds, C. R., & Fletcher-Janzen, E. (Eds.). (1997). *Handbook of clinical child neuropsychology* (2nd ed.). New York: Plenum.

Riccio, C., & Reynolds, C. R. (1998). Neuropsychological assessment of children. In M. Hersen & A. Bellack (Series Eds.) & C. R. Reynolds (Vol. Ed.), *Comprehensive clinical psychology: Vol. 4, Assessment* (pp. 267–301). New York, NY: Elsevier.

Riccio, C., Reynolds, C. R., & Lowe, P. A. (2001). *Clinical applications of continuous performance tests: Measuring attention and impulsive responding in children and adults.* New York, NY: Wiley.

Riccio, C., & Wolfe, M.E. (2003). Neuropsychological perspectives on the assessment of children. In C. R. Reynolds & R. W. Kamphaus (Eds.), *The handbook of psychological and educational assessment of children, Vol. I, Intelligence, aptitude, and achievement, second edition* (pp. 275–304). New York: Guilford.

Salthouse, T. (2012). Consequences of age-related cognitive declines. *Annual Review of Psychology, 63*, 201–226.

Santini, A., Bullen, J. C., Zajic, M. C., McIntyre, N., & Mundy, P. (2022). Brief report: The factors associated with social cognition in children with autism spectrum disorder. *Journal of Autism and Developmental Disorders*, 1–7.

Schretlen, D., Testa, S., Winicki, J., Pearlson, G., & Gordon, B. (2008). Frequency and bases of abnormal performance by healthy adults on neuropsychological testing. *Journal of the International Neuropsychological Society, 14*(3), 436–445. doi: 10.1017/S1355617708080387.

Schroeder, R. W., & Martin, P.K. (Eds.). (2021). *Validity assessment in clinical neuropsychological practice: Evaluating and managing noncredible performance.* New York, NY: Guilford Press.

Schurgin, M. W., & Flombaum, J. I. (2018). Properties of visual episodic memory following repeated encounters with objects. *Learning & Memory, 25*(7), 309–316.

Sheslow, D. V., & Adams, W. V. (1990). *Wide range assessment of memory and learning*. Wilmington, DE: Wide Range, Inc.

Sheslow, D. V., & Adams, W. V. (2003). *Wide range assessment of memory and learning* (2nd ed.). Wilmington, DE: Wide Range Incorporated.

Snyderman, M., & Rothman, S. (1987). Survey of expert opinion on intelligence and aptitude testing. *American Psychologist, 42*, 137–144.

Squire, L. R. (2009). Memory and brain systems: 1969–2009. *Journal of Neuroscience, 29*(41), 12711–12716.

Squire, L. R., & Schacter, D. L. (Eds.). (2002). *Neuropsychology of memory*. New York, NY: Guilford Press.

Squire, L. R., & Wixted, J. T. (2011). The cognitive neuroscience of human memory since H.M. *Annual Review of Neuroscience, 34*, 259–288.

Steidl, S., Mohiuddin, S., & Anderson, A. K. (2006). Effects of emotional arousal on multiple memory systems: evidence from declarative and procedural learning. *Learning & Memory, 13*(5), 650–658.

Takehara-Nishiuchi, K. (2021). Neurobiology of systems memory consolidation. *The European Journal of Neuroscience, 54*(8), 6850–6863.

Tombaugh, T. N. (1997). The test of memory malingering (TOMM): Normative data from cognitively intact and cognitively impaired individuals. *Psychological Assessment, 9*(3), 260–268.

Toplak, M.E., West, R.F., & Stanovich, K.E. (2013). Practitioner review: Do performance-based measures and ratings of executive function assess the same construct? *Journal of Child Psychology and Psychiatry, 54*(2), 131–143.

Uttl, B., & Kibreab, M. (2011). Self-report measures of prospective memory are reliable but not valid. *Canadian Journal of Experimental Psychology, 65*(1), 57–68.

U.S. Census Bureau. (2017). American community survey, 2017 1-year period estimates.

Vardalaki, D., Chung, K., & Harnett, M. T. (2022). Filopodia are a structural substrate for silent synapses in adult neocortex. *Nature, 612*(7939), 323–327.

Wechsler, D. (1945a). A standardized memory scale for clinical use. *Journal of Psychology*, 19, 87–95.

Wechsler, D. (1945b). *Wechsler Memory Scale*. San Antonio, TX: Psychological Corporation.

Wechsler, D. (2008). *Wechsler Adult Intelligence Scale* (4th ed.). San Antonio, TX: NCS Pearson.

Wechsler, D. (2009). *Wechsler Memory Scale* (4th ed.). San Antonio, TX: NCS Pearson.

Wechsler, D. (2014). *Wechsler Intelligence Scale for children* (5th ed.). San Antonio, TX: NCS Pearson.

Wechsler, D. (2020). *Wechsler Individual Achievement Test* (4th ed.). San Antonio, TX: NCS Pearson.

Weissberger, G. H., Strong, J. V., Stefanidis, K. B., Summers, M. J., Bondi, M. W., & Stricker, N. H. (2017). Diagnostic accuracy of memory measures in Alzheimer's dementia and mild cognitive impairment: A systematic review and meta-analysis. *Neuropsychology Review*, 27(4), 354–388.

Weniger, R., & Adams, W. (2006, November). *Differences in performance on the WRAML2 for children with ADHD and reading disorder*. National Academy of Neuropsychology Annual Meeting, Tampa, FL.

Wilkinson, G. S., & Robertson, G. J. (2017). *Wide Range Achievement Test* (5th ed.). San Antonio, TX: NCS Pearson.

Zhang, X., Liangliang, L., Min, G., Wang, Q., Zhao, Y., & Li, Y. (2021). Overview of the complex figure test and its clinical application in neuropsychiatric disorders, including copying and recall. *Frontiers in Neurology*, 12, 680474.

Zillmer, E. A., Spiers, M. V., & Culbertson, W. (2008). *Principles of neuropsychology* (2nd ed.). Belmont, CA: Wadsworth.

ABOUT THE AUTHORS

Wayne V. Adams, PhD, earned his degree in developmental/clinical child psychology from Syracuse University. After teaching at Colgate University, he received postdoctoral training in pediatric psychology at Memorial Hospital, UNC-Chapel Hill. Thereafter, he was Chief Psychologist at duPont Hospital for Children (Wilmington, DE) that has academic ties to Jefferson Medical College. After working 24 years at the hospital, he assumed chairmanship of an APA-accredited clinical psychology program at George Fox University located just outside of Portland, Oregon; there he also taught courses in cognitive and neuropsychological assessment. He retired from the university with Professor Emeritus status after 23 years of service. He has published more than 40 articles, co-authored several nationally used test instruments, and made more than 80 presentations at national conferences and workshops. He is a Fellow of APA's Division of Clinical Psychology as well as the National Academy of Neuropsychology and holds diplomate status within the American Board of Professional Psychology. He was a recipient of a Fulbright scholarship to conduct memory research in China and a Lifetime Achievement Award from the School Neuropsychology Institute. He and his wife, Nora, have two grown children and four grandchildren—all charming. He enjoys the leisure activities of hiking, reading, jogging, photography, pickleball, gardening, and piano.

Essentials of WRAML3 and EMS Assessment, First Edition.
Wayne V. Adams, David V. Sheslow, and Trevor A. Hall.
© 2024 John Wiley & Sons, Inc. Published 2024 by John Wiley & Sons, Inc.

ABOUT THE AUTHORS 277

David V. Sheslow, PhD, earned his degree from the University of North Carolina at Greensboro. After completing his internship in pediatric psychology at the University of Maryland School of Medicine, Dr. Sheslow joined the staff of Nemours Hospital for Children, where his long collaboration began with co-author, Wayne Adams. Dr. Sheslow worked at the hospital for over 35 years, where his role changed many times, including serving as a team member in the Divisions of Developmental Medicine and Rehabilitation (where he trained in neuropsychology). Ultimately becoming Chief of the Division of Behavioral Health, he saw psychology firmly placed in most hospital divisions and outpatient pediatric practices. While Dr. Sheslow enjoyed his clinical and research collaborations as well as administrative experiences, he is perhaps most proud of his role teaching residents and fellows, ending his hospital career as Director of Resident Training. Among the most professional fun Dr. Sheslow had was working with his friend Wayne and colleagues at Wide Range, Inc, and then Pearson Publishing. Together, they developed the Wide Range Intelligence Test, the Wide Range Assessment of Visual Motor Abilities, and the three editions of the Wide Range Assessment of Memory and Learning. Throughout most of his career, Dr. Sheslow maintained a private practice and continues to do so in his semi-retirement. Dr. Sheslow mostly lives at the beach when not traveling. His best achievements include marriage to his wife Liz for over 35 years, his son Paul, who is a nurse practitioner in psychiatry, and his daughter Annie, who is a social worker.

Trevor A. Hall, PsyD, is a Professor of Pediatrics in the Divisions of Pediatric Psychology and Pediatric Critical Care at Oregon Health & Science University (OHSU), where he serves as the Associate Director of the Pediatric Critical Care and Neurotrauma Recovery Program (PCCNRP). Dr. Hall is a board-certified pediatric neuropsychologist who specializes in providing care for children and adolescents with central nervous system complications. He primarily provides neuropsychological evaluation and treatment services to pediatric critical care survivors; he does this longitudinally from regular consultations in the pediatric intensive care unit (PICU) to attending the multiple follow-up clinics associated with the PCCNRP. In addition, Dr. Hall is recognized for his ongoing clinical research that has collaboratively produced over 60 peer-reviewed publications related to the development, validation, and methodological utilization of contemporary baseline and outcome measures for use in medically complex populations. He is also actively involved in the training of neuropsychology practicum students, interns, and postdoctoral fellows. In his personal life, Dr. Hall enjoys spending time with his family and friends! He also enjoys backpacking/camping, mountain climbing, snowboarding, and all things related to science fiction!

Index

abbreviated formats, 167,
179–180
Brief format, 169–170
case illustration, 171–179
cautionary note, 171
Screener format, 167–169
age equivalent scores, 52, 53,
219, 260, 261
age trajectories, 261–265
Alzheimer's disease, 5, 15–16,
30, 59
amnesia, 29
anterograde amnesia, 29
astrocytes, 26
Attention Concentration Index
(ACI), 42–44, 119–121,
255–256
Finger Windows subtest,
121–122
administration errors, 124
administration procedure,
122–123
observations, 123
rubric, 124–125

Number Letter subtest,
125–126
administration errors, 128
administration procedure,
126
observations, 126–128
rubric, 128–129
subtests, 120–121, 129–130
attention deficit/hyperactivity
disorder (ADHD), 4–5,
58
case study
clinical impressions,
185–186
comments, 187–188
history, 183–184
informal writing task, 185
reason for referral, 183
recommendations, 186–187
test administered and
results, 184–185
WRAML for, 252–253
Autism Spectrum Disorder
(ASD), 258–259

Essentials of WRAML3 and EMS Assessment, First Edition.
Wayne V. Adams, David V. Sheslow, and Trevor A. Hall.
© 2024 John Wiley & Sons, Inc. Published 2024 by John Wiley & Sons, Inc.

280 INDEX

Bender-Gestalt Test, 20
Benton Visual Retention Test,
19, 20
Binet, Alfred, 13
brain anatomy, 25–26
Brief format, 169–170, 190–193

case study
abbreviated formats, 171–179
ADHD
clinical impressions,
185–186
comments, 187–188
history, 183–184
informal writing task, 185
reason for referral, 183
recommendations, 186–187
test administered and
results, 184–185
dementia
Design Learning and Verbal
Learning subtests, 208
everyday memory, 209
history, 205–206
interpretation of results, 209
PVI, 206
reason for referral, 204
WRAML3 evaluation,
206, 207
hepatic encephalopathy, 196,
203–204
current status, 197
Delis-Kaplan Executive
Functioning System, 198
EMS, 199

history, 197–198
interpretation of results,
199, 201–202
MMPI-2 RF, 198
reason for referral, 197
test administered, 198–199,
200
Test of Memory and
Malingering, 198
WAIS-IV, 198
Wisconsin Card Sorting
Test, 198
WRAML3, 200
learning disability
Brief format, 190–193
comments, 195–196
Design Learning subtest,
194, 195
history/current status,
189–190
rote subtests, 190, 194
traumatic brain injury,
243–247
Commission Errors, 77, 80
conditions with likely memory
deficits, 3, 4
confirmatory factor analysis, 149

Delayed Memory subtest, 45, 46
dementia
case study
Design Learning and Verbal
Learning subtests, 208
everyday memory, 209
history, 205–206

interpretation of results, 209
PVI, 206
reason for referral, 204
WRAML3 evaluation,
206, 207
impact on memory, 14–16, 30
Design Learning (DL) subtest,
73, 82–83
administration errors, 91–93
administration procedure,
83–84
Brief format, 169–170
case study
on dementia, 208
on learning disability, 194,
195
DL Delayed, 84–85
DL Recognition, 85
observations, 90–91
process score, 85
performance analysis, 85–89
quadrant analysis, 89–90
slope analysis, 89
rubric, 93–94
developmental trajectories in
memory, 261–265
discrepancies, 151–157,
160–163

Ebbinghaus, Hans, 12
ecological validity, 221
emotional valence, 31
everyday memory, 220–221
Everyday Memory Survey (EMS),
10–11, 220

administration, 228–230
applications, 222, 226
case example, 243–247
embedded PVI, 223, 225
general description, 224
Hall's research, 256–257
interpretation, 236, 247–248
additional factors, 265
contextual factors, 241–242
critical items, 234–236
individual items, 240–241
integrating objective and
subjective findings, 237
low scores, 238
multiple responders, 238
re-evaluation, 238
results, 236–237
T score, 237
Manual, 227, 228, 230, 240
Observer form, 222–223,
226–229
overview, 221–224, 232
Q-global, 239
reliability, 226
scoring, 231–232
scoring profile, 238, 239
Self-report form, 222–223,
225–227, 240
standardization, 225–226
user qualifications,
responsibilities, and
cautions, 227–228
uses, 233–234
validity, 226–227
executive functioning, 187, 188

282 INDEX

Finger Windows (FW) subtest,
    121–122
  administration errors, 124
  administration procedure,
    122–123
  observations, 123
  rubric, 124–125
forgetting curve, 12
Freud, Sigmund, 13
frontotemporal dementia,
    15–16

General Immediate Memory
    Index (GIMI), 149
gist, 101–102

Hall, Trevor, 256–257
Halstead-Reitan
    Neuropsychological Test
    Batteries, 20
head injury, 60
hepatic encephalopathy, case
    study on, 196, 203–204
  current status, 197
  history, 197–198
  reason for referral, 197
  test administered and results
    Delis-Kaplan Executive
      Functioning System, 198
    EMS, 199
    interpretation, 199, 201–202
    MMPI-2 RF, 198
    Test of Memory and
      Malingering, 198
    WAIS-IV, 198

Wisconsin Card Sorting
    Test, 198
  WRAML3, 200
hippocampus, 25–28
historical foundations, 12–24
horizontal interpretive model,
    158–160

immediate memory, 12, 38
immediate memory subtests, 45
implicit memory, 28
individual educational plan
    (IEP), 209–210
  academic achievement,
    211–213
  comments on, 218–219
  interpretation of results,
    215–216
  psychological evaluation, 211
  recommended accommodations,
    217
  speech/language evaluation,
    210–211
  WRAML3, 213–214
intellectual disability, 58,
    189–196
International Conference of
    Practical Aspects of
    Memory (1978), 221
interpretation, 148–165
  cautionary comments on
    discrepancies, 160–163
  horizontal interpretive model,
    158–160
  vertical interpretive model

contributing indexes, 150
decision-tree, 152, 153
global indexes, 149–150
index and subtest
    discrepancies, 151–157
pyramidal/top-down
    approach, 148–149
subtests, 149
Interpretive Report (IR), 253
intrusion errors, 112
IQ tests, 21

Lashley, Karl, 13
learning disability
case study on
    Brief format of, 190–193
    comments, 195–196
    Design Learning subtest,
        194, 195
    history/current status,
        189–190
    rote subtests, 190, 194
in reading and/or written
    expression, 58–59
Lewy body dementia, 15–16
long-term memory, 23–24, 30,
    257–258
Luria, Alexander, 13

major depressive disorder, 59
McCarthy, Dorothea, 21
McCarthy Scales of Children's
    Abilities, 21
memory
anatomy, 24–31

developmental trajectory of,
    261–265
immediate, 12, 38
implicit, 28
long-term, 23–24, 30,
    257–258
phenomena, 21–23
research, 13
verbal, 25
visual, 20, 25
working, 48
memory assessment
historical foundations, 12–24
need for, 2–6
memory loss, 14, 17, 45, 221
mild cognitive impairment,
    5, 59
Miller, George, 13

neurobiology of memory, 29
Number Letter (NL) subtest,
    125–126
administration errors, 128
administration procedure,
    126
observations, 126–128
rubric, 128–129

Pearson, 61, 62
pediatric traumatic brain injury,
    59–60
Performance Validity Indicator
    (PVI), 38, 41–44, 206,
    223, 225, 255–256
phonetic errors, 111–112

Picture Memory (PM) subtest, 74–75
administration errors, 79–80
administration procedure, 75–76
Commission Errors, 77, 80
observations, 77–79
PM Delayed, 76
PM Recognition, 76
process score, 77
rubric, 80–81
posttraumatic amnesia (PTA), 29
primacy, 113–114

Q-global, 62
quadrant analysis, 89–90
qualitative descriptors, 259

reading disorder (RD), 4–5
recency, 113–115
recognition memory, 47–48
Recognition subtest, 45–46
repetition errors, 113
retrograde amnesia, 29
Rey Auditory Verbal Learning Test (RAVLT), 19–20
Rey-Osterrieth Complex Figure Task, 19, 20

Screener format, 167–169
Selective Reminding Test, 20
semantic errors, 111–112
Sentence Memory (SenM) subtest, 130–132
administration errors, 133

administration procedure, 132
observations, 133
rubric, 134
slope analysis
DL subtest, 89
VL subtest, 111
Standards for Educational and Psychological Testing, 64, 227
Story Memory (SM) subtest, 96–97
administration errors, 104–105
administration procedure, 97–99
Brief format, 169–170
comparison of two stories, 103
observations, 103–104
rubric, 105–106
SM Delayed, 99–100
SM Recognition, 100–101
verbatim and gist, 101–103

traumatic brain injury, 243–247

vascular dementia, 15–16
Verbal Immediate Memory Index (VerIMI), 96
Story Memory subtest, 96–97
administration errors, 104–105
administration procedure, 97–99
comparison of two stories, 103
observations, 103–104

rubric, 105–106
SM Delayed, 99–100
SM Recognition, 100–101
verbatim and gist, 101–103
Verbal Learning subtest,
106–117
Verbal Learning (VL) subtest,
106–107
administration errors, 116
administration procedure,
108–109
case study, 208
intrusion errors, 112
observations, 115–116
performance analysis, 111
phonetic errors, 111–112
primacy, 113–114
process score, 110–115
recency, 113–115
repetition errors, 113
rubric, 117
semantic errors, 111–112
slope analysis, 111
VL Delayed, 109–110
VL Recognition, 110
Verbal Working Memory
(VerWM) subtest,
141–142
administration errors,
144–145
administration procedure,
142–143
observations, 143–144
rubric, 145
verbatim, 101–102

vertical interpretive model
contributing indexes, 150
decision-tree, 152, 153
global indexes, 149–150
index and subtest discrepancies, 151–157
pyramidal/top-down approach,
148–149
subtests, 149
Visual Immediate Memory Index
(VisIMI), 73–74
Design Learning subtest,
82–83
administration errors, 91–93
administration procedure,
83–84
DL Delayed, 84–85
DL Recognition, 85
observations, 90–91
performance analysis, 85–89
process score, 85–90
quadrant analysis, 89–90
rubric, 93–94
slope analysis, 89
Picture Memory subtest,
74–75
administration errors,
79–80
administration procedure,
75–76
observations, 77–79
PM Delayed, 76
PM Recognition, 76
process score, 77
rubric, 80–81

286 INDEX

visual memory, 20, 25
Visual Working Memory
    (VisWM) subtest,
    135–137
    administration errors,
      139–140
    administration procedure,
      137–138
    observations, 138–139
    rubric, 140–141

Wechsler-Bellevue intelligence
    test, 19
Wechsler, David, 19
Wechsler Memory Scale (WMS),
    2, 19
Western psychology, 19
Wilkerson, Gary, 251
working memory, 48
Working Memory Index (WMI),
    134–135, 146
    VerWM subtest, 141–142
    administration errors,
      144–145
    administration procedure,
      142–143
    observations, 143–144
    rubric, 145
    VisWM subtest, 135–137
    administration errors,
      139–140
    administration procedure,
      137–138

observations, 138–139
    rubric, 140–141
WRAML
    ADHD assessment, 252–253
    development, 252
    standardization efforts, 251
WRAML2 vs. WRAML3,
    36–41
WRAML3, 10–11
    additional contextual factors,
      265
    Administration manual, 64,
      66, 259–261
    age equivalents, 260–261
    clinical groups findings,
      57–60
    Delayed Memory subtest,
      45, 46
    diversity issues, 63–64
    immediate memory subtests
      and indexes, 45
    interpretation, 148–163, 200
    Interpretive Report, 253
    learning, 250–251
    major changes made to, 38–40
    objectives, 37–38
    on-line assists, 61, 62
    partial assessment, 261
    publication information
      for, 62
    qualitative descriptors, 259
    re-administration, 253–255
    Recognition subtests, 45–46

reliability, 55–56
scores available in, 50–54
standardization, 54
structure of, 45–46
Technical manual, 54, 64
test forms, 60–61, 66
test kit components, 61
timing details, 48–50

transition from WRAML2, 36–41
user qualifications, responsibilities, and cautions, 64–68
validity, 56–57
working with special populations, 67